Damien Fleming is a former Australian cricketer, regarded as one of Australian cricket's premier pace bowlers, a recognised expert in the art of swing bowling. Since leaving cricket Flemo has worked on TV and radio as a commentator, is a popular figure on the speakers' circuit and has refined scientific coaching principles to help developing bowlers – otherwise known as Bowlology. He lives in Melbourne with his wife and family.

DAMIEN FLEMING
BOWLOLOGY

CRICKET, LIFE & STORIES FROM THE AVENUE OF APPREHENSION

The Five Mile Press

The Five Mile Press Pty Ltd
1 Centre Road, Scoresby
Victoria 3179 Australia
www.fivemile.com.au

Part of the Bonnier Publishing Group
www.bonnierpublishing.com

Copyright © Damien Fleming, 2013
All rights reserved. No part of this book may be reproduced, stored in a retrieval system, or be transmitted by any form or by any means, electronic, mechanical, photocopying, recording or otherwise, without the pior written permission of the publisher.

Damien Fleming asserts his moral rights to be identified as the author of this book.

First published 2013

Printed in Australia at Griffin Press.
Only wood grown from sustainable regrowth forests is used in the manufacture of paper found in this book.

Page design and typesetting by Shaun Jury
Cover design by Luke Causby, Blue Cork
Front cover photo by Melanie Faith Dove
Back cover photograph Hamish Blair © Getty Images
Internal photographs: p4 © Newspix; pp82-3 *Pakistan vs Australia* tour booklet, 1994; p130 Pradeep Mandahani; p175 Kamal Sharma; p183 Phil Hilyard © Newspix; p220 Howard Burditt/Reuter's Pictures/Picture Media; p240 golden albatross, right, ryanhellyer.net; p240 seagull, left, www.abbotsweld.co.uk/classes-2/seagull; p257 *The Ashes* magazine, 2001; p263 *Tour Guide 1989/90*; p294 Pitchmap courtesy Hawk-Eye Limitations Limited; p302 © Sabine Albers Photography; p308 ©Foxsports; p325 courtesy Fox Footy.
Photos on pp189, 257 (top), 306, 318, 332 and 339 © Melanie Faith Dove.
All other internal images from the Damien Fleming collection.
Caricatures © Greta Waring.
Thanks to Pete Hanlon and Fairfax for permission to use the material on pp319–21.

Every attempt has been made to trace and acknowledge copyright of the internal photographs. Where an attempt has been unsuccessful, the publisher would be pleased to hear from the copyright owner so any omission or error can be rectified.

National Library of Australia Cataloguing-in-Publication entry
   Fleming, Damien, author.
   Bowlology: cricket, life and stories from the avenue of apprehension/
   Damien Fleming.
   ISBN: 9781743463581 (paperback)
   Fleming, Damien.
   Cricket players–Australia–Anecdotes.
   Cricket–Bowling.
   Bowlers–Australia–Anecdotes.
   796.358092

A late swinging outswinging dedication to this book to my beautiful wife Wendy, and great supporting act, my crazy kids Braydo, Jazzy and Izzy. 'I wanted the best and I've got the best. The hottest family in the world. The Flemings.'
Love you, guys.

Di and Ian Fleming, I know I didn't end up an accountant, but I did work with statistics to a certain degree. Thanks for all your support and love.

To my bro Justin, keep rocking!

Contents

Foreword by Warwick Todd		1
Chapter 1	Four Life Goals	3
Chapter 2	Kickstart My Heart with the Vics	15
Chapter 3	The Seven O'Clock Bandit Pays his Dues	21
Chapter 4	To Be or Not To Be a Nightwatchman	25
Chapter 5	Swerve Merv	31
Chapter 6	A Hot Dog Salute for Lord Sheffield	43
Chapter 7	Welcome to Harp's Nightmare	49
Chapter 8	'New Sensation' Debut with Supermodels	57
Chapter 9	AB and Me	61
Chapter 10	Tubby Ruins a Test Debut Hat-trick	67
Chapter 11	Slats the Matchwinner and Juniorisms	85
Chapter 12	Boxing Day with Billy, Warnie and Boony	91
Chapter 13	Danny and Aussie Mac	99
Chapter 14	Lara, Lara, Laraaa!!!!!	109
Chapter 15	The Rommates XI	113
Chapter 16	We're Not the Champions of the World	119
Chapter 17	Sympathy for Gilly	133
Chapter 18	Stuck in a Rut, and Freddy Krueger vs Predator	135
Chapter 19	Cochin – Our Papillon	141
Chapter 20	Tendulkar and Our Sharjah Birthday Bash	147
Chapter 21	Haggle Up	155
Chapter 22	Reverse Swing	159

Chapter 23	Nerds and Julios	169
Chapter 24	Devil Worship	181
Chapter 25	World Cup, Cardiff, No Regrets	187
Chapter 26	You're So Dizzy	213
Chapter 27	Junior, Nicho and Nine Slips in Zimbabwe	215
Chapter 28	Dominators	221
Chapter 29	Streakers and Albatrosses in New Zealand	237
Chapter 30	AC/DC Caught Backstreet Boys Bowled Kenny Rogers	241
Chapter 31	Foccor	253
Chapter 32	Sackings	259
Chapter 33	Coaching Cricket Academy	265
Chapter 34	Bowlology	273
Chapter 35	Transition from Player to Commentator	279
Chapter 36	The Corridor of Uncertainty	285
Chapter 37	The Fast Bowlers Cartel	287
Chapter 38	ABC Radio, Richie Benaud and the Chinamen XI	297
Chapter 39	Beach Cricket	301
Chapter 40	Pitch Reports, Aussies with Hat-tricks and Test 70s Club	307
Chapter 41	A Bit Like My Bowling, eh, Steve!	315
Chapter 42	My Mate Oscar	319
Chapter 43	After the Bounce	323
Chapter 44	Finish Life Goals Review	329
Chapter 45	Australians with Hat-tricks on Test Debut Club	335
Acknowledgements		337

Foreword

Warwick Todd

CRICKET'S A FUNNY game. When Flem asked me to pen a few words for his latest book, I was a little surprised. I'd made the same request to him back in 2007, only to be told by his 'media manager' (in other words, his missus) that 'Damien is a little too busy to help out at the present time'. Too busy doing what? Calling Ryobi Cup matches with Mark Waugh? I don't think so.

But Warwick Todd is not a man to harbour a grudge. Unless it involves Arjuna Ranatunga. And I'm big enough to let bygones be bygones. So once we had settled on the terms (a mention in the thankyous and cash up front), I was happy to oblige. Here it is then.

Flem is a top bloke. Amongst the very, very top. What's more, he's an Aussie cricketer who always gave his all – 110 per cent, no matter what the circumstances. In fact, the only time I saw Flem drop his work rate was during a one-dayer in '98, and that was probably due to some arrangement he had with an Indian bookmaker.

He's also a good writer, and I'm sure this latest publication will be full of fascinating insights, along with another retelling of that bloody hat-trick in Adelaide. Anyways, I wholeheartedly endorse this book of humorous anecdotes/coaching tips/wistful recollections/angry complaints (strike out whichever are not applicable), and I urge you to buy a copy before they're all dumped in a discount bin at some school fete.

Good on ya, mate.

Toddy

P.S. We did say 'cash up front' . . . Still waiting.

Chapter 1
Four Life Goals

WHEN I WAS a kid, Dennis Lillee was up there with Superman, Batman and Muhammad Ali – he was a cricketing superhero. He didn't leap tall buildings in a single bound or drive a batmobile, but his superpowers involved a fast outswinger, cutters, yorkers, bouncers, amazing endurance, determination and charisma. Who cared if he batted with an aluminium bat? If Dennis did it, it was all right by me – and every other kid in Australia.

The first day of Test cricket I attended was with my dad, Ian, back on 27 December 1981. Australia was playing the West Indies at the mighty MCG, and I was hoping to see DK break the world record number of Test wickets, then held by Lance Gibbs with 309.

The night before, after a classic hundred from Kim Hughes and his Slazenger Ton – which was my first ever bat (Dennis didn't endorse bats . . . well, not wooden ones), Australia had just a few overs to bowl, but it was enough for Dennis to demolish the West Indian top order. When he bowled Viv Richards with the last ball of the day – a leg-cutter dragged onto the stumps – the West Indies was 4/10 and the entire country went berserk. It was one of the greatest moments I can ever remember in cricket. People were screaming, dancing, celebrating long after the ball was bowled, and waiting for the next day was like waiting for Christmas.

Getting to the world's greatest sporting colosseum, the mighty MCG, the next day (very early) was a dream. The atmosphere

BOWLOLOGY

My hero, Dennis Lillee, had that much self-belief he was already clapping his delivery in mid-action.

was like nothing I had ever experienced. It was pure euphoria watching my idol bowl a ball in the 'Doorway to Departure', and we didn't have to wait too long before he had mustard man Jeffrey Dujon out. This was fast bowling at its best. Superman live.

Then Larry Gomes nicked a ball to Greg Chappell, who effortlessly took the catch.

That dismissal was Lillee's 310th and made him the highest wicket-taker in Test history. Sorry, Lance. The thing that stood out most for me, as an 11-year-old, was the crowd noise. The chant of 'LILLEE, LILLEE!' was famous and ubiquitous in those days, but I swear it went on for 15 minutes after he got Gomes out. It was unbelievable. Like being at an enormous rock concert with the crowd demanding an encore.

The fans didn't let up, chanting through every ball of Terry Alderman's next over. The great man was so overcome by having reached the milestone that he walked down in front of us at third man even though he was fielding at fine leg.

So my idol, with his thinning hair held in tight by his yellow headband, and the famous golden cricket bat dangling on his hairy chest, was standing RIGHT IN FRONT OF ME. It was like a religious experience, and I knew there and then what I wanted to do with my life. I was going to be a Test cricketer. A fast bowler just like DK, although maybe with just a bit more luck in the hair department.

I recently reviewed the life goals I wrote for myself on returning from the MCG that day, and I gave myself a performance review to see whether I had achieved them.

BOWLOLOGY

Life goals at 11	Results at 2013
1. Take the most Test wickets.	Fail. Currently 756 short.
2. Kick winning goal for Hawthorn after the siren in the grand final.	Fail. Trained with the Hawks' under-19s.
3. Become lead guitarist for Kiss.	Fail. Can play the lead riff of 'God of Thunder'.
4. Win an Academy Award.	Pass. *Slumdog Millionaire* (more about this later).

Batting-wise, I loved Greg Chappell and Alan Border – and, for some reason, Kepler Wessels, the South African opening batsman who debuted for Australia in World Series Cricket with his unique crab-like technique. Kepler would slide back toward leg slip and nail anything on the stumps or wider to the off-side boundary. He cut his way to a hundred on Test debut against England, but later in the series the Poms worked out that you could tie him down on leg stump as he couldn't get his bat around his front leg to hit the ball.

In one dry batting spell for the Springvale South under-16s I reverted to the Kepler backlift technique, so I could be ready to smash any ball pitching on or outside off stump for four through the point region. I was promptly bowled for a duck – bowled leg stump, Wessels-style.

* * *

Like all kids of that era, I played footy in the winter and cricket in the summer. Mum's side of the family were all passionate Carlton fans, while Dad's family were Footscray. Naturally, therefore, I picked Hawthorn, which must have been on top of the ladder when I started taking an interest.

FOUR LIFE GOALS

We didn't book holidays in September between 1974 and 1994, as the Mighty Hawkers didn't make the finals only three times in these years. Seven premierships came in that era. Michael Tuck played in them all, along with stars such as Leigh Mathews, Peter Knights, Dermott Brereton, Johnny Platten, Robert 'Dipper' DiPierdomenico and 'the Chief' Jason Dunstall. But my favourite was Gary Buckenara. I tried to play like Bucky, who was a dangerous half-forward with a booming kick. He took big screamers and could run in the midfield as well.

TOP FIVE HAWKS

- *Leigh Mathews*: Nicknamed 'Lethal' because of his bulldozing, shirtfronting style. A possession-gathering, goal-kicking superstar.
- *Peter Hudson*: Flat-punt exponent who, in just 130 games, banged through 727 goals. Some with his ear half torn off, some after flying to the game in a chopper so he wouldn't miss the Friday-night shift in his family's Tassie pub (a fair distance from the ground in Melbourne).
- *Jason Dunstall*: The Chief. A strong mark and kick, he used to lose backmen with his pace over the first 10 metres (although he fatigued by the 11th metre).
- *Dermott Brereton*: Flamboyant and tough centre half-forward who strutted around like the WWF wrestler Brutus Beefcake. Actually, strike that – Brutus strutted around like Dermie.
- *Buddy Franklin*: Physical freak. A 196 centimetre athlete who is quick on the lead, has great touch at ground level, too good for any back. Unfortunately, on a bad day (like the 2012 Grand Final, sob) his kicking tends to be about as accurate as Steve Harmison's first ball of the Ashes in 2006/07.

BOWLOLOGY

One of my earlier favourite players was full-forward Michael Moncrieff. He wore the number six on his guernsey and was a bit like Stuart MacGill in that his timing was terrible. MacGill arrived around the same time as Warnie, while Moncrieff was sandwiched between Paul Hudson and Jason Dunstall – two of the game's best ever full-forwards.

Moncrieff was a good goal-kicker, though, and part of his appeal for me was that he slotted 97 goals in the 1976 and 90 goals in the 1978 premiership seasons.

Also, he was part of one of the great VFL commentary calls of all time: Peter McKenna, a legendary full-forward for Collingwood, was not so good behind the microphone, once saying, 'If you put Michael Moncrieff's head on that guy's shoulders . . . he'd look exactly like . . . Michael Moncrief!'

Everybody knows Shane Warne tried out for St Kilda, but I'd like it on record that I too had an equally brief and inglorious flirtation with the second-greatest game on earth. My budding VFL/AFL career came to a close after I debuted for Victoria in the 1988/89 cricket season.

In 1988 I'd had a run with the Hawks Under 19s, although I didn't manage to play a game. Clearly, they were keeping me on ice, waiting for the right time to bring me in. (Probably for a grand final so I could kick the winning goal after the siren.)

Not put off by my modest efforts the previous year, in early 1989 they called me up and I dusted off my boots, ready for even bigger things. Going straight from cricket to a full-on Aussie Rules practice match was going to be tough, given that the other players had been training all summer. It was only an intra-club game but I ran around like a headless chook.

Umpiring the game was the late, great Allan Jeans, the Hawks' messiah and one of the greatest coaches of all time.

FOUR LIFE GOALS

THE WISDOM OF ALLAN 'YABBY' JEANS

- 'Footballers are like sausages – you can fry them, grill them, bake them, but they're still footballers.'
- 'Are you prepared to pay the price? WILL YOU PAY THE PRICE?' *Jeans at three-quarter time of the 1989 Grand Final, relating the story of a boy who wanted some shoes that were too expensive for him.*

Jeans had a surprisingly booming voice, which I'd never noticed while he was doing his 'coaching corner' segment on the Sunday TV show *World of Sport*. I certainly noticed it as I flapped about during this game.

This was when I realised Jeansy and I had different footballing philosophies. He felt I should 'show some courage, put your head over the ball and get it out to a teammate!' I was what is called, in AFL circles, a 'receiver', and so I thought my teammates should show some courage, put their heads over the ball and get it out to me so I could show off my exquisite kicking skills under no pressure. Maybe I could also take a hanger or two, just to give the crowd something else to marvel at.

Despite my best efforts to be an outside player and not get in the way of any physical stuff, I got belted from pillar to post. All I could think was, *If I get off this ground alive, I will never play footy again!* (Actually, that shows you exactly how confused I was. After all, if I *didn't* get off the ground alive, I wouldn't play again either . . .) I was shitting myself and Jeans just kept yelling at me.

Two weeks later, I had footy's version of a diamond duck – a no-stat debut for Noble Park Footy Club seniors – and that sealed the deal. I was told not to come back on Monday, which suited me fine as I had things to do, but it turned out that they didn't want me to come back on any other day either.

Handballing – something I never did.

* * *

I loved music from an early age, and I was lucky that Mum and Dad had a good collection of rock-n-roll records. I remember getting up early in the mornings, partly to watch the *Thunderbirds* on TV, but also to go through the record collection and pull out the Chuck Berry, Rolling Stones and Beatles LPs. The romance of the covers and the sound of the needle dropping was magic for me as a kid. The guitar sound was amazing on these albums, and that forged my love of guitar-based bands.

If Dennis Lillee was Australian cricket's superhero, well, Kiss had *four* musical superheroes. With their make-up, characters and hard-rock tunes – such as 'I Was Made for Loving You' – they were musical nirvana for kids in Australia during the late 1970s and early '80s.

They were made up of the Starchild (Paul Stanley), the Demon (fire-spitting blood-dripping bassist Gene Simmons), the Catman (Peter Criss, drumming in the background), and – my favourite – the Spaceman (Ace Frehley, who provided the guitar riffs).

There were Kiss cards, Kiss icy-poles, Kiss dolls and even Kiss comics. Of course, when you become so famous there are always detractors, and some people enviously accused them of going 'commercial'. Jealousy is a curse. And frankly, my 11-year-old eyes just didn't see it.

One of the major disappointments in my early life was not seeing Kiss at Waverley Park in 1980 – my parents deemed me too young. 'But isn't rock ageless?' I pleaded, to no avail. I swear I could hear Peter Criss's drums from my bedroom.

In 1996, the Triple M radio station got me tickets to the Kiss concert that year, and I took my brother, Justin (who is the lead singer of the Australian metal band Pegazus). It was a childhood dream for us, even though we were both well and truly out of short pants by then.

As it happened, that was Kiss's first reunion comeback concert series, which continues to this day. But this one was with the original members. Since then, they've had so many reunions that I'm starting to wonder when they get the time to break up . . . But who cares, baby? When you are Kiss, you can do no wrong.

BOWLOLOGY

The next day Triple M rang and asked me to do a review for them. I agreed, and told them that the members of Kiss actually reminded me of some cricketers. Peter Criss, the Catman, reminded me of David Boon. Both had some serious facial hair – Boony's was a bushy moustache, and Criss's was whiskers. They both went about their business with a minimum of fuss but got the job done. Cult heroes.

Ace Frehley reminded me of Mark Waugh: laconic, laid-back and classy – did have a couple of soft glitches on his guitar, but overall a crowd favourite.

Gene Simmons, meanwhile, was like Merv Hughes – a larger-than-life character who loved the crowd's attention and was loved in return. Both were very adept with their tongues.

And Paul Stanley, Kiss's lead singer, reminded me of Dean Jones: he wanted to be the centre of attention but was a bit of a tryhard.

My brother Justin and me. Combining rock with cricket.
I'm surprised Kiss didn't come up with this concept.

12

FOUR LIFE GOALS

The next day at Victorian training, I said g'day to Deano, who didn't give me much as he ran past me with a stony face.

Oh, well, I thought, *Deano's having one of those days.*

Eventually, he ran past me again and said, 'What are you, a psycho-fucking-analyst these days?'

He was obviously a Triple M listener.

Anyway, if you grew up in Springvale in the mid-1980s and didn't listen to heavy metal and didn't have a mullet, you were asking for trouble. I fell into line and did both.

Although it was quite a contradiction, the popular metal bands of the day – Motley Crue, Poison, Twisted Sister and co. – all wore make-up, used hairspray and wore glam clothes, while us supporters in Springvale wore no make-up and had mullets and grunge clothes more like those of Pearl Jam and Soundgarden, icons of the grunge explosion of the early 1990s.

I never could figure that out. Maybe the Springvale bogans were trendsetters. Grunge's advance party. They don't call it 'the Seattle of the South' for nothing.

The longer I grew my mullet, the more wickets I seemed to take for Springvale South, my rep teams and South Melbourne. I saw myself as a fast-bowling Samson, cutting a swathe through batting line-ups. He used the jawbone of an ass, I used a Kookaburra. You can see the similarities immediately.

All cricketers are superstitious, and as my mullet grew longer and longer I began fearing that if my locks were cut, my bowling figures would be too. By the time I debuted for Victoria, it was halfway down my back.

BOWLOLOGY

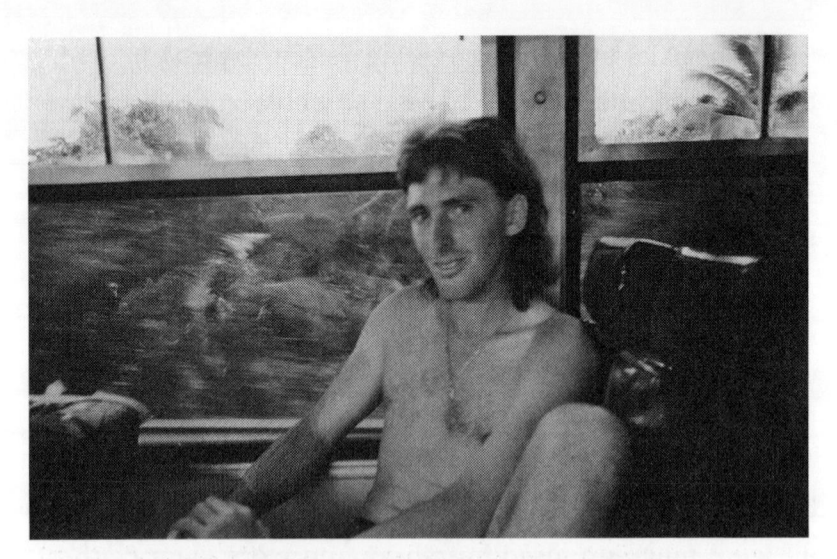

My Samson superstition stayed with me until the 1991/92 season, where a poor return of 15 wickets at an average of 49 saw me revert to short back and sides.

Chapter 2
Kickstart My Heart with the Vics

WITH MOTLEY CRUE blaring in the headphones of my state-of-the-art and ever-present Sony Walkman, I may not exactly have walked from the pages of the cricket manual. In fact, Adam Gilchrist reckons I looked more like Otto Man, the bus driver from *The Simpsons*, than a cricketer – but what would a nerd from Deniliquin know?

I remember walking nervously into the dressing rooms for the first time at the MCG and rubbing shoulders with Australian cricket legends such as big Merv Hughes – along with self-proclaimed legends such as Dean Jones, and also fine cricketers such as Simon O'Donnell, Jamie Siddons, Tony Dodemaide.

I played domestic one-day cricket straight away, but I was 12th man for the last three Sheffield Shield games of the season. It seemed like three years. As I was young and naive, it is fair to say the boys took the mickey out of me. In fact, that's an understatement. Guantanamo detainees were treated with more respect.

In cricket, 12 is the loneliest number. In *This Is Spinal Tap* the amplifiers went to 11, but not 12. From day one, it became clear that there was no task too menial, that no ask went unasked, and that no one was lower than the Victorian 12th man.

BOWLOLOGY

My duties included (but were not restricted to) the following:

1. On arrival at the ground, make sure the beers are on ice, and prepare for a long night of providing personal butler service, delivering the little cans of personality to teammates desperately in need of it.
2. Stay in my cricketing whites all day, ready to perform other man-servant tasks for the aforementioned players. They may have lacked personality but they didn't lack anger, spite or bloody-mindedness.
3. Take drinks onto the field every hour – and at any random minute in between, should somebody bat an eyelid in a manner that indicates thirst.
4. Remain vigilant at every moment for player requests for sunscreen, jumpers, towels, gloves, ice, toothpicks and any other passing whim of the first XI. Non-delivery within a moment leads to a dressing-down of blistering proportions by a person I will soon be serving drinks to. Should you miss a micro-signal from a player – say, Deano, who may have to wait an extra over for the gloves he so desperately needs – you will be scrubbing his pads with a toothbrush, or he'll sit you down after the day's play and tell you about his 200 in Madras (again), only pausing for breath while you dash off to fetch him another beer.
5. Run beers to the showers while players are in there after the day's cricket. The 12th man is Not To Shower until everyone else has, lest they need a beer.
6. Make sure the beers are cold.

I remember thinking, in between checking the temperature of beer, running gloves, doing throw-downs and finding lost socks, *Give me the pressure of bowling any day.* War hero and cricketer Keith Miller was once asked about pressure in cricket and famously replied, 'Pressure is a Messerschmitt up your arse,' but I don't think Keith was ever 12th man to Deano or Merv.

It was a bizarre culture back then. I was in the playing Eleven one minute as part of the one-day team and definitely one of the boys, but the next minute, when I was 12th man for the Shield team, I was suddenly a second-class citizen!

Maybe the lads were toughening me up, and maybe I needed it. Let's face it, I hadn't seen a lot of the world. I hadn't even managed to get my driver's licence by then, so it was public transport all the way for me around this time. The 8.30 a.m. train from Springvale to Richmond Station – the closest stop to the MCG – was packed with business people who struggled to squeeze in with their briefcases, so you can imagine how tough it was when I lugged my massive cricket coffin onto the train. And how popular I was.

Once off at Richmond Station, the 2 kilometre trek to our dressing rooms was a long haul for a 63 kilogram teenager, especially as no one had thought to stick wheels on the bottom of a cricket coffin. How could it take thousands of years to figure that out? And why did they wait until after I had bought a car?

Sometimes a kind-hearted teammate would see me as he was driving by on Brunton Avenue and would stop and wait for me. When I'd get a metre or so away, he'd shout out, 'Make sure the fucking beers are cold!' and drive off.

I could have copped being 12th man if the humiliation had started and ended with the above set of tasks, but there was always more. Playing Western Australia in the last Shield game of the 1988/89 season, I remember walking into the dressing rooms after hitting a thousand catches to our loveable but not overly skilled left-arm orthodox spinner Paul Jackson to find that my cricket gear had disappeared. It didn't take long to realise that it had taken up residence in every nook, cranny, toilet and rubbish receptacle in the dressing room.

It was like finding Wally. I'd look up and see my bowling boots sticky-taped to the roof. After 10 minutes I found my pads and bat in the heater, and my batting gloves in the spa. The worst thing was that Merv had gotten a big black texta and signed his name on all my gear. Even sadder, Merv still hadn't learnt to spell his name correctly.

For the next 12 months, every time I walked out to bat in a first-class game the opposition would snigger – and not for the obvious reasons. I was the only person in the world with a full kit of *misspelt* Merv Hughes autographed gear. How that never outsold Michael Jordan's Nikes I'll never know.

Nevertheless, it was still less painful than receiving a sloppy moustached kiss in the ear when you got a wicket.

Cricketers are very much creatures of routine, and when I was 12th man I was no different. After some time I had settled into a pattern of sitting upstairs in the viewing area and watching the game, but my vision was trained like a hawk on the players so I could detect any request from the ground.

Here's how a good day might progress for me if our two star batsmen were making a fist of it:

1. Make sure beers are cold.
2. Grab Deano's and Jamie Siddons' spare batting gloves and caps.
3. Grab Coke and peanuts.
4. Bring Walkman and two cassettes – some pump-up music (Metallica, Anthrax, etc.) and something mellow (AC/DC, Angels), depending on my mood.
5. Have one TV on the cricket feed at ground, and another on the WWF wrestling on the Sky channel for a bit of Hulkmania.
6. Check beer temperature.

KICKSTART MY HEART WITH THE VICS

In this match, Deano was not out overnight, so I was keen to get up into the viewing area nice and early to look out for anything he might need. People think the batsmen and keeper have to concentrate hard, but few understand the anxious hyper-vigilance of the 12th man. I didn't want to be even a millisecond late in seeing a call for some fresh gloves or a cap, or I knew the pad-scrubbing and Madras torture routine would ruin my night again.

Having lugged my gear into the rooms, I put the beers on ice, did the throw-downs and whatever other task was requested. Of course, my teammates expressed their thanks for my efforts in the usual way and hid all my gear, which I had to find before settling in. The last part of the puzzle fell in place when I found my Walkman sticky-taped behind the door. I removed it, grabbed my Coke and peanuts and made it upstairs just as Deano walked out to bat.

I watched the first two overs with no requests from Deano, so I relaxed a bit, opened my Coke, ate some peanuts, put my headphones on and pressed play, ready to listen to some hard rock. Nothing happened. Instead of the pounding of drums, all I could hear was the familiar knock of leather on wood, and Deano telling the nearest fielder how he'd played a similar cover drive early in his Madras 200. I pressed play again. Nothing. I repeated half a dozen times, each time becoming more frantic. Always the same result. My Walkman was broken.

Well, I completely lost it and gave the boys a spray: 'You can write on my cricket gear but you don't mess with a man's [that got some sniggers] Walkman!' They were stunned. Until now, most of them had assumed I was mute.

I was in a frantic state and ran downstairs, thinking there might be a key piece of my music machine stuck somewhere, but the toilets were flushed, the ceilings inhabited only by flies and the bins empty. The thought of a whole day's cricket without music filled me with dread.

Then I heard a shriek from upstairs. It was uncanny how that could happen the very second a 12th man left his post. *Shit, I hope it's not Deano*, I thought.

I ran back up to my teammates. 'Who is it?' I asked meekly.

'Deano,' they all said.

'Shit. What does he want?'

'Don't know,' someone replied. 'But he doesn't look happy.'

I frantically looked out to see Deano, hands on his hips, looking like he'd been waiting for hours. He was not happy. Mr Teapot appeared to have steam coming from his spout.

I ran out as quickly as possible. Normally, he'd meet me halfway, but this time he stood right on the pitch, staring at me. Forgetting all my anger from moments before, I cleared my throat to apologise but he cut me off.

'Hey, champ,' he said – and he threw the two batteries from my Walkman at me.

Chapter 3
The Seven O'Clock Bandit Pays His Dues

RICHARD 'BANDIT' MCCARTHY was a wonderfully skilled fast bowler for the North Melbourne and Victorian cricket teams. He swung and cut the ball both ways, bowled a dangerous bouncer, had a good yorker and ticked all the boxes of the Bowlology skill set. He also had tattoos, which back in 1989 meant he was tough.

Not that he was a ruffian, mind you. Bandit was part of North Melbourne's socially mobile set – he had his own teeth. In those parts, a teardrop tattoo was a bloke's way of showing his soft side. AFL fans will know about the reputation of the Shinboners. Those of you unfortunate enough to have been born on the other side of the Murray may never have visited the area, where every business was a butcher shop and the only historical landmark was the gasworks (now demolished). Can I just point out that Ricky Ponting and Peter Siddle both support the local footy team, and that Sam Kekovich played for them?

McCarthy earned the nickname 'the Seven O'Clock Bandit' because of his habit of turning up late for training, grabbing a new ball in the fading light and then doing maximum damage to the all-rounders and his fellow bowlers. The top order had all had a hit by that time and were safely in the rooms getting a gentle rub or enjoying a hot bath.

The Bandit's pace was a nightmare in the half-light. He would get countless wickets, but he'd also provide a colossal amount of body bruises, particularly around the very tender inner-thigh area.

When not bullying his own kind, the Bandit was an extremely laid-back character, often sleeping while the top order was batting. He only played a few games for the Vics, but one incident left a mark (or a 'brain tattoo') on all his teammates.

We were playing against Queensland at the MCG in the 1989/90 season. I was, it won't surprise you to know, 12th man, and I remember the game for it being Carlton AFL superstar Craig 'Braddles' Bradley's debut outing for Victoria.

Sometimes waiting to bat is like being a prisoner awaiting execution. It can produce anxiety and genuine fear – fear of failing, fear of getting hit by a fast bowler, fear of looking foolish in front of teammates, the crowd and those members of the media not still at lunch. It was one thing to back away in the nets or fall to the ground in agony, furiously rubbing a sore spot, but quite another to do it out in the middle of the pitch.

At the MCG everyone can hear you scream . . .

The Bandit was one of those 'only speak to him if you can improve on silence' sort of guys, so while he waited to bat he didn't say a word. He just puffed on cigarette after cigarette. If he was nervous, he hid it well . . . but not well enough.

Anyway, on this day a wicket fell and his number was up. Bandit didn't say a word, just had one last puff of nicotine, closed his eyes to savour the buzz and then squashed the butt into the ashtray. Yep, he was ready to go and do his thing in the middle. Not nervous at all. Well, not unless you studied him closely. And as 12th man, I was watching everything.

Bandit grabbed his helmet, sighed as if it was all a bit of an imposition, and then walked out the dressing-room door to the batting crease as casual as you like.

THE SEVEN O'CLOCK BANDIT PAYS HIS DUES

I don't want to appear a smartarse here, or some sort of expert on everything, but I think we would all agree that when a batsman walks out to bat, probably the most important piece of equipment to take out there is your bat. After all, it is called BATting – bit of a clue there, I reckon.

But there was Bandit, strolling down the race without his bat, and about to walk out onto the MCG. Ever alert and eager to do the right thing, I pointed out what was happening to my teammates and grabbed his bat, ready to race it down to him. Alas, the milk of human kindness had curdled in the veins of my fellow Victorians, who yelled as one, 'Don't you dare!' and jumped to their feet to restrain me.

In team sport, these are the moments players treasure most. For some, there is nothing funnier than seeing one of your mates humiliated, and for the rest there's just relief it isn't happening to us.

We watched as Bandit strode out onto the MCG unarmed and vulnerable. He took his helmet from under his arm, placed it on his head and then reached for the bat that should have been under his other arm.

His double-take was priceless. He put his hand on his head in shock, and then turned and began to sprint back toward the dressing rooms.

Ever the good Samaritan, I met him halfway with the missing piece of equipment and placed it in his hand. As I did so, the scoreboard showed a replay of the Bandit realising at the crease that he didn't have his bat. He was like a man trapped in a dream in which he gets to work only to realise he has no pants on. (You do know the one . . . don't you?) The Queensland players were in the middle of the pitch pissing themselves with laughter.

Not surprisingly, the blushing Bandit was bowled by Dirk Tazelaar for a duck, so maybe his bat was indeed excess baggage

BOWLOLOGY

The incident was probably payback from the cricketing gods (a philosophical concept of Boony the Buddha) for the 1352 inner thighs he corked in the nets at training. In the chapter on ethics in the Bowlology handbook, it clearly says that crimes don't pay – especially crimes inflicted in the half-light against fellow bowlers.

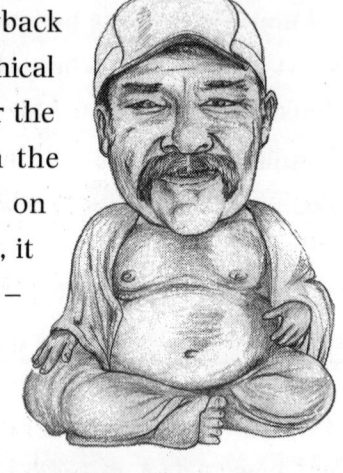

My vision of the cricket god – a Boony Buddha-looking supreme being.

Chapter 4
To Be or Not To Be a Nightwatchman

EVENTUALLY, I PROGRESSED from being 12th man to being selected for a first-class game for Victoria. And as I was still without a driver's licence, the public transport system continued throwing up doosras to my budding cricket career. Two days before my first-class debut I was riding the 814 Springvale bus to the train station.

I'm a 'give the seat to females and the elderly' sort of guy, and I prefer to stand up like Keanu Reeves in the *Speed* movies, perusing the scene. On this day, the bus hit a car and came to a screeching halt, and I was thrown around (like Keanu Reeves in *The Matrix* movies) into a railing, which broke the pinkie finger on my left hand.

Now, that hurt on a few levels.

A fitness test was arranged by our coach, former Australian batting great Ian Redpath, in an indoor centre imaginatively named 'Bat and Ball'. It was a

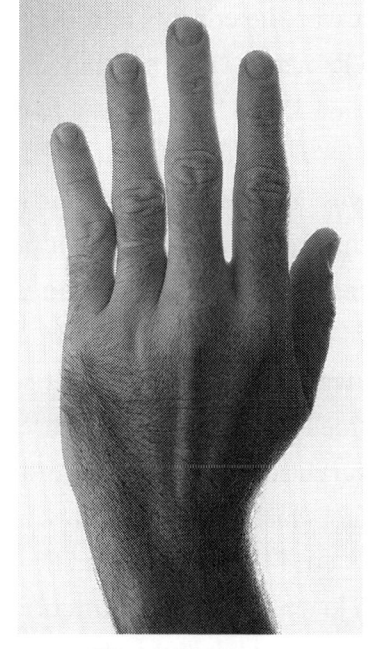

While my other fingers are straight, my pinkie's shaping for an inswinger.

pretty rough joint with synthetic wickets laid on concrete that had started to crack and buckle. There were areas on the pitch from which the ball would spear straight into your ankle or your nose. A centimetre either side and its trajectory would leave you singing like the Bee Gees for the rest of the session (not a comfortable place to ice).

Batting with a busted hand in such circumstances is not pleasant, particularly as our tough-nut assistant coach, Keith Stackpole, was ready to cancel my Shield debut at the first sight of a wince. Any backward step or grimace of pain would see me ruled out of the team. I'd been 12th man for so long, and I'd taken so much crap in that time, that I was determined to get through the session, no matter how much it hurt. I wasn't going to quit.

Still, cricketing bastardry takes all forms, and on this day it was the coach's and the selectors' turn. Stacky had invited Victoria's – and possibly Australia's – quickest bowler at the time, Denis 'Reg' Hickey, to come along and bowl to me. Facing him at any time was not fun, but facing him with a broken finger was definitely not fun. Facing him when he has just been told that you've taken his spot in the state team if you get through the net session is just plain misery.

Reg, like all our quicks, liked to bowl from about 14 yards away, and I reckon he let some go from so close that I could smell the leather and his breath simultaneously. Yet somehow I survived one of the shortest and fastest sessions and made my first-class debut a few days later, on 17 November 1989.

And I was extra-glad that I did, because we bowled first on a kryptonite-green Junction Oval wicket. Geoff Marsh edged my second delivery straight to Tony Dodemaide at slip. It went straight into his ever-reliable hands – and then straight out. After that, however, things went my way that day, maybe my reward for my chivalrous act on the bus, and I finished the innings with 6/37.

My next hurdle as a first-class player was to deal with being the team's designated nightwatchman. The role of nightwatchman is an interesting one in the game of cricket. A nightwatchman is usually a lower-order batsman who is not a 'rabbit' or a 'ferret' but a tailender with a competent defence. (A rabbit is a particularly incompetent batsman, who is expected to be dismissed cheaply almost every time. A ferret describes a batsman who is even worse, because 'a ferret goes in after a rabbit'.) Because I was a budding all-rounder in those days, I played with a pretty straight bat and was therefore earmarked as nightwatchman material.

A nightwatchman is sent out to bat about half an hour before the end of play, in order to protect the top-order batsmen. So you're often facing the quickest bowlers (Rackemann, McDermott, Reid, Holdsworth, etc.) with a new ball, sometimes in faltering light, and they are trying to hurt you. The last bit I wasn't keen on. Despite my heroics at the Bat and Ball, I am allergic to pain – more specifically, to pain inflicted on me!

Despite this, I used to acquire the job a fair bit when I first started playing for Victoria. I absolutely hated it, and I tried not to be around when the late afternoon arrived and the 'nightwatchman' word started to be slated around.

Once we were playing New South Wales at the Junction Oval in the 1990/91 season. Jamie Siddons and my fellow ex-Springvale South player Warren Ayres were batting well.

I was feeling pretty content with myself, having taken 5/50 in the first innings. Merv sensed this and, knowing how much I hated being nightwatchman, turned to our captain (and future fill-in host for Ray Martin's show), Simon O'Donnell, who was also the next man in to bat. 'Simon, it's very close to the tea

FIVE FAMOUS FERRETS

- *Chris Martin* (230 Test wickets, 123 runs at an average of 2.41): A ferret hall-of-famer. It's still a great debate as to who is a better bat – Chris Martin the Kiwi quick, or Chris Martin the lead singer of Coldplay.
- *Phil Tufnell* (121 Test wickets, 153 runs at an average of 5.10): Still the only batsman I have seen laughing as he walked out to bat.
- *Courtney Walsh* (519 Test wickets, 936 runs at an average of 7.54): Scored his 100th first-class duck against Victoria in 2000.
- *Bruce Reid* (113 Test wickets, 93 runs at an average of 4.65): The best state bowler I ever faced – and the worst batsman. He was once bowled middle stump by Merv at the WACA as he was backing away; he was quoted as saying, 'I'm prepared to play for Western Australia but I'm not prepared to die for Western Australia.'
- *Glenn McGrath*: A controversial selection, this one, because Pigeon became a very reliable number 11, hanging around while Steve Waugh and Mike Hussey reached hundreds. But I can't overlook that after 21 Tests he had scored 38 runs at an average of 2.11. Around this time, Steve Waugh was floating rumours that Pigeon was getting paid by more than one bat manufacturer. He then added that they were paying him *not* to use their gear.

---

break,' he observed. 'Maybe it's time for a nightwatchman – should Flem put the pads on?'

Simon was an authoritative captain who didn't like being told what to do, and to my relief he said no.

Ten minutes later, Merv again suggested to our skipper that he should protect himself and send me in to face the new ball,

TO BE OR NOT TO BE A NIGHTWATCHMAN

and that I loved doing the job. I was thinking, *Merv, just shut the fuck up!* But again Simon said no.

After the tea break, Ayresy was run out by Michael Bevan. Simon walked out to bat, and soon he and Siddons were smashing the New South Wales attack everywhere. Jamie was probably the best player I played with who did not play Test cricket. He was an exhilarating batsman to watch, with his cutting and pulling and the best cover drive of the era. We saw plenty of that through this innings as he bludgeoned his way past 150 and neared his double-ton.

It was about 30 minutes to the end of play, and Merv piped up again, suggesting that I should go in as nightwatchman to protect our debutant – and future England Test player – Craig White. (Interestingly, he had replaced Darren Lehmann on our 1990 youth tour to the West Indies as 'Boof' was getting married. Many years later, Boof got married for a second time – to Whitey's lovely sister Andrea!)

Dean Jones, our vice-captain, agreed, and I was sent downstairs to pad up. I was absolutely spewing at Merv for getting me into this situation. I padded up slowly, and in that time we didn't lose a wicket. As cricketers are a superstitious bunch, I therefore decided to stay downstairs in our dressing room. I couldn't see the play from there, but the crowd would usually give you a hint as to what was going on.

Soon there was an almighty roar, and then I heard the dreaded noise of feet running down the stairs. It was our wicketkeeper, Darren Berry, saying, 'Jamie is out.' I was disappointed not only because now I had to go out there and face Wayne Holdsworth and Geoff Lawson and co., but also because Jamie had just missed his 200.

I slammed on my Victorian helmet and slowly made my way up the stairs and pushed my way through the Friday after-work crowd that had built up as the afternoon progressed. All of them were standing to applaud Jamie's majestic knock. A few people gave me a strange look, but I dismissed it. Hadn't they ever seen a nightwatchman before?

I got to the wooden gate and the nerves were swirling around in my stomach. I then made my way to the pitch, head down and dragging my feet. I felt like a zombie in the land of the living dead.

Halfway to the wicket, I heard a massive burst of laughter from the crowd behind me. I looked up towards the pitch to see Jamie raising his bat for his 200, then I looked back to see hundreds of spectators laughing. There, in the middle of them, laughing harder than anyone else, was big Merv Hughes.

I drew a line in the sand after that game. I never, ever wanted to be nightwatchman again.

FLEMO'S ADVICE FOR GETTING RID OF THE NIGHTWATCHMAN'S CURSE

- Build a reputation as an erratic, unorthodox strokeplayer
- Play plenty of shots, particularly pulls and hooks
- Drive in the air
- Slog the captain's and the coaches' bowling in the nets

After taking my own advice, my days as a nightwatchman were soon behind me.

Chapter 5
Swerve Merv

MERV HUGHES PROVIDED four things for his cricket teams: courage, determination, charisma and plenty of laughter. I first roomed with him in January 1989, when I was an 18-year-old mulleted kid straight out of high school on my first trip with the Victorian cricket team.

Merv was probably Australia's most famous and charismatic sporting identity at the time, coming off 13 wickets and hat-trick in a Test match against the West Indies.

I began to grow nervous about my roommate when I was in the Brisbane Hilton's lift with Tony Dodemaide and Michael Dimattina. They wished me good luck when I headed towards my room and said they were thinking of me. *What is waiting for me up there?* I thought.

I opened the door, and there he was: big Mervyn Hughes. 'Single or double bed?' he asked.

'S-s-s-single,' I eventually blurted out, sounding a bit like Noosha Fox from the 1976 classic single. Cough. Splutter.

'Shit, you're good to room with,' he

said, and then he shook my hand.

Merv and I hit it off straightaway, and he became like a big brother to me. In those days, the Victorian players used to switch roomies every second trip. I don't know what I did wrong but I roomed with Merv for six years!

Still, nothing prepared me for seeing him naked for the first time. There was no 'manscaping' back then – he was like a cross between a Hell's Angels bikie and a Yeti. He was big, hairy and proud of it. If a Christian creationist met Merv, he'd abandon all faith and side with Darwin – one look at him and he'd know for sure that we're all descended from apes. (Well, Merv was, at least. If the great Charlie Darwin had seen my weedy, hairless young frame, he might have assumed we'd evolved from the earthworm.)

MERV AND FLEM'S TOUR ROUTINE

Elite sportsmen always have routines that revolve around a special diet, plenty of rest and bursts of intense physical activity. Merv and I were no different.

1. We would arrive at our hotel, and Merv would stretch out on his double bed and grab the TV remote. I would be sent to get food, generally a couple of hamburgers – he could eat a Big Mac in one bite. Merv always instructed me to get a Diet Coke with his fast food as that would even things out! I would also buy a Big M and Picnic each, to be saved for later on that night. Food was a good way to tame the beast.
2. I'd then 'Bat Cave' our room by closing all the curtains so no light could enter, and we'd have a couple of hours' siesta.
3. We'd wake up, then go out to a pub or nightclub. Hopefully, there'd be drink cards in Merv's name and direct entry so we could miss the queues. He was a Test icon at the time and recognised all over Australia. Once we pulled up at a nightclub

and were directed around the queue to go straight in by a fawning bouncer. Ever polite to the small people, Merv thanked the guy, who turned, smiled and said, 'No problems, Dipper.' The bouncer had mistaken Merv for the equally heavily moustached Hawthorn Brownlow medalist Robert DiPierdomenico. Evidently all men with moustaches look the same. Merv's pride was shattered especially when for the rest of the night we told him 'Your shout, Dipper.'

4. Merv normally left earlier than me. Being a single bloke, I would stay and work my charm with the ladies, but always end up heading back home alone and ready to comfort myself with a Big M and a Picnic. Outside the room, I'd usually be greeted by a demolished room service tray with two Picnic wrappers and two drained Big M cartons.

5. There was no need to set an alarm, since we could rely on Merv's natural alarm clock. All I will say is that it was loud and could be smelt in Russia. And it was very consistent, always going off 30 minutes before we had to leave for the ground.

It's fair to say that pubs and nightclubs were part of the routine back in the late 1980s and early 1990s. If you happened to bowl the opposition out on day one, the bowlers and 12th man would generally go out and have a good night.

This was one 12th man duty I didn't mention before. Basically, it was your job to stay out until the last of the boys had finished drinking – and often that meant being out later than Charlie Sheen with a bloke who drank more and was considerably less interesting.

We never did well against Western Australia in Perth in those years. The trip across the continent just didn't suit us Victorians. It was a hostile and strange environment, with a pitch that could crack up like Kerry O'Keeffe hearing one of his own jokes.

BOWLOLOGY

During our match in 1990/91, the WACA pitch was so bad that Geoff Marsh put his bat in a crack on a good length and it stayed bolt upright, like Excalibur. Needless to say, this was not a welcoming sight for any batsman. It was double jeopardy. If the ball didn't fly off the edge of the bloody thing, there was every chance you could get on the front foot and fall into it.

We ended up winning that game, and Merv and I got 14 wickets between us and contributed almost as many runs with the bat. Looking back, there was plenty going on. One Darren 'Boof' Lehmann was playing for Victoria in those days, and it was the first state game of a young Damien Martyn.

Western Australia had a bowler called Ken MacLeay, who seemed a lovely bloke. But every time he came out to bat, Merv just wanted to kill him. It didn't matter if it was a Shield game or one-day game, but whether Kenny was batting at number six or number 11 Merv would just bombard him with bouncer after bouncer.

When asked why he hated Kenny so much, Merv replied, 'I played against him in an under-23 game. He walked out in a helmet and I just didn't like the look of him.'

Tough school!

Kenny also bowled lovely little outswingers, which rarely pitched on the stumps. He bowled a foot outside the off stump, just tempting batsman to size up his outswingers, play a cover drive and then nick the ball to Timmy Zoehrer or one of the waiting slips.

MC Hammer was massive at the time, and his second single, 'Pray', was in the charts. Having too much time in the dressing rooms, I made it into a song about Kenny:

They have MacLeay (Claaay)
They'll bowl MacLeay (Claaay)
Kenny won't make you play today . . .

SWERVE MERV

Anyway, in that match Merv got his 200th Shield wicket, I got my 50th first-class wicket and we won a close match. Since it was the first time any of the Vics could remember winning over that side of the world, there was plenty to celebrate. I was young and it was only my second time at the WACA, but blokes like Merv, Deano and Gary Watts had been travelling over and crawling back defeated their whole careers. I would like to tell you something about that night but I can't. If anybody can fill me in, please do.

The next season at the WACA we put on 500 in our first innings, thanks mainly to Deano, who knocked up a beautiful double-hundred. This was the game in which a passionate little bloke called Justin Langer made his debut. He scored a neat 59, opening the batting against a Victorian attack featuring a bloke called James Sutherland (now better known for running Cricket Australia). We managed to knock them over for 330 in the first innings and force the follow-on, but we still needed 11 wickets on the last day to win the match and get home for Christmas.

We felt we had no chance of a win, so we held a team meeting at a nightclub called Gobbles. There were a few West Coast Eagles boys there too, and the Vics were flying and having a great night.

Around this time there was a bizarre story about a nightclub singer, Fairlie Arrow, who went missing on the Gold Coast; it later emerged that she had done it as a hoax, to gain some publicity for herself. It's fair to say that didn't go down all that well on the world stage. Nonetheless, Perth is a small town, and when she showed up at Gobbles that night she was a gold-plated star. Centre of attention.

We had been sipping a fair few 375 millilitres of bottled personality that night and were getting charged up. Merv took one look at Fairlie and said, 'Fairlie Arrow . . . Fairlie fucking ordinary!' That got a laugh from us, which was a big mistake, because if Merv reckoned he was on to a joke he would not let it go. The big fella repeated it over and over again – if he said it once, he said it a hundred times.

Fairlie was within earshot and clearly got a little sick of this buffoon, and for the second time in her career she made a planned disappearance.

As did the West Australian batsman the next day. Despite our late night and counterintuitive attempts at rehydration, we took 11 wickets, chased down a small target and had consecutive wins at the WACA. It was straight back to Gobbles that night, but I'm sorry to say there was no second sighting of Fairlie. In fact, has anyone seen her since?

Our next Shield game was in Tasmania, and we saw a great example of Merv's love of the contest. Whenever he was coming back from playing Tests for Australia, he'd limp around and ice himself up in the rooms, but once the Shield game started he'd regularly bowl 40 to 50 overs per day and then go off to another Test match. In those days that was the rotation system – you rotated from Test to Shield to Test to Shield to ODI to club cricket.

Merv, along with Tony Dodemaide, really showed Paul Reiffel and me the level of competitiveness, hard work and never-say-die attitude that we needed if we were going to take the next step and play for Australia.

In this Shield match in Hobart, it came down to the last session on day four, and we were bowling to win the game. Merv bowled 30 overs in the first innings and 26 in the second. I was fielding at silly mid-off on that last afternoon, and I remember looking at Merv as he hobbled back to his bowling mark. You could see how much pain he was in, and I could only imagine how tired he was, but when he reached the top of his mark he turned around and charged in like a bloody great Mallee bull, snorting and grunting and full of rage as if it was the first ball of the game. I was in awe of the Big Fella.

As Merv told me, 'If you are mentally fresh and physically tired, you can still get through. Practice it at training.'

Sean 'China' Young, who later played one Test for Australia, was batting. He was copping bouncer after bouncer from Merv, and a verbal assault after every ball. Poor bugger was under fire. I was waiting for a Red Cross person to jump the fence and save him, but China saved Tassie in the end. Still, I will never forget the mighty efforts of Big Merv.

※ ※ ※

It's fair to say Merv was a dietician's nightmare. Once we had a dietician presenting to us about our eating habits. Someone asked about fast food, and she explained there were smart options even with fast food – tomato-based sauces on pasta, seafood and wholemeal options, for example. She also mentioned that quantity is crucial to cutting down skin-fold fat levels.

'What about if I'm going to have a pizza?' Merv enquired.

'That depends,' she replied. 'How many slices do you have, Merv?'

'That depends how many slices they slice the pizza up into,' Merv answered.

Merv was the king of the one-liner and, like all good comedians, his timing was excellent. He just knew how to make a joke and release the pressure in situations where things were starting to close in on us.

He was at his best against South Australia in the 1991/92 season at the MCG. Deano again scored a double-century – he was such a great batsman. When he was in his batting zone, he seemed totally in control of his game and the match situation.

BOWLOLOGY

We bowlers loved him when he was like that. Being in the dressing room was like being on a summer holiday, just watching the waves come in without a care in the world. Well, at least that's the way we saw it.

We were building an imposing total and were in a great position to win outright. Now, players behave very differently while waiting to bat. Mark Waugh used to sleep, and if he woke up he'd throw a squash ball against a wall with his headphones on. Some batsmen were like Maxwell Smart and used a cone of silence, mentally preparing for that first ball.

Merv had a fair bit of nervous energy, so he'd be telling jokes and funny stories, reminiscing about how many batsmen he had hit in the head and what grounds he had sixes on. If he got bored with that, he would throw in a bit of WWF wrestling too.

Simon 'Scooba' O'Donnell, as I've already explained, was a dominating captain who told you exactly what he wanted you to do when you went in to bat. As the score passed 400, Merv announced that he was going to go out there, slog a few sixes and get the game wrapped up early. Simon didn't like that idea at all.

'No, Merv, when you get out there push the singles, and I'll give you the signal to start lifting the run rate,' he said, with a hint of annoyance in his voice.

Twenty minutes passed, and as many runs were scored, and in that time we heard more of Merv's batsmen scalpings and I copped a couple of Hulk Hogan headlocks. Then he turned to the captain again.

'Scoob, what do you reckon if I get out there, slog a few sixes for quick runs, we declare and then we knock them over and be on the piss celebrating tonight?'

SWERVE MERV

Being Merv's captain or coach must have been like Chinese water torture.

'Mate, I'm not sure you heard me last time,' Simon said. 'If you get out there, get your head down, work the ball around and I will give you a signal when to accelerate.' He was angry this time.

Eventually, a wicket fell. Paul 'Pistol' Reiffel had been run out after compiling a neat 34. Merv let me go, got up, grabbed his tree trunk of a bat and trod out to the crease. The score had us well placed at 7/473.

Tim May was bowling his off-spinners for South Australia, with the field spread to cut down our ever-increasing total. At the sight of Big Merv approaching, it spread even further. This left plenty of gaps for the singles and twos that the captain had ordered.

Merv took centre. There was air of expectancy from our dressing room, as we knew Merv had a natural attacking game, but our captain had told him to curb that. You may as well have asked him not to breathe.

Tim May strolled in and looped up a juicy off-spinner, and Merv swung himself off his feet as he tried to launch the ball to the moon. All he managed to do, however, was sky the ball high in the air, and he was caught by the always beautifully groomed Glenn Bishop. Out first ball for a duck.

With that, Simon O'Donnell banged his fists against our dressing-room windows, which do well not to break. 'What the fuck was that?' he yelled, and he started cursing Merv. He was, it is fair to say, a little upset.

Meanwhile, up the back of the room, us younger blokes were trying not to laugh – if one broke, we would all be gone. Warnie had the luxury of being next in, and he looked to be pissing himself all the way to the middle.

Merv walked off the field with his head down and his shoulders stooped, like a kid who knows he is in trouble.

Eventually, he put his hand up to open the dressing-room door, but before he could, Scoob had swung it open and given him a bake. 'What the fuck was that shot? I told you to put your head down and push the singles. What sort of example are you to our young blokes? What the fuck where you thinking?' (And that's the censored version . . .)

Merv looked up sheepishly and said, 'What – you never got a good ball early?'

※ ※ ※

As I mentioned earlier, quantity control wasn't one of Merv's strengths in jokeology. His theory was that if it was funny the first time, it'll be just as funny the 100th time.

We were once playing a charity game in Tasmania. The cricketing celebrities were Merv, Colin Miller, Zoe Goss (right after knocking over Brian Lara in another charity game) and Trevor Chappell.

Trevor was a lovely fella, but even years after the underarm incident he couldn't escape it. He batted away every enquiry about his infamous underarm delivery in a very dignified manner.

After the game, we were in the dressing room and all the locals were hovering around Merv, who was going through his whole list of jokes and stories. They were loving him. He had a quick shower and walked out with his towel around his midriff – looking a lot like Obelix drying himself off.

In front of the packed audience, he mimed spraying under his hairy armpits and yelled across the room to Trevor Chappell, 'Hey, Trev, have you got any underarm?'

There was a little pause, then everyone cracked up. Even Trevor had a little smirk.

SWERVE MERV

Then Merv's quantity vs quality dilemma started to kick in. 'Seriously, Trev, have you got any underarm?' He repeated this a few times over the next hour, to less and less laughter. Already people were dropping off.

Trev took it all with a great deal of grace. But every man has his breaking point.

At 2 a.m. in the Hobart casino bar, Merv trotted it out for the 43rd time. 'Seriously, Trev, have you got any underarm?'

'Right, that's it,' Trevor said. 'I've fucking had enough.' He got up and stormed out of the bar.

'What's his problem?' Merv enquired, oblivious to the carnage he had created.

* * *

Merv was a massive sledger on the field as well, of course. I reckon he was one of those players who needed to release the pressure on himself by unsettling the batsman with verbals. Mike Atherton said that whenever Merv sledged him, he couldn't understand too much – but he knew when the sledge had finished since Merv ended every sledge with the same word: 'Arsewipe!'

Merv was at his sledging best in 1993/94 at the MCG, during a match in which Greg Blewett played a blinder of an innings against our attack, which included Merv, Tony Dodemaide and me.

Blewy got to his first milestone, raising his bat to acknowledge his half-century. Merv walked up to him and said, 'Put down that bat, champ, that's the worst 50 I've ever seen at the MCG . . . Arsewipe.'

Blewy was a bit taken aback but he got on with the job and stroked his way to 100 – his first at the MCG. After raising his bat and helmet to the applause and admiration of his teammates, he turned around and found Merv waiting for him. 'Jeez, you're carrying on a bit, aren't you, considering that's the most embarrassing 100 I've ever witnessed . . . Arsewipe.'

Undaunted, Blewy continued to pass through milestone after milestone – 150, 200, 250 – and Merv was always there to let him know just how bad an innings he was playing.

Finally, he got out for 268 and was clapped off the ground. Who should be at the gate to see him off the field? It was the big man. We all knew Merv was a tough but fair man who appreciated great cricket. As he opened the gate for the fatigued Blewett, he shook his hand and said, 'That was the worst fucking 268 I've ever fucking seen at the MCG . . . Arsewipe.' This time with a big smirk on his face.

The next year the teams met again at the Adelaide Oval. On a very flat pitch, Blewy was facing a fired-up Merv. When Merv pitched short outside off stump, Blewy cut it to the fence like a tracer bullet. Merv followed through and stared at him from a metre away, furious, but he didn't say a word.

The next delivery was on the same line but fuller, and Blewy drove it through the covers for four. Again Merv followed through all the way down the pitch, staring daggers at the batsman. Blewy was waiting for the inevitable spray but Merv just glared at him and turned back to his bowling mark.

Merv charged in harder and bowled a fast bouncer, trying to dislodge Blewy's head, but the skinny South Australian was up to the task and hooked it to the square-leg fence for his third boundary in a row. When he looked up, Merv was face-to-face with him, slobbering like a Doberman. Blewy braced himself for a gobfull.

Merv looked at Blewy, then looked where the ball went, 80 metres away, and then looked back at Blewy. 'Fuck, you're good,' he said, and trod back to his mark.

Chapter 6
A Hot Dog Salute for Lord Sheffield

IN 1892 LORD Sheffield donated £150 to fund a trophy for an annual tournament between the three colonies of New South Wales, Victoria and South Australia, and this became the Sheffield Shield. In the early years, it seems, you could finish last and third in the same season!

A Polish immigrant named Phillip Blashki won the competition to design the silver shield trophy. Blashki was the first in a long list of Polish influences on Australian cricket, with one little flat spot – between 1892 and 1989, when Michael Kasprowicz debuted for Queensland.

The ladder leader at season's end took the title until 1982/83, when a Sheffield Shield final was finally introduced. Victoria first hosted a final in Melbourne in the summer of 1990/91, against their traditional rivals New South Wales. Anticipation was high for the Vics as, up to this stage, we had won as many finals as Papua New Guinea, who obviously didn't contest in the Sheffield Shield.

Day one of the 1990/91 Sheffield Shield final. No other sport has to bow so deeply to the weather gods, and it was bucketing down so hard in Melbourne that animals were starting to pair up. Both teams were missing their stars, as the Aussie team members were tanning themselves calypso-style in the West Indies at the time.

The experienced players knew not to stress out too much, so they immersed themselves into the regular poor weather routine of cards and cigarettes. I was a nervous 20-year-old in his first Shield final. I had my trusty Walkman on, trying to control my butterflies with some late 1980s hair metal like Def Leppard, Motley Crue and my new favourite band, Faith No More.

Another youngster Darren 'Chuck' Berry was (along with Craig McDermott) the most anal cricketer I ever played with. He was calming his nervous energy by organising his gear into specific groupings. Shirts had to be folded correctly, pants hung straight, and he was even labelling his socks 'left' and 'right'. Finally, the umpires popped their heads in to say the match was abandoned for the day.

The next morning, Simon O'Donnell, our TV glamour-boy captain, won the toss and without hesitation decided to bowl on a straw-coloured pitch that had been sweating under its covers for a couple of days. There was enough swing and seam to keep the ball up and let the pitch work its magic.

I relished the sweaty conditions early, snaffling the first three wickets – including Michael Bevan, who had just come off a 1000-run season as a 20-year-old – with the bowling dynamic duo of swing and his trusty sidekick seam. We did well to knock New South Wales over in the face of a fierce onslaught from the 36-year-old opener Steve Small, who was always a handful to bowl to.

Not unlike a young Phil Hughes, he possessed an unusual batting technique and tactics. He wasn't a big rap for defence, moving to square leg to open up his stumps. This invited the bowlers to zero in on his stumps, then he'd back his dead-fish eye and smash you through the off side. He did exactly this in the final, to the tune of a run-a-ball 82.

A HOT DOG SALUTE FOR LORD SHEFFIELD

Despite this, Tony Dodemaide, Simon O'Donnell, Paul 'Action' Jackson and I shared the wickets between us, bowling New South Wales out for 223.

Our innings began with our openers, Wayne Phillips and Gary 'Killer' Watts, walking out to face the New South Wales pace attack. Wattsy was the veteran of the team – although I am stunned to see now that he was only 32 years of age! He was a member of the Watts cricketing dynasty from Fitzroy, along with his brothers, Rod and Leigh.

Wattsy was one of the finest hookers and cutters in Australia at the time – he was absolutely dynamite square of the wicket. This made it all the more perplexing that his one mission in his last two years was to drive New South Wales paceman Wayne 'Cracka' Holdsworth though the covers every ball. Holdsworth's 90-mile-per-hour inswingers knocked over our nuggety left-hander five times in his last two years, and each time Killer walked off shaking his head in disbelief that he hadn't nailed that elusive cover drive. So it came as a surprise when the 200 centimetre goliath Phil Alley dismissed him at the other end, which triggered a massive batting collapse.

There is nothing like the fall of a cluster of wickets to cause a pall of silence over the dressing room as each batsman walks out to face the executioner. I remember watching our chunky boom recruit from South Australia, Darren 'Boof' Lehmann, walk out to bat. Boof was fortunate to play in the final, having needed facial surgery prior to the match after being struck in the nose during a training session. His droopy eye socket could have got him a part-time job in a haunted house scaring kids, but it was a brave effort all the same.

Like the cool Melbourne weather, not one Victorian batsman reached 30, and we were dismissed for a lacklustre 119. The fast, sliding outswingers of Holdsworth and the bounce and pace of Alley were too much for us.

New South Wales increased their lead early in their second innings, getting to 26 without loss by the end of the day. They progressed to 2/81 the next morning, and our chances of winning the match were as likely as me buying a Michael Bolton CD.

When your team is 185 runs behind with eight wickets in hand in a low-scoring game, you need players to rise to the occasion. That's what finals are all about. Our man was Tony Dodemaide. 'The Professional One' was revered for having the meticulous reliability of a bookkeeper in both his preparation and his trimmed moustache. His accounts were awry early in the season, as he missed three-quarters of our matches with injury, but he came back powerfully, bowling fast and getting his outswinger to move late. And he helped himself to a five-wicket haul to put his season's ledger in the black.

Future star horse-owner (then medium-pacer) Simon O'Donnell liked the look of the track, and he galloped in and claimed Michael Bevan dead in front lbw despite a protest from Bevo. Our best bowler of the summer, former carpenter Paul Reiffel, then 'chipped' in for a couple of wickets.

We started our second innings requiring 239 to win the match. We started badly – but not surprisingly – when Wattsy tried *another* ill-fated cover drive off Holdsworth and nicked one behind. Next in was our sporting prodigy, Geoff Parker, who had played VFL for Essendon at the tender age of 16 and state cricket at 17. Tragically, Parksy's sporting career peaked before he could legally drink or drive. He made up for the latter in his post-peak career, but today he's a non-drinking, Coke-guzzling development officer for Port Power in the AFL. He was knocked over cheaply to leave us at 2/27 and in dire trouble.

A HOT DOG SALUTE FOR LORD SHEFFIELD

By the close of play on day four, we had edged to 2/102, with Wayne 'Rowdy' Phillips on 41 and Jamie 'Spanner' Siddons on 42.

The VCA picked an unusual time for us to have our team photo the next morning. There was a fair bit of nervous tension around, and it was tough to get much of a smile out of us when we said 'Cheese'.

Well, if you can't stand the heat, get out of the kitchen, as they say, and one man who always looked like he needed a good feed was Wayne Phillips. Rowdy was the toughest Victorian cricketer I played with, possessing a sound technical game topped up by enormous courage.

In some ways, he was the complete opposite of Merv Hughes. While Merv was physically imposing, hairy, loud and the dressing-room pest, Rowdy was just five-foot-eight. Merv could have used him as a toothpick, and ET could have out-benchpressed him. But one thing they both had in abundance was physical courage.

And Rowdy used every inch of that, alongside our much-loved country boy Jamie Siddons, to get us home. As Rowdy played straight for his five-and-a-half-hour 91 not out, the flamboyant Siddons hooked, cut and cover-drove his way to a match-winning hundred. They put on 212 runs to take Victoria to its 25th Shield title – and its first for 13 years.

It was pure euphoria when the winning runs were hit. It had been a long nine-month slog to get to the final, and to turn a 100-run first-innings deficit around was incredible – especially since we had won the wooden spoon the previous two years.

Thousands of fans converged onto the MCG as we accepted the Shield and the celebrations started. We later progressed to the Silvers nightclub in Prahran, and the evening ended in classy fashion when we used our $50 drink cards at the infamous

BOWLOLOGY

Tunnel nightclub in the city. The night finished with a tasty 3 a.m. hotdog with 'Chuck' Berry.

Lord Sheffield would have been proud.

Chapter 7
Welcome to Harp's Nightmare

SPORTING TEAMS HAVE always prided themselves on playing hard on the field but also having a bit of fun off the field. One of the ways the Victorian cricket team used to lighten up the mood in the dressing room and on tour was known as 'the art of cranking' (also known as 'taking the piss', 'taking the mickey', 'winding someone up' or 'pulling someone's leg').

The Victorian teams were noted crankers. Merv Hughes, Paul Reiffel and co. loved nothing more than to get a teammate to respond to a question/statement that was sometimes true and fairly believable purely for the purpose of ridiculing his response. This become rife in the early 1990s, as teammates tried to catch each other responding to obvious leading questions. The US rapper MC Hammer was huge at the time with his song 'Can't Touch This', and instead of responding to a possible crank players would just say, 'Can't touch that.'

As teammates become wiser to potential cranks, we refined the art into what we called 'reverse cranking'. I would pair up with, say, Merv Hughes, and get Merv to say an obvious wind-up. Then I would gullibly answer his questions, and a third teammate – often our straight-down-the-line country boy Ian Wrigglesworth – would say, 'Merv, you really cranked Flem there,' oblivious to the fact that he was part of the reverse crank set-up from the start.

In hindsight, we really did have too much time on our hands when waiting to bat.

BOWLOLOGY

Things got so out of hand that some teammates were refusing to speak to each other in the dressing room for fear of being cranked. Our coach, Les Stillman, went to the extraordinary length of making Wriggles a 'protected species'. He was granted a crank-free status, which helped him start speaking in the rooms again.

At the start of one pre-season, Stillman tried to change the cranking culture by announcing at our first training session, 'Cranking is now banned within the squad.'

This comment met with a deafening silence, until Merv put his hand up.

'Yes, Merv?' Les asked.

'Les, was that a crank?'

The cranking ban was already over.

*　*　*

In the early 1990s, Bill Lawry was our cricket manager. Bill's mantra was that his 'door was always open' – which was a great sign of an open leadership management style, but unfortunately once you went through his door, he was never there! In hindsight, then, the following incident may have been a brilliant crank by Cricket Victoria that *all* the players fell for.

After being 12th man during a match in Sydney, I received a letter from Bill in the mail. The contents are shown on pages 51 and 52.

Victorian Cricket Association

President: Jack E. EDWARDS • Executive Director: K.W. JACOBS
"VCA House" 80 Jolimont Street, Jolimont, Vic. 3002 • Telephone: (03) 654 5511 • Facsimile: (03) 650 5896

16 November 1992

Mr Damien Fleming
Australian Cricket Board
90 Jolimont Street
Jolimont 3002

Dear Damien,

Please find enclosed an invoice regarding VCA cricket balls misplaced during the recent Victoria vs New South Wales Sheffield Shield Match.

As you are no doubt aware practise balls are the direct responsibility of the twelfth man during all matches. A total of 38 balls were supplied to the team for the match in Sydney. Only thirteen balls returned.

The executive committee have insisted on a retention rate of no less than 80% for each match during the season. Thirteen balls represents a total of 35%. The invoice relates to those balls lost. You may wish to ask the team for assistance in paying this invoice as I'm sure the loss was not totally your fault. However given the tough times the Association is facing the executive have asked us to take a harder line on wasteful expense and unfortunately they must make an example of this match.

If you have any queries regarding this matter please do not hesitate to call me.

Yours faithfully,

Bill Lawry.

RECEIVED 18 NOV 1992

EASTON
High Performance Sports Equipment

BOWLOLOGY

```
                VICTORIAN CRICKET ASSOCIATION
                    86 JOLIMONT STREET, JOLIMONT 3002
                         Telephone: 654 5511

                                              17 November  19 92

                                                        GENERAL
    To   Mr D Fleming
         A.C.B.
         90 Jolimont Street              INVOICE No.   2545
         JOLIMONT   VIC   3002

              VCA Cricket Balls

              25 misplaced match balls              $ 1,250  00



    E & O E                                 TOTAL   $ 1,250  00
```

I wasn't sure if this letter was serious or another crank, so I focused on the last paragraph where Bill suggested I get some help from my teammates in recovering the lost money. The next night at training at the Junction Oval I read the letter out, as well as a letter from me detailing the money owed by each player.

Dear Teammates,
I am not solely responsible for the missing balls as our cricket manager points out. So I have worked out each player's percentage of the $1250 they owe according to how much slogging they did in the nets and how many balls were thrown at them by myself at the ground after each day's play in my duties as 12th man.
Warne 18% = $225
Berry 15% = $187.50
Ayres, Lehman 12.5% = $156.25
O'Donnell, Jones 10% = $125
Phillips, Nobes, Dodemaide, Fleming 5% = $62.50
Hughes, Reiffel 1% = $12.50

WELCOME TO HARP'S NIGHTMARE

Regards

Flem

P.S. If you would like to discuss this with Bill you know his door is always Open!

It is fair to say a few noses were out of joint, others weren't sure if I was taking the piss or not.

I wasn't sure myself until a few days later when I heard no more from Bill Lawry. He'd cranked me. Anyway, there was no need to be defeated as there was always a better crank around the corner.

I didn't tell any of my teammates as they were avoiding me for fear they would have to give me the money they owed me. Cricketers are the tightest people on earth, but state cricketers are by far and away the worst. Moths were more likely to fly out of wallets then $20 bills.

* * *

At the next Sheffield Shield match, down in Tasmania, I was back in the team to bowl my outswingers. Our young Deniliquin-born left-hander Laurie Harper was the new 12th man. I was probably the only person who knew Harps well, so when we arrived at the Grand Chancellor Hotel in Hobart I wasn't surprised to find us rooming together. It was a smart move rooming the new player with someone he was comfortable with, which was a bonus for me as well: as the experienced player, I would get the double bed. It was a great start to a trip that was about to get even better.

Harps was a very conscientious individual and wanted to make a good impression, so in the elevator he asked me some questions about his role as 12th man. To be honest, the job still hadn't really progressed a long way from keeping the beers cold and running out the batsman's new gloves.

'Do they take the money out of your bank account for the lost cricket balls, or do you have to write them a cheque?' Harps enquired.

Now, I knew he played for the St Kilda Cricket Club – the home of noted crankers Warren Whiteside and Peter Cox. 'No, you have to write them a cheque,' I said, feeling the beginnings of a crank.

'How much again do the balls cost?' he asked.

'50 dollars per ball,' I told him.

'Mate, I'm on $12 a day Austudy – I can't afford that! I'm going to lose all my match payments . . . I won't eat this week,' he said, seriously stressed.

Shit, I've got a live one here, I thought. *He is bloody genuine! I can have a bit of fun with this.*

I didn't tell any of my teammates for fear of giving it away but sat back and watched what Harps would do. By the next day, 'HarperGate' was ready to be implemented.

At training I watched him count how many balls were in the bag. He was determined not to lose a single one. Now, that's like attempting to staple water to a tree – it's just *impossible* not to lose a ball on tour.

We started with a fielding session on the oval, and balls were flying everywhere. Harps was running himself ragged, chasing balls like a faithful dog. One minute he was chasing a ball over to the other side of the ground, and the next minute he was under the grandstand taking on spiders and snakes, then he was chasing the kids who were trying to flog some of our cricket balls.

The Victorian team members were very impressed with Harps, who continued chasing cricket balls with the energy of chocolate-addicted kids at an Easter egg hunt, but they were oblivious to his true financial motivation. Each ball was four weeks Austudy to the poor bugger.

WELCOME TO HARP'S NIGHTMARE

We finished the fielding session and walked over to the nets. 'Already lost four fucking balls – that's $200 bucks!' Harps said angrily.

Of course, our teammates were oblivious to what was going on, and they were having a usual net session, which meant slogging balls left, right and centre. Harps usually bowled a little slow-medium pace, but on this day he was charging in and trying to bowl as fast as he could. Even the coaches were surprised. 'He's bowling 15 kilometres an hour quicker!' Every ball launched out of our nets was like a dagger in his heart, as he weighed up the cost of battling the snake-infested scrub in the hope of saving himself some money.

'Fuck this – I'm going to bowl bodyline,' he said at last, cleverly noting the higher netting on the leg side of the right-handers.

'Gee, the 12thy is bending his back,' teammates were saying.

If they only knew.

Then our wicketkeeper, Darren Berry, launched a shot out of the nets and out of the whole practice facility. It went miles.

Now, until this stage Harps had not uttered a word. As a new player, you just don't want to bring attention to yourself. But the money debt volcano had been building, and he couldn't control it anymore. He began spewing Deniliquin-ese lava. 'Chuck!' he screamed. 'Any fucking chance of keeping the ball in the fucking nets?'

Training came to a screeching halt. The other players looked at Harps and shrugged their shoulders, rolling their eyes. Everyone was stunned by how passionate Harps' outburst was – none more so than Chuck.

I was pissing myself. This moment was close to the highlight of my cricket career at this stage.

'What's up with the 12thy?' I heard from a few teammates. 'Jeez, the 12thy's a bit uptight.'

By the time we finished training Harps looked like he had run a marathon in Madras. He was physically and mentally drained. In the dressing room he continued searching for cricket balls in every nook and cranny, much to his teammates' bemusement.

We drove back to the hotel in the team bus, and when Harps and I got up to our room he was frantic about how he was going to pay for the lost balls.

'Jesus Christ!' he moaned. 'Four hundred dollars' worth of balls gone! I'm going to owe money after my first fucking game.'

I saw the cuts and scratches all over his body – he was a beaten man. There was clearly no need to draw this out any further – it was a clear victory. ('He's gone!' Bill Lawry would have cried out if he was commentating.) So why I waited until the end of day three to break it to him, I'm not sure . . .

For the next two days Harps looked for the lost balls until he was exhausted. I noted he was developing what Vietnam veterans' term 'crawling': he was seeing balls flying from the nets that had not even been hit! His tertiary education money was slipping away – he soon wouldn't have to worry about his HECS debt because was amassing such a huge cricket ball debt that would put a small country out of business.

Back in our hotel room after day three, I came clean. 'Harps, you might not want to hear this, but Bill Lawry was *cranking* about the lost balls,' I said, casually flicking the TV remote. 'I didn't have to pay anything back.'

He stared at me with the look of that spooky kid from *The Sixth Sense*, and I wasn't sure if he was going to high-five me or hit me.

Eventually, the stingy uni student kicked in and the relief of saving so much money won out, and he came through with a high-five. 'You're a prick,' he gasped, 'but what a relief.' Later, over a beer (I paid), he added, 'Jeez, I was expecting a bit more support from my roommate in my first game.'

Chapter 8
'New Sensation' Debut with Supermodels

IN EARLY 1994 I was back home in my birth city of Perth with the Aussie cricket team on the eve of my one-day international debut against South Africa. My parents had owned a fish-and-chip shop in Bentley, a suburb of Perth, which they told me was up the classy end of Gosnells. (Adam Gilchrist tells me there's no such thing . . .)

Perth was generally a happy hunting ground for me over my career in Tests and Shield games. I really enjoyed playing at the WACA, with the 'Fremantle Doctor' breeze aiding my swinging deliveries. The parochial local media relished the fact that I'd been born in Perth; any time I got wickets they'd write: 'Western Australian–born fast bowler Damien Fleming (Man of the Match in the 1998/99 WACA Test vs England)'. If I didn't get wickets it was: 'Victorian medium-pacer Damien Fleming'.

I checked in at Perth's Hyatt Hotel and learned that Aussie rock legends INXS were playing in Perth, touring their latest album, *Full Moon, Dirty Hearts*. The first single from that album was 'The Gift', which was appropriate, as INXS – being huge cricket fans – had left the Australian team some merchandise bags full of goodies like T-shirts, hoodies and CDs. Better still, they'd offered us tickets to watch them in concert that night.

After a quick team meeting, we got a bus to the concert and rushed backstage to meet the band. I was talking to bassist Garry

BOWLOLOGY

Plenty of 'Swing' when INXS catch up with the Aussie cricket team.

Beers and mentioned how much I loved the tour's opening band, Urge Overkill, whose album *Saturation* was one of my prime CDs in 1993. Michael Hutchence happened to be walking past and said, 'Yeah, Urge Overkill rock, man!'

'Yeah,' I replied, 'they're *positively bleeding*' – a witty reference to *Saturation*'s first single.

Michael just stared at me blankly and walked off. I don't think he got the reference.

Still, I was pretty chuffed that I was probably the only cricketer – besides our team's own 'Suicide Blonde', Warnie – who spoke to Hutchence. I felt I had rock cred.

We got shuffled towards the concert, hoping for some good seats – only to find that we didn't actually have any seats, since we were *on the stage*, with eskies full of beers. We looked out at 40 000 screaming people.

My head was spinning the next day from this amazing rock experience, and I hadn't even begun my ODI debut for my country. I was realising my childhood dreams.

'NEW SENSATION' DEBUT WITH SUPERMODELS

We bowled first, and it's fair to say that, with a record WACA crowd watching on in intense heat, I ended up 'Melting in the Sun' (*The Swing*, track 2, 1984). In any debut game, it's important that you 'Don't Change' (*Shabooh Shoobah*, track 10, 1983) your routine. I should have known this.

1. I committed the 'Original Sin' (*The Swing*, track 1) of bowling in new boots that weren't worn in, and I was slipping around everywhere.
2. I was bowling from the wrong end for my outswingers, and the Fremantle Doctor now became my enemy pushing the ball to the batsman.
3. My worst moment almost came when Mark Waugh was bowling. I was in the circle for one batsman and then on the fence for the another, and Junior was rushing through his overs. As I was running from the circle to the boundary I heard an awful cry – 'Catch it!' I swivelled around but luckily the ball wasn't coming to me; if not, it would have been the most embarrassing moment and the end of my career.

So I trudged off the ground pretty disappointed with my efforts. We had our lunch, then got up to our 'viewing area' to support our batsman as they chased down South Africa's total. The viewing was top-class, but what served to 'Mystify' (*Kick*, track 10, 1987) us was that our viewing area was chock-full of supermodels!

The INXS boys had brought their wives and girlfriends to the cricket. Helena Christensen and her fellow rock WAGs were there, and it was mindboggling. That quickly took my mind off my bowling, and I thought, *Jeez, if this is the standard for international cricket – backstage passes and supermodels – then I'm in!*

Unfortunately, we collapsed with the bat. While I was batting, I edged an Alan Donald delivery into my pads and was given out lbw. I fought the urge to tell the umpire to 'shove it, brother' and had to 'Just Keep Walking' (*INXS*, track 3, 1980) completing a dismal day on the field. But it was still a quality day of viewing off the field.

My cricket career got going in the next ODI and I started taking wickets. We had plenty of rock bands grace our dressing rooms over the years, but there was a criminal lack of supermodels from then on.

Chapter 9
AB and Me

DENNIS LILLEE WAS my all-time cricketing idol for his charisma and his wicket-taking ability in all conditions, but my second-favourite cricketer was Alan Border. AB is criminally underrated in our cricket history, but he was an incredible captain and a man who led by steely example. His determination and concentration were superhuman. Thor had his hammer, and AB had his square cut. He also had a look that could kill a man on the other side of a brick wall. If he was cranky with you, life was not worth living. Strangely enough, he developed the nickname 'Captain Grumpy'.

I reckon that between 1984 and 1989 he was our only truly world-class Test match player. A lot of people forget that, back then, he had to play the West Indies every six months, with an attack containing Malcolm Marshall, Joel Garner, Curtly Ambrose, Courtney Walsh and co. This was the best bowling attack ever, and it lived by the motto: 'Kill the captain and the rest will die.' They were mean, they bowled 12 overs an hour, four

AB: ' I remember getting my overs wrong, with Warne and McGrath bowling out their 10 too early, so really Flem was my last resort.'

bouncers per over and offered a batsman three balls of driving length every session.

AB was the perfect captain for such a time. He didn't flinch, didn't give an inch. He was as tough as a cockroach and continued to average over 50 in that period. He began to have more team success after 1989, when Boon, Taylor, Jones and the Waugh twins came aboard to provide some batting support, and McDermott, Alderman, Reid, Hughes and Warne started to take wickets. It also helped to have the irrepressible and equally tough Ian Healy behind the stumps.

In 1994, I replaced the injured Craig McDermott for the one-dayers in South Africa, but I didn't look like playing a game. Basically, I was on a Contiki tour with the injured Merv Hughes. The pair of us spent a lot of time investigating the sports cafes in various towns.

Captain Grumpy had a massive presence in the group. He was our Don Corleone and had everyone's respect. Being a new player, I didn't know how to address him. Most of the team were calling him 'AB' or 'Pugsley', but I started with 'Mr Border', and I had tentatively progressed to 'Alan' by the later stages of the tour.

I was picked to play in Bloemfontein in a match that was a turning point for Australian cricket. Deano was dropped and promptly retired from international cricket, but there was more to come. We didn't know it at the time, but it was also Alan Border's last game of international cricket. And he was about to make me an offer I couldn't refuse.

We needed to win the game to tie the one-day series. What a time to learn that I would be bowling the last over – also known as the 'death over' – for Australia in a one-day match. I had done it for Victoria plenty of times over the previous four years so I had a fair bit of confidence. I loved the responsibility of containing or winning the game at the do-or-die stage.

AB AND ME

Death bowling really is an extreme sport and an adrenaline rush. You're walking on the wild side, with baying crowds, short boundaries and batsmen wielding tree trunks. I must admit, it's as big a rush as being in a Metallica mosh pit. You get the chance to play hero and build your reputation as a 'cool under pressure' bowler, which means your stocks can rise with your teammates and the selectors and fans alike.

The downside is that you might dribble out some short-of-a-length crap or waist-high full tosses that end up in another postcode. If you want to see what I mean, check YouTube for Mick Malone's last delivery to Wayne Daniel in an early World Series Cricket match at 'Arctic Park' and watch the ball being sent into orbit by the big West Indian. Or look up Allan Lamb smashing Bruce Reid for 17 runs in the last over to win another game.

It's also one of the few specialist positions in cricket. If I could be the best death bowler for Victoria, I knew I'd be a good chance to get the same job for Australia.

So, with three overs to go, AB, who was clearly aware of my excellent death bowling for Victoria over the past couple of years, threw the ball to me.

(A quote from AB: 'I remember getting my overs wrong, with Warne and McGrath bowling out their 10 too early, so really Flem was my last resort.')

My 48th over had been pretty good, but still it had gone for 10 runs, including a misfield for four and a French cut that also reached the boundary. That's the way things sometimes go in 50-over cricket.

I always liked to have at least eight runs to defend, but on this occasion South Africa only needed six so there was a bit of extra pressure to execute well. Tim Shaw and Dave Richardson were at the crease.

THE KEYS TO DEATH BOWLING

1. *Develop Your Skills*

To become more attractive to the selectors and the skipper, you have to show them skills that sparkle. With more skills, you have more ways to bowl dot balls or to dismiss batsmen.

You must be able to call on a bouncy stock ball, a toe-crushing yorker, and a fast and a slow bouncer. Several changes of pace are vital. Your off-spinning slower ball might be effective against left-handed batsman, as it turns away from their bat, but a right-hander might smoke you over cow corner for six. Leg-cutters, split-fingers and knuckle balls will be your friends in times of need.

2. *Practise Your Skills*

In archery, the archer has different cues for different targets, and so do most elite bowlers. Where you look while you deliver your stock ball might be totally different to where you look while you bowl your yorker. For my stock ball I looked at the sponsor's sign three-quarters of the way up off stump, but for my yorker I focused on the top of the bails. This helped me bring my length up fuller, and if I got reverse swing I was hoping to york leg stump.

Be proactive in creating match intensity at training. Grab your best batsman – think Bevan as opposed to McGrath – send him into the nets and create a scenario of the last couple of overs in a match. Set your fields and test your skills under pressure.

3. *In-Game Tactics*

When Tiger Woods has a big putt to win a major, do you think he wonders about what would happen if he misses? No way. It's the same with bowling at the death. You have to want the ball in your hand and enjoy the excitement of the moment.

AB AND ME

You should already have practised different game scenarios at training and therefore ruled out the chance of being surprised in the game. When you feel in control of the situation, your confidence rises and so do the chances of a good outcome. Elite sport is all about confidence. You need to keep the little man in your head happy.

Always work with your captain to get your field right, and to cut off potential boundaries. Don't worry so much about run targets, just plan to bowl the best ball you can. Take a couple of deep breaths, go through your pre-ball cues and back your skills and preparation.

Remember to continually upset a batsman's timing by subtly varying your velocity, moving the ball in the air or off the wicket. For spinners, adding more backspin or overspin or sidespin presents more variables that the batsman must consider.

The ever-alert Ian Healy noticed that I had really charged in during the previous over, and he told me I looked like I was over-striding. A quick check of my run-up showed that he was right – I had been running in from Glenn McGrath's bowling mark!

The last over progressed pretty well, and by the final ball South Africa still needed four runs to win. AB jogged over to me and said, 'Good luck, mate. Just execute your plan as best as you can.'

I was pumped up but I could sense something odd in the skipper's manner – there seemed to be a little extra emotion in his urging. Maybe he knew that the cricketing Grim Reaper was waiting for him in the dressing room. Or maybe he didn't think I was up to it and was cursing his own stupidity in bringing me on.

Anyway, sensing something big was riding on this, I knew I had to bowl the perfect delivery. Unfortunately, I let go a screaming full toss, but it proved to be pure genius as Richardson was so surprised that he only managed to noodle it away. We won by two runs.

It wasn't the best six balls I ever bowled at the death, but we got home. That set the precedent for me, and I generally bowled the last overs for the rest of my career.

The skipper was rapt. 'You fucking beauty, Flemo,' he said.

'Cheers . . . AB.'

I'd just called him AB for the first time and it felt great! Now I really felt part of the team. The seal had been broken, and soon I was throwing around 'ABs' like they were going out of style. I was now a *peer*.

We had our tour celebration at an Irish pub with plenty of beers and exotic spirits. Unfortunately for us, it also had a karaoke machine, which was used and abused by most of my teammates. To be fair, Michael Slater did a couple of reasonable Elvis Presley covers. A few boys sang 'You're so Vain (Shane)', an ode to Warnie, which was pretty funny.

I relaxed enough to socialise a bit, particularly with the legendary AB. Everyone was having a good time, and I thought I'd test my new relationship out a bit.

'AB, seriously,' I said, 'any chance of you getting your hands out of your pockets and buying us a beer?'

He looked a bit taken aback but he did go to the bar.

We were equals!

That didn't last long, however, because the great AB retired just before our 1994 tour of Pakistan. He became a selector, so I quickly reverted back to addressing him as 'Mr Border'. Needless to say, it was me buying the drinks from then on.

Chapter 10
Tubby Ruins a Test Debut Hat-trick

MY CHILDHOOD DREAM was finally coming true when I got an invitation to become Australian Test player number 361 in the Second Test of our 1994 tour of Pakistan. Glenn McGrath had torn his quad muscle in the First Test, which we lost by one wicket, thanks to an amazing 98-run partnership between Inzamam-ul-Haq and Mushtaq Ahmed (and a very unlikely missed stumping by Ian Healy).

I admit that my dream usually had my Test debut taking place on a green seamer at Lord's, or on a perfect swinging day in Perth – or, better still, on my home turf at the MCG in front of 80 000 fans. But no, I was debuting on a flat pitch in the thriving metropolis of Rawalpindi, a city near Islamabad, the capital of Pakistan. In fact, Osama bin Laden was later found and killed about 135 kilometres away from Rawalpindi – which, freakily, was about my average bowling speed throughout my career.

I must admit, I didn't know a lot about Pakistan before the tour. Sure, women loved their former superstar all-rounder Imran Khan, and they had some great players like Waqar Younis, Wasim Akram and Salim Malik in their team, but my knowledge of Pakistan the country was a bit like my knowledge of . . . something I have no knowledge of.

On the flight there, I overheard some horror stories told about the previous tour to Pakistan, in 1988, during which the talented batsman Jamie Siddons contracted a food bug from some dodgy seafood and was sick for the next 18 months (and never played Test cricket for Australia).

There was an even more disturbing story from the 1988 tour. In the Third Test, the Aussies were trying to get a breakthrough. A lot of lbws were given not out (it was a time before neutral umpires).

Finally, Tim May spun one through Pakistan's gun batsman, Javed Miandad, who ran down the pitch and missed it, then Heals neatly stumped him. The Australian team ran up to Maysy to congratulate him, then all reeled away.

'Maysy, have you shit yourself?' Alan Border asked in disbelief.

'Yep,' came the reply.

'Well, get off the ground!'

'Nuh,' Maysy replied. 'I shit myself three overs ago and it's dried up now.'

It was true that in Pakistan I got a lot more runs off the field them I did on it. In fact, that was not hard, as I didn't bat once on the entire 10-week tour!

A GUIDE TO PAKISTAN FOR AUSSIE CRICKETERS

If you get magically transported back in time to the 1994 Australian tour of Pakistan, here are some top tips to get you through:

- *Alcohol*: The Britpop band Oasis might have been singing about 'Cigarettes and Alcohol' around this time, but they obviously hadn't toured Pakistan. Their song 'The Importance of Being Idle' would have been more appropriate. Pakistan is a military dry state – it was easier to get a submarine-launched ballistic missile than it was to get an ice-cold beer! In some hotels,

TUBBY RUINS A TEST DEBUT HAT-TRICK

if you signed in as an alcoholic they would serve you alcohol, which was a bonus. And you didn't have to go to all their meetings or follow the seven steps. I don't know the stats, but David Boon always seemed to get runs in those games. I cunningly packed a bottle of Bundaberg Rum in my cricket coffin to sip through the tour, but unfortunately it leaked on the trip over. So not only did I have to find some new whites to wear in Pakistan, for the rest of the tour I could smell the Bundy but couldn't drink any of it.

- *Pubs and nightclubs*: These were part of an Aussie cricketer's routine when playing at home, and we held drink cards like badges of honour. In Pakistan, there was no chance of being knocked back by a 'door bitch' for having inappropriate attire as there weren't any nightclubs or pubs.
- *Women*: Females in Pakistan were like a botched CIA plan — covered up — but unlike botched CIA plans, there were not that many of them.
- *Diet*: Only bottled water for drinking and brushing your teeth, and no ice cubes in your drinks or your water pistol. No salads — and if you 'seafood', don't eat it.
- *Fast food*: Back then, I wasn't exactly a worldly young man so I didn't know about the western world, the developing world or the third world. In my mind, there was only one distinction between countries: those that had McDonald's and those that didn't. For me, McDonald's symbolised music, movies and commercialism — basically, fun. Pakistan didn't have a McDonald's.
- *Movies*: The only thing more lacking than the nightlife in Pakistan in 1994 was the day life. We spent a lot of time in the 'team room' having a few beers, playing cards and watching videos. Comedy movies dominated the VCR and always lifted team morale on subcontinental tours. Quotes from *Dumb and*

Dumber, There's Something About Mary, Austin Powers and so on — on and off the field — created a good team vibe.

Comedy movies have always had a big influence on me. I remember as a very young boy my parents, Di and Ian, coming home and telling me about the Black Knight scene – 'None shall pass!' – from *Monty Python and the Holy Grail*. I think that changed my life.

Glenn McGrath reckons I don't actually have my *own* personality. Instead, I'm a comedy movie Frankenstein, he says, with my personality made up of different bits of Ace Ventura, Austin Powers and Ford Fairlaine and co. (Note to self: return Pigeon's Andrew Dice Clay CD.) I reckon he's right. (Let's hope I stick to comedies and not movies like *Natural Born Killers* or *American Psycho*.)

Our comedy movie preparations weren't great, however, and I was the only one to bring a movie on the tour – *Ace Ventura: Pet Detective*. (Mark Taylor says that's the reason they gave me a Test.) We must have watched it 50 times through the tour. I thought I was him so much that Ian Healy still calls me 'Ace'.

✷ ✷ ✷

Anyway, I accepted my invitation to become Australian Test player number 361 and we batted first. Pakistan had an awesome attack, led by Wasim Akram and Waqar Younis, who were damaging batsmen's batting averages and toes with fast, reversing, swinging full balls.

As was generally the case with Pakistani cricket, however, the team was in turmoil and contained eight past, current and future captains in its line-up. Wasim and Waqar weren't communicating with each other at this time, as each felt that the other had shafted him over the captaincy. Like a scene from the movie *Step Brothers*, Wasim and Waqar communicated through their captain, Salim Malik. Even more bizarrely, they refused to field off each other's bowling unless the ball came directly to them. A metre either way and it was four!

We batted first, and thanks to a brilliant 110 from Michael Slater and 50s from the Waugh twins, Heals and Michael Bevan, we made an imposing 9/521 and I wasn't required to bat. A shame really. I felt in great form and reckon we could have pushed on to, say, 10/522.

Late on the second day, then, I was feeling plenty of nerves as I ran in to bowl for the first time in Test cricket – particularly when Aamir Sohail and Saeed Anwar tried to chase down the total that night. Sohail and Anwar were both ultra-attacking players, and it was a real eye-opener for me to see the way they attacked the bowling. Anwar, in particular, was in the top tier of batsman that I bowled to. He rarely resorted to defence, and a good length ball could be driven or pulled or cut, such was his wonderful eye and quick handspeed.

I must admit, I was a bit shell-shocked that first night. But I had a good chat to our coach, Bob Simpson, who was very positive. It fair to say I didn't have a lot in common with Simmo due to the gap in our ages, but cricket-wise he was the best coach I played under. He was his own cricket computer: he watched a lot of matches and got to know your game very well. He also tried to improve your game, which in my case mainly meant fielding and batting. He was a very good technical coach and also good at role definition.

His pep talk helped, and the next morning Craig McDermott and I ripped through the Pakistan batting line-up, picking up four wickets each. I had a few dropped catches, but the inswinger that knocked over Sohail's stumps more than made up for them.

Getting four wickets really gave me confidence. *Hey, maybe I'm up to the level*, I thought.

After knocking Pakistan over for 260, we sent them in again. They had to make another 262 runs for us to bat again, while we had two and half days to bowl them out and get some retribution for our First Test loss.

Fast-forward 48 hours and we were still bowling, and the Test was heading for a boring draw. By then Pakistan was 2/336 and their batsmen were smashing our attack to all parts of the ground. Their captain, Salim Malik, was batting like a man possessed and we were at long odds to get him out. He was a fine batsman, but was later banned for life for match-fixing and spot-fixing.

The day-five pitch was now as flat as a pancake, and we were dishing up syrupy bowling. And the heat was stifling. I had only one more goal in my Test debut, and that was to not bowl *another* ball on my Test debut.

I somehow avoided Mark Taylor's gaze for a good couple of hours. If I thought he was looking towards me, I would try to be tying my shoelaces or interacting with the few spectators that were at the ground. A bit like waiters in those modern restaurants who have turned avoiding eye contact into an art form.

Finally Tubby tried to talk me around with some clever leadership psychology.

TUBBY RUINS A TEST DEBUT HAT-TRICK

Tubby: You're bowling.
Fleming: Sorry, you talking to me?

With that he threw me a piece of tattered leather and assured me it was the ball. Softer than a marshmallow (the ball not me).

Tubby was the best captain I played under, always remaining composed and unflappable. Although he'd made a pair in the First Test of this tour – his first Test as skipper – he didn't change his demeanour at all, keeping us focused on winning the game and captaining the best he could. Sometimes he might have been having a bad day off the field, but he just stood at first slip and chewed his gum with positive body language, and made clever bowling and fielding changes. Like all great leaders, he gave you confidence that he was always in control of himself and the situation.

He was his own man as well. I remember our old coach Geoff 'Swampy' Marsh saying with admiration that during Tubby's great batting slump, Swamp would offer to face a press conference on his behalf, but Tubby always said it was his responsibility, whether he'd had a good or bad day. He had real character (which is more than you can say for his dress sense; more about that later).

Like our next captain, Steve Waugh, I really appreciated the definition he gave to players' roles, which gave you a lot of confidence – firstly, that you had a role in the team, and secondly, that you were clear to prepare that role and plan to execute it in the game. For example, in one-day cricket Tubby always emphasised to me that I should maximise my ability to swing the ball and get early wickets. I didn't have to be too concerned about the run rate, as long as I was getting driven and my bowling was full enough to let the ball swing.

Tubby gave me some great advice during that tour to Pakistan in 1994. I was a bit paranoid about what I ate as I didn't want a dodgy belly. Tubby mentioned to me one night at a team dinner that he drank six beers a night and had never been crook on the subcontinent.

What a great idea, I thought. *The beer probably kills all the food bugs and you're safe!* Great advice from a truly health-conscience athlete.

However, I watched Tubby for the next few years and noticed that he drank six beers a night *every* night, whether we were in England, Pakistan, the West Indies or India. So he wasn't drinking beer to kill any food bugs, he was just a pisspot!

Anyway, after Tubby threw the ball to me I bowled a couple of maiden overs. Then, on the fifth ball of my third over, I ran in to bowl to Aamer Malik (no relative of Salim). I'm pretty sure this was Aamer's last Test match (although he didn't know it yet), so as I ran in to bowl, he was very much in the *twilight* of his Test career.

I pitched the ball on middle stump, hoping to draw Aamer into a drive and swing it away to get a nick to Heals. But the ball didn't swing and ended up being a half-volley on leg stump, which he hit straight to Michael Bevan at square leg, who duly took the catch.

You beauty! I had 1/81 and Pakistan was 4/469. We might even get off the ground this session!

The next Pakistan batsman was the slowest-walking incoming batsman in the history of cricket. It was Inzamam-ul-Haq. All the Aussies had aged a few years by the time Inzy marked centre.

Although he was a non-drinker, Inzy always walked out to bat as if he was suffering from a massive hangover, and he ran

INZAMAM-UL-HAQ

Talking about Inzy, he provided one of the best one-liners I ever heard on a cricket field.

In the build-up to a series, Glenn McGrath and Shane Warne liked to target top-class opposition batsman like Michael Atherton, Brian Lara, Sachin Tendulkar and co., in order to provide a bit of publicity for the series and also to show a bit of intimidation.

It's a little-known fact that I used to target batsman as well. I was a bit more conservative with my targets, however. I chose tailenders like Phil Tufnell, Devon Malcolm and Allan Mullally.

Anyway, in a press conference before a series against Pakistan, an Australian pressman asked Inzy what he felt about Glenn McGrath targeting him during the series.

Inzy's response was: 'Isn't that what bowlers do?'

Gold!

---

between the wickets like he was fucking smashed. But he was as powerful a timer of the ball as I had ever played against.

I knew he wasn't always the finest starter early in his innings so I decided to bowl a quicker yorker, hoping to deceive the so-called 'King of Multan'. It wasn't a perfect yorker but it was quick and full, and it hit Inzamam on his pads dead in front of his stumps. I turned to appeal and the *neutral* umpire's finger went up. Inzy was on his way.

I was on a hat-trick – and I was the first Australian to get a lbw in Pakistan!

The only thing slower then Inzy's walk to the crease was his walk from the crease. Play continued for half an hour before Inzy was completely off the ground.

So, I was a Test hat-trick on debut! It was the end of my over, however, and then we took a drinks break. And because there was now no chance of a result, there was no urgency as we lazed on the field. Gradually, the tea break turned into a shortened lunch break.

I knew there was one big factor in me getting this hat-trick: I didn't want to bowl to Salim Malik, who was on 236 not out and was seeing them like beach balls. I wanted to bowl my hat-trick ball to Rashid Latif, the incoming batsman, who hadn't faced a ball. I needed the bowler at the other end to bowl a maiden to Salim so I could have a crack at Rashid.

Big Jo Angel was bowling at the other end. He was a giant, big-hearted fast bowler who took hundreds of wickets for Western Australia but played only a few Tests for Australia. He was also a loveable guy who used to wear his Aussie rock tour T-shirts around with pride, but in life he could sometimes get caught between FM and AM radio, if you know what I mean.

During the tour, for instance, our team was invited to a BBQ and beers with one of Pakistan's top officials, and we jumped at the chance. At the end of the night, Mark Waugh, Tim May, Jo and I were joined by some of the keener cricketing guests, who hovered around us, keen to know what was happening to some of their favourite former players.

One guy enquired about 'big, fiery Merv Hughes'. I told him that Merv had missed the tour with a knee injury but was keen to keep playing and get back in the team.

'What about Deano? Dean Jones, where is he?'

I responded that he was still scoring a mountain of runs for Victoria.

Then another guy asked about his favourite player: the 'Big Whit', Mike Whitney.

Mark Waugh told the guy that Whit had retired but was now a celebrity on TV – and that he'd also had some good news lately. Whit and his wife had gone on the IVF program and had recently had triplets. Mark said, 'He's actually the only Test cricketer to get a hat-trick with two balls!'

Everyone roared with laughter – except Jo. He was actually trying to work out how Whit had got his hat-trick with two balls!

***

Back to the Test. Big Joey bowled five beautiful deliveries to Salim outside off stump, and he couldn't score. On his last ball, however, he pitched on leg stump and Salim leg-glanced his 237rd run down to me at fine leg, thus retaining the strike.

Shit! There goes my hat-trick, I thought.

As I got ready to bowl, Tubby came up to me and asked what I wanted for my hat-trick ball.

'Let's jazz it up a little bit,' I said. 'Get a few slips in place, and a gully, and get Boony back in his helmet and under Salim's nose.'

If someone had wandered into the stadium, seen that the score was 5/478 and then looked at our field – four slips, a gully and bat-pad – he would have thought, 'What the hell is going on here?!'

Before I ran in for the hat-trick ball, for some ungodly reason I turned to Craig 'Billy' McDermott at mid-on and said, 'Billy, Salim doesn't know it yet but he's going to be part of history.' Not even Arnie Schwarzenegger has said a cheesier line then that.

I had actually taken many hat-tricks in underage cricket for Springvale South, in school cricket and for South Melbourne firsts. I'd even taken one in my first 'Youth Test', against the West Indies in Jamaica in 1990. I knew I had to bowl it full and fast to make Salim play.

Usually when you are on the verge of taking a hat-trick, it's against a batsman facing his first ball. I momentarily reflected that there wouldn't have been too many taken when the third batsman was on 237!

Finally, I got into my shortened run-up and released the ball. It started gun-barrel straight, then landed on a good length that caught Salim on the crease. Then it ever so slightly shaped away, and Salim nicked it through to Heals behind the stumps.

The next minute I was getting bench-pressed in the air by big Jo Angel. I had a hat-trick on debut! I didn't know it at the time but I was the first Australian to take a hat-trick on Test debut, which was a huge honour considering the previous 360 Australian players who had basically failed to achieve this feat, including in no particularly order here Ray Lindwall, Denis Lillee, Glenn McGrath and Ian Healy!

After this massive high, however, the cricketing gods showed me exactly how cruel they could be. Within an hour, I was brought crushingly back down to earth when Mark Taylor and then Michael Slater took Test wickets, totally devaluing my earlier hat-trick. It was the lowlight of my cricketing career – and, some would say, the lowest day in Test cricket history.

Mark Taylor had the worst bowling action I saw in any cricket. And that includes John Howard and the bloke who played Harold Larwood in the *Bodyline* series on TV. He had two styles, actually: right-arm extra-slow drifters, and right-arm wrist-spin. Following is my comparison of his bowling action with that of leg-spinning great Shane Warne.

TUBBY RUINS A TEST DEBUT HAT-TRICK

I expected the elation after dismissing Salim Malik for my hat-trick on Test debut. I didn't expect this to be followed by Jo Angel slam dunking me WWF-style.

BOWLOLOGY

	Warnie	*Tubby*
Run-up	Short but flowing and powerful	Stuttering, no momentum
Action	Side-on, momentum going to the target	Mixed action, body parts going away from the target
Release	Strong wrist ripping leg-spinners	Limp wrist floating the ball out
Result	Gatting ball	Harmison ball

Whenever a Test is snoozing towards a draw, you see, part-timers and casual bowlers have a trundle. So when Tubby brought himself on to bowl there were no complaints. We just wanted to get off the field. He started his run-up (sorry, *stutter-up*), barely got through his action and shot-putted a warped leg-spinner down the pitch.

Because of his lack of momentum through the crease, the ball barely reached halfway down the pitch. I was wondering whether Tubby might run down and grab the ball and bowl it again. It was that slow I swear I saw the ball yawn!

The batsman, Rashid Latif, pulled the short half-tracker straight to Michael Bevan on the leg side. I reckon Bevo had time to drop it but he didn't. And the only defence I would allow Rashid was that he might have fallen asleep by the time Tubby's ball got to him.

'Excuse me, Flemo, I think you will find that magnificent delivery was my cleverly disguised zooter ball!'

TUBBY RUINS A TEST DEBUT HAT-TRICK

So Mark 'Tubby' Taylor had just got his first Test wicket. He quickly stopped bowling so he could keep his figures to an impressive three overs, one wicket for 11 runs, including a maiden.

Slats then grabbed the new ball and caught Waqar Younis on the crease lbw. For me, it was like watching a horror movie car crash. Even now, it's hard to reflect the utter disappointment I feel, and Waqar Younis and Rashid Latif must be held accountable.

At the end of their careers, Tubby's Test bowling average was 26, while Slats' was 10! And, years later, when Salim Malik was banned for life for match-fixing and spot-fixing, some boys did mention they thought they saw him running off punching the air like he'd won something when I dismissed him, and questioned me 'Do you reckon you *really* took a Test hat-trick?'

I tell you what, I fucking well did take it!

But to Tubby, the best captain I played under, but who selfishly bowled himself and then also had the audacity to take a wicket and thus call my hat-trick into question, all I can say is this: 'As Ace Ventura would say, on that occasion, Tubby, you were a "Looo-hooo-zuh-her!"'

'Looo-hooo-zuh-her!'

Indian cricket fans are fanatical about their cricket heroes, knowing every tiny detail of their heroes' lives. Pakistani fans, however... check out Shane Warne and our quick Meck Garth.

1994 Pakistan vs Australia tour booklet player bios

Robertson

Robo, the team's poet. Brought quotes like, 'Hats off, lads,' after a good session; 'Swim between the flags,' when we needed to settle down a bit.

Mecdermott
One day	-	117
Runs	-	49
Ave	-	7.35
Catch	-	
Wkts.	-	172
100's !	-	Nil
50's !	-	Nil
H.S	-	37

Billy, the greatest red-haired Aussie quick.

Mark Taylor
One day	-	60
Runs	-	1798
Ave.	-	13.45
Catches	-	73
100's !	-	Nil
50's !	-	16
H. S	-	94

Our skipper, averaging an impressive 13.45

Shane Warne
One day	-	25
Runs	-	140
Ave.	-	16.66
Catch	-	19
Wkts.	-	51
50's !	-	1
H.S	-	55

Warnie in his dark-brown-hair phase.

S. Waugh
One day	-	170
Runs	-	3454
Ave.	-	30.56
Catch	-	58
100's !	-	Nil
50's !	-	16
Wkts.	-	157
H.S	-	86

The Iceman.

Michael Bevan
One day	-	6
Runs	-	174
Ave.	-	58.00
Catch	-	2
Wkts.	-	Nil

Bevo looking a lot like a future Channel Nine cricket commentator.

Langer

One day	-	4
Runs	-	65
Ave	-	32.50
Catch	-	1
H.S	-	36

A lanky Justin Langer.

Meck Garth

Combining two former Aussie greats, Ian Meckiff and Graham 'Garth' McKenzie. Both not on this tour.

Jo - Angel

One day	-	1
Runs	-	Nil
Wkts	-	1
Catches	-	Nil

Giant-hearted quick whose bowling manta was 'Hip to heart', which he later released as a single.

Timothy May

One day	-	35
Runs	-	36
Ave.	-	9.00
Catches	-	1
Wkts.	-	26
H.S	-	15

Maysy my tour roomy. A tour marred by match-fixing allegations, with Salim Malik offering $200,000 to Maysy and Warnie to bowl poorly. Maysy's classic response: 'Imagine offering me $200,000 to bowl shit. I bowl shit anyway!'

Fleming

One day	-	4
Runs	-	65
Ave.	-	32.50
Catch	-	1
H.S	-	36

Happy with my batting average. Wouldn't mind the wickets of the bloke in ths photo.

S. Waugh & Mark Tailor

Tour leaders Tugga Waugh and Tubby Tailor, who did some handy clothing repairs on tour.

Chapter 11
Slats the Matchwinner and Juniorisms

AFTER MY DEBUT Test, my shoulder flared up in a one-day game in Multan and I missed the Third Test in Lahore – which, as Greg Baum wrote, 'set the pattern for his career'. I had missed virtually a whole season when I was 16 thanks to a shoulder complaint similar to this one, but no one at the time could really diagnose what was wrong.

I didn't have any discomfort in my shoulder again until I was 23, just before I was picked for the Australian one-day team. I had just completed my first season of league cricket in England, and perhaps the volume of deliveries and my predisposed lax joints meant I overstretched the ligaments.

Before my shoulder reconstruction, I actually used to feel my right shoulder stretch slightly when I bowled my quick deliveries – a bit like Mr Fantastic from the Fantastic Four. I didn't mind as I felt it gave me more leverage to catapult the ball with extra pace. But I was stretching the ligaments past their limit and doing damage, and eventually my shoulder didn't snap back, which was not all that fantastic.

As we entered the home series against England in 1994/95, I was advised that I urgently needed surgery but I decided to back myself. I'd worked hard to get here. Even though I'd only played seven days on the Pakistan tour, I'd had a good debut Test and was the leading wicket-taker in the one-day series. It was too hard to take a break now.

For the First Test against England, played at the Gabba, I was 12th man. Our brains trust thought England was vulnerable to off spin, and with memories of the 'spin twins' creating havoc on the 1993 Ashes tour, they picked both Shane Warne and Tim May. Craig McDermott and Glenn McGrath formed the pace attack.

I might not have been on the field, but I had the best seat in the house to witness Michael Slater and Mark Waugh at their classic best – in slightly different ways.

It was a beautiful morning for Test cricket, with the sun shining and the England team brimming with optimism as they took the field. They wanted a crack at the Aussies and were hoping that our nervous batsmen might make a mess of the first session. Phil DeFreitas took the new ball and stood at the top of his mark. At the other end, young Michael Slater took block and looked up, ready to start just his second Ashes series.

DeFreitas was no doubt planning to get the new ball up on a full length, give it plenty of time to swing and hope that Slater's eyes lit up. Then, if all went to plan, the keeper and the slips cordon would accept an outside edge.

There was a lot riding on this first session. England's coach, Keith 'Gnome' Fletcher, had been talking up the Poms' pace attack in the lead-up to the game. But the England players were having about as much luck as one of their backpackers in a Bondi rip. Alec Stewart broke a finger in practice, Shaun Udal broke a thumb, and then Devon Malcolm got chickenpox a couple of days out from the Test. You had to feel sorry for the poor bastards . . . well, in public, at least.

In fact, things were about to get worse. The ever-aggressive Slater wanted the ball like his height – short – and his chest size – wide. He loved to free his arms and cut through the off side. As it turned out, he got exactly what he wanted with the first delivery, which he crashed through the off side for four. A nightmare start for the Poms.

With every ball and every boundary, you could see English shoulders droop. Their supporters were so quiet that you could hear a chin drop. 'Here we go again . . .'

Sure enough, England lost the first battle, and their resolve was swept away like the aforementioned backpacker. Thanks for coming. It was typical counterattacking by Slater, who was at his best when he set the tone early. He had belted a furious 176 by end of day one, helping Australia to 4/329. Just three sessions, but it already felt like the series was over. And that was only the first instalment of the day's entertainment.

Mark Waugh is one of the funniest men I have ever met. Like Jim Carrey's character in *Liar Liar*, he can't sit on the fence, and he instinctively and sometimes naively says exactly what is on his mind without a thought for the consequences. This provided some golden moments in the dressing room, and to this day in the Fox Sports commentary box.

Come to think of it, Junior's compulsion to say the first thing that came into his head was a little bit like the reflex that made Slats swipe at anything wide of off stump. Both actions were fraught with danger and could often be as calamitous as they were entertaining.

Junior was at his best in the Gabba Test of 1994/95. In our second innings we were 398 runs ahead. Steve's little brother came to the wicket hoping to join in, but was getting frustrated by Phil Tufnell's tactics of bowling into the rough outside his leg stump. It was a negative approach, and Junior's game was all about entertaining and giving the paying public something to cheer about. He certainly didn't think much of this English trick, and was probably bored more quickly by it than the youngsters in the outer.

In attempting to liven up proceedings, Junior played an outlandish reverse sweep, which he guided straight into his stumps. He was out for 15, and his 140 in the first innings had been erased in a moment. Critics have a short memory.

Outrage broke out in our dressing room. His tenacious brother Steve muttered, 'What sort of shot is that? It's a bloody Test match!' He added a few expletives as he donned his helmet to walk out to bat.

Junior's shot was like a live-action horror movie – it was *Texas Chainsaw Massacre* on replay, getting worse with every viewing. Our captain, Mark Taylor, watched a replay with the wide-eyed expression of a passer-by at a car crash, then slowly shook his head. The younger players were huddled up at the back of the dressing room, trying not to break out laughing. We were all anticipating the inevitable spray Junior would get from our bemused captain – and we were looking forward to witnessing the fireworks.

Junior finally reached the dressing room. He walked straight over to the television, had a look at the reply and moaned, 'How unlucky am I?'

That did it and we all cracked up laughing. Even the horrified Tubby found it funny, but he soon wiped the smile from his face and replaced it with that disappointed dad look. (It's this homely, caring nature that today makes him one of Australia's great air-conditioner salesmen.)

'Have you ever played the reverse sweep in a game before?' he asked.

'No,' Junior replied.

'What about at training?'

'No,' Mark said. He was incapable of telling anything but the truth when he was put on the spot like this.

'Well, do you think it's a high-percentage shot to play in the first Ashes Test match of the summer?' Taylor asked.

'Settle down,' Junior said. 'Tufnell was boring me – and anyway, how many more runs do you want us to get before you declare?'

You had to hand it to the younger Waugh. In his mind, it was the captain's fault for making him go out and bat when the game was all but won. He is a unique character, although I suspect that if you were his defence lawyer you would advise him not to take the stand in a trial.

We did eventually declare, and thanks to Warnie's mesmerising 8/71 we were soon 1–0 up in the series. Back in the dressing room, as we sang our victory song – 'Beneath the Southern Cross I Stand' – Junior was still blaming Tubby for not declaring earlier.

Chapter 12
Boxing Day with Billy, Warnie and Boony

ON 26 DECEMBER 1994, I walked out to bat for the first time for Australia in a Test match. It was early on the second day of the Boxing Day Test match against England. Hearing my name announced as I walked out to bat, and getting a massive roar from the 51620-strong Victorian crowd, was a magic moment. Hearing it announced when I walked out to bat at number 11 did take a bit of the magic off! But to be fair, I was only batting at number 11 because Glenn McGrath was 12th man (and averaging a paltry 2.14 runs per innings at this stage in his career).

The adrenaline was flowing, and I was pumped to slog the Pommy bowlers all round the MCG. But it's a long walk out to the middle, and the further I walked, the more indecision entered my mind.

What if I trip over my feet right now?

What if I get a first-ball duck in my first bat for Australia in a Test match?

Why don't the Waugh twins talk to each other?

Somehow, I got to the batting crease, asked for centre and took block to Phil 'Daffy' DeFreitas. He pitched my first ball onto my pads and I whipped it away for two through square leg. *You beauty*, I thought. *I can't make a duck so I'm definitely going to start slogging now.*

My batting partner was the Iceman, Steve Waugh, who had compiled 78 runs by this stage. He gave me a nod of reassurance, which gave me extra confidence. Later I realised that Steve just used to nod a lot, whatever the situation.

Mostly I was playing and missing like an out-of-form baseball slugger, but I managed to hit a couple of fours off Darren Gough and Devon Malcolm. As my confidence lifted, so did my estimations of my batting talent – so much so that I attempted an adventurous hook shot off the express pace of Malcolm and gloved it through to Steve Rhodes, England's wicketkeeper. The Englishman appealed and I started to walk – then a Vincent Price–like voice in my head said, 'Stay!'

So I waited for the umpire's decision. (Sorry, Gilly!)

Steve Bucknor, the West Indian umpire, looked like he'd just awoken from a siesta and took his time to make his decision. After a while he adjudged me not out!

I was relieved at first, then I thought about the possible consequences. The year before, in a game for Victoria against the South Africans, I had been given not out in a similar situation and they had sledged me for the next couple of hours – and at a function later that night. They left me in no doubt that they played the game hard and tough.

The end of the over arrived but no Englishman has said a word, so I walked up towards Steve Waugh. I sensed someone running up to me. It was Rhodes. *Here we go – typical mouthy wicketkeeper*, I thought. *They're never short of a word.*

'Flem, did you get a little tickle on that?' he asked.

'Yep,' I said.

'We thought so,' he laughed, then he ran off to his position.

I wasn't sure that Heals would have been that friendly to a young English player.

BOXING DAY WITH BILLY, WARNIE AND BOONY

A couple of classic back-foot drives from Steve and a few ungainly ones from me accelerated the scoring. In no time we'd put on 37 for the last wicket, and Tugga had progressed from 78 to 94.

Now, I was a knowledgeable young man (in cricket terms), and I knew that Steve had been left stranded in the 90s by an irresponsible tailender in Test cricket many times before. That wasn't going to happen on my watch, I decided. No way. I made it my focus to get the big man to his 100. I decided to suppress my own attacking tendencies, play defensively and straight, and get Steve his *first* Boxing Day century.

I tried to block the next ball – a Devon Malcolm thunderbolt – but only managed to nick it straight into Graham Hick's waiting hands at second slip. I was out for 16.

Having got out playing defensively, my first thought was that I should have kept slogging. Then I looked over at Steve, his head down, left not out in the 90s again.

Once we were back in the MCG dressing rooms, I plucked up the courage to walk over and apologise. 'Sorry about that, Tugga,' I said. 'I was trying to play straight and get you your 100!'

'Don't worry about it,' he said, putting me at ease. 'If Glenn McGrath had walked out at number 11, I would have been 78 not out.'

Steve went straight to the top as my favourite Waugh brother.

When we took the field, our two gun bowlers – the ginger-headed banana-bending Queensland paceman Craig 'Billy the Kid' McDermott and the spin king Shane Warne – ran through the Poms, dismissing nine batsmen between them.

Billy was one of my favourite teammates. An underrated outswing bowler, he was big, fast, strong and aggressive but strangely neat and obsessively tidy. He was the only cricketer I've seen eat alphabet soup in alphabetical order.

BOWLOLOGY

The only thing holding Billy back was his insecurity about himself. I never met a happier man when we won the toss and were batting. He'd launch into a big song-and-dance routine with great gusto (à la Ricky Martin in the film clip for 'She Bangs'). At the other end of the scale, when we lost the toss and bowled, he was deflated like an old balloon.

By the time Tubby was walking out to toss the coin, Billy would already be in his whites, zinc cream on, saying to everybody, 'We're bowling today,' as if hoping to fool the cricketing gods that he was keen to bowl. If Tubby lost the toss and we were bowling, this was reliably followed by two statements:

You're not fooling me, Billy.

1. 'Fucking Tubby! He never wins a fucking toss. Heals [our vice captain] should be tossing.'
2. 'Hooter!' (Our trusted physio, Errol Alcott, would then have to work on Billy's body, soul and mind to get his fast outswingers ready for action.)

During the Melbourne Test in the summer of 1994/95, however, he was flying and in career-best form. As Chazz from the movie *Wedding Crashers* would say, 'He was just living the dream.' Billy took 31 English wickets for the summer, and during this Test he took his 250th Test wicket, passing Richie Benaud to sit second behind the great Dennis Lillee as Australia's greatest wicket-taker. Soon afterwards, he said at a press conference that he was chasing Lillee's record, and that there was no room for number two, only number one.

Now, Billy was McGrath-like in his ability to know exactly how many wickets he had taken through his career. This used to give us a good laugh in the dressing rooms. Billy always knew exactly where he stood on the wicket-taking lists. but he'd still ask loaded questions in a naive way.

After we bowled England out at the Gabba, we came off the ground and Billy started to ask very innocently, 'Who's Statham? Who's Statham?'

A few boys, suspecting where this question was leading, said they didn't know.

'Simmo, who's Statham?' Billy asked our veteran coach, Bob Simpson.

'Brian Statham,' Simmo replied. 'He was a great English bowler from the 1950s. Real workhorse, accurate and seamed the ball a great deal. Why, Billy?'

'Oh, I just passed him on the all-time Test wicket totals!' Billy said with wry smile.

We had another hit, declaring at 7/320, which included a beautiful 131 from our nuggetty number three, David Boon. This left the Poms a target of 388 runs in the fourth innings, so the game was alive. I decided to back myself and let things happen. I planned to bowl fuller and give the ball a chance to swing.

I had struggled a bit with the ball in the first innings, probably trying a bit too hard in front of my home crowd. The thing about being a home-town player at the MCG is that you are so pumped up to perform in front of your family and friends. And you've already dealt with the inevitable requests for free tickets for everyone you have met since kindergarten. There's increased media scrutiny when you're a local player, and peripheral things can distract you from just playing the game. Brad Hodge made his Boxing Day debut against the South Africans, coming off scoring 200 against them in Perth. He told me everything was a blur from the moment he left the dressing rooms to the sound of the ball hitting the bat as he faced his first ball.

Anyway, I took the new ball and had Graham Gooch out nicking an outswinger to Heals, then I got Graham Hick with a late outswinger, squaring him up and bowling him through the gate. The Great Southern Stand went crazy.

Once we got back into the dressing rooms, our lovable team manager Ian McDonald came up to me and said the press wanted to talk to me after the captains had spoken.

'No worries,' I said.

Forty minutes later, I was in the medical room getting some shoulder treatment from Hooter. Billy was there too, waiting for treatment, with his back to the door.

Macca put his head in the door, looked at me and said, 'Are you ready for your press conference, mate?'

Before I could say a word, Billy let out a massive sigh, like he'd been asked to donate a leg, and said, 'Not another bloody press conference! Can't they leave me alone?' He was trying to pretend it was a chore but he loved the press.

Macca laughed. 'Not you, Billy, you idiot,' he said. 'It's for Flem.'

Billy got really embarrassed. 'Flem! Flem!' he spluttered. 'What's he done? He's only got two wickets in the whole Test match!'

* * *

That night I was dreaming of a five-wicket haul – and of singing the team song, which I hadn't experienced yet. But the next day, Billy, probably stung by his non-invite to the press conference, launched into the Poms, knocking over their middle order and getting another 'Michelle Pfeiffer'.

Then Shane Warne, who was at the height of his powers,

BOXING DAY WITH BILLY, WARNIE AND BOONY

knocked over DeFreitas and Gough in consecutive deliveries. The Aussie players all huddled together, discussing what Warnie should bowl for his hat-trick ball.

Of course, it was the batsman who were offering most of the suggestions, including our skipper, Mark Taylor, who had the worst bowling action I've ever seen, in any form of cricket. He suggested to Warnie that he should bowl his flipper – a ball that pitched halfway down the pitch, kept low and usually trapped the batsman bowled or lbw.

The next batsman to offer some advice was our 'keg on legs', David Boon. Boony played 107 Tests for our great nation and didn't get one Test wicket, but he still felt he should tell our great leg-spinner what to bowl. He suggested the wrong'un, which would spin in to the new batsman, Devon Malcolm. Then Boony would take the catch at bad-pad.

As we were walking back to our positions, I was thinking, *It's only Devon Malcolm – he's legally blind! You could underarm a basketball and he wouldn't be able to hit it. Just bowl the ball on the stumps!*

(To illustrate just how well English cricket was going at the time, Devon was actually batting at number 10 – they still had Phil Tufnell to come!)

I could see that Warnie was a little bit confused about all the advice he had received. Should he bowl the flipper, the wrong'un or a leg break? So I thought I would help him out. I walked over and said, 'Warnie, do you really want to know how to get a Test hat-trick?'

He looked at me, still confused.

'Well, I've already got one,' I said immodestly.

He laughed.

And I told him how I'd thought about bowling a bouncer or a yorker to Salim Malik for my hat-trick ball, but I ended up going back to my stock ball, the outswinger, the ball I bowl eight times out of 10. And it had worked for me.

History shows that Warnie went back and bowled his top-spinning leg break to Malcolm, who gloved the ball to Boony, who – on his 34th birthday – took an amazing one-handed catch. After a quick induction ceremony from me at mid-on, Warnie joined the exclusive Test hat-trick club.

Soon afterwards, we made our way into 'the Dungeon' – our name for our dressing room in the bowels of the great MCG. I'd been waiting for this moment since I made my Australian debut the previous summer. We gathered into a circle, then Boony propped himself up on a bench and said a couple of words about each of us. Then he started singing, and we ripped into 'Beneath the Southern Cross I Stand'. I felt shivers down my spine as we screamed it out at the top of our lungs. Five days of Test match cricket were behind us and this was the reward.

Later on, I was sitting down with a beer, letting it all soak in, when Boony came and sat next to me. We started chatting about cricket, and I thought, *If I use this advice, I'm going to be such a good player. And if I continue to drink with Boony for the rest of the night and pump him for all his cricketing gold, I will be a great player much more quickly.*

I woke up the next day with a massive hangover. I reflected in an almost dreamlike way on the past few days. I'd played for Australia in a Boxing Day Test, and we'd beat the Poms. Finally I'd been able to sing the team song.

And I tried to remember what the fuck Boony had been saying last night!

Chapter 13
Danny and Aussie Mac

SYDNEY, NEW YEAR'S Day, 1995. Australia versus England in the Third Test of the series. As I walked onto the field, I slipped my game face on.

Craig McDermott bowled the initial over to Michael Atherton, and I had the second over with a beautiful new ball. It was shiny red and with a big seam – as far as new balls go, this one was Elle Macpherson, it was glamour. I was sure the Kookaburra would swing (not so sure about Elle).

Before the first ball, I reminded myself of my first-over Bowlology tactics:

1. *Get your game going from ball one.* My game is built on my stock ball, an outswinger in the Corridor of Uncertainty.
2. *Assess the pitch and conditions quickly.* Is there swing, seam, pace or bounce? Am I going to attack or defend?
3. *Read and plan for each batsman.* How is the batsman's footwork? Is he getting caught on the crease or playing forward or back? Is he leaving the ball or flashing outside off stump?

The Bowlologist

BOWLOLOGY

My first ball pitched outside off stump and swung away from the droopy-moustached English legend Graham Gooch, who tentatively played and missed. The ball died on the way through to Heals behind the stumps.

The ball was swinging but I needed to attack off stump more, with a bit more power through the crease and a higher ball release so I'd get the ball through to Heals at around hip height.

My second ball was a wide outswinger. It carried through to Heals better but Goochy left it easily. After two balls I quickly realised this was a green light – I had to attack and make Goochy play in these swinging and seaming conditions.

Ball three was an outswinger close to off stump. Goochy contemplated playing a shot but left it late. I was happy with the swing and length, but I had to get my line on off stump.

Ball four was a beauty, an outswinger on off stump that swung late, drawing Goochy into the drive. The ball just missed his outside edge.

Ball five was a fuller outswinger, which Goochy tentatively blocked to cover. This was significant. If he had smashed the half-volley through the covers for four, I'd have backed away a bit, bowling a bit wider and trying to encourage him to come at me. But when he blocked that half-volley, I knew he wasn't going to hurt me. It was swinging a fair bit and I decided to attack the stumps even more.

FLEM'S TRAFFIC LIGHTS BOWLING PLAN

1. SWINGING LOTS? GREEN LIGHT – GO! Get it up there and encourage the batsman to drive on the up. Aim for lbw, bowled or a nick behind to the wicketkeeper or slips. (Hope that the slips can catch it.)
2. SLIGHT SWING/SEAM? ORANGE LIGHT – WAIT! (GO OR DEFEND) Bring the length back a little to hit the splice of the bat. Get the batsman pushing forward tentatively. Bowl the odd delivery up to encourage the drive. (Hope that the slips can catch it.)
3. NO SWING? RED LIGHT – DEFEND! Flat pitch, red alert! Bowl faster, hit the deck hard. Use changes of pace, up and down. The odd bouncer must be faster, slightly higher and outside the batsman's back ear. (Hope that fine leg can catch it.) Bowl to your field; bring in a catching cover for slower balls. (Hope he can catch it.)

Ball six was a peach. Starting on middle stump, it drew Goochy into the shot then swung very late and caught his outside edge. The ball flew straight into Heals' waiting gloves. I felt like I'd climbed my personal outswinging Everest – it was the best over I'd ever bowled.

I strode down to the Doug Walters Stand euphorically, feeling like my feet weren't touching the ground. Unbelievably, I received a standing ovation from the Sydney crowd. I was overcome – here was a Melbourne boy being recognised by a parochial Sydney crowd.

❋ ❋ ❋

Fast-forward to day five. By then we were having a red hot crack at winning the Test, with Michael Slater and Mark Taylor getting us off to a flyer. Then rain dampened our run chase, and with wickets lost we needed our lower order to defend well in order to save the game.

Our spin twins, Tim May and Shane Warne, were in the middle, and I was next in to bat. I was very nervous. The thought of batting to save the Test while on a king pair didn't fill me with a lot of confidence.

I realised that I had to distract myself from the match scenario, so I put my headphones on and started playing my Nintendo Game Boy. I wanted to do anything apart from think about going out to the middle of the SCG to bat to save the Test match.

Amid all the swirling anxieties was a little voice needling away, saying, *You're going to make a pair.*

With the noise of 'Midlife Crisis' by Faith No More in my ears, and immersed in Donkey Kong, I vaguely heard the dressing-room phone ring. *Who the hell would be ringing at this stage of a Test match?* I wondered vaguely. *It must be important.*

Our normal room attendant was away for some reason, and his young assistant answered and yelled out to me, 'Flem, phone call for you.'

I was totally perplexed. Who would possibly be ringing me in the middle of a tense Test match? I tentatively took off my headphones and put down the Game Boy. I was very wary of a crank. I looked around as if someone was playing a practical joke and walked to the phone.

I grabbed the phone and said, 'Hello?'

A voice on the other end said, 'Flemo, Danny here. Are you guys still going for the runs? I'm with a few mates in Melbourne, drinking a slab, and we just want to know if we are still trying to win the game.'

It was one of the first times in my life I was totally speechless. I had no idea who this bloke was, and I was struggling to comprehend what I had just heard. 'How the hell did you get through to the rooms?' I asked.

'I said I was your brother,' said Danny, 'and they just put me straight through.'

I was dumbfounded. I called Heals over and quickly explained the situation. As I went back to my seat I heard him explaining the match situation to my newfound brother.

Luckily for me, Warnie and Maysy batted bravely and managed to save the Test.

A couple of weeks later I was having a drink with a few mates at the Depot Hotel (now the Precinct) in Richmond. A bloke came up to me and said, 'You don't know who I am, do you?'

His voice was vaguely familiar but I didn't know him.

'I'm Danny,' the bloke said. 'I rang you in the dressing rooms during the Sydney Test!'

I had a laugh, got him a beer and we had a chat. It turned out that Danny had popped up at different stages through my life, including years earlier at a Hoodoo Gurus concert in Lorne. Merv had lifted me up to crowd-surf, and the man who had helped Merv lift me up was my old mate Danny.

* * *

Our next Test, in January 1995, was in Adelaide, one of the great cricket venues. Our coach, Bob Simpson, finished our team meeting by saying that he felt we'd lost focus in the Sydney Test. Headphones and video games would now be banned from the dressing rooms.

As we left the room, Steve Waugh said to me, in his dry way, 'Do you reckon he was talking about you there, Flem?'

Two South Australians (and good mates) were making their Test debuts in the match: the classy middle-order bat Greg Blewett, and the leg-spinner Peter McIntyre.

AUSSIE MAC

Peter 'Macca' McIntyre was true character, a really funny man who, later in his career, was known as 'Aussie Mac'. The story goes that Macca and his South Australian teammate (now a media superstar) James Brayshaw were in a pub talking to a few people. Bray overheard someone ask Macca what he did for a job, and Macca replied that he played cricket for South Australia and sometimes for Australia.

Bray pissed himself. Macca had in fact played for Australia – once! Not 'sometimes', just the one time! By Macca's definition, man sometimes lands on the moon. Bray quickly told his South Australian teammates the story, and Macca was quickly nicknamed 'Aussie Mac'.

The sequel to this came in 1996, when Macca replaced the injured Warnie on Australia's tour of India. Macca, Dizzy and I were at the opening of the Delhi McDonald's (I loved the Maharaja Burger and the vegetable nuggets! 'You want parsnip fries with your order, sir?') Macca was trying to take the opportunity to recreate his nickname history by telling Dizzy and me that his nickname was in fact after McDonald's 'Aussie Mac burger'. Knowing the original story, we looked at each other and started pissing ourselves. 'No, Macca, we're not falling for that,' we told him. After that episode he was sometimes known as 'Indian Mac'.

He finished his South Australian career known as 'Fourth Day Mac'. He actually believed that he grew an extra spinning finger on day four whenever he was playing on Adelaide's turning pitches. This was apparently invisible to the human eye.

DANNY AND AUSSIE MAC

Greg Blewett batted with typical class in his debut innings, hitting cover drives and sweetly timed pulls and hooks, to reach 96 not out. Then I let him down by scoring a duck (trying to hook Devon Malcolm), which left only 'Aussie Mac' Peter McIntyre and the injured Craig McDermott to bat to help him get his hundred.

There are three categories of lower-order batsman:

1. Lower-order batsmen who are expected to score some useful runs, e.g. Paul Reiffel, whose Test batting average was 26.
2. 'Rabbits', who are incompetent batsman who are usually knocked over cheaply.
3. 'Ferrets', who go in after the rabbits. They rarely survive long or score anything. Examples are early Glenn McGrath and Peter McIntyre.

But remarkably, in his debut Test innings, Macca showed remarkable determination and saw Blewy to wonderful hundred. He joined a select club of players to have scored a century on Test debut.

When we bowled, the cricketing gods turned back the clock for me. I'd had a couple of weeks off before the match to strengthen my shoulder, and I bowled my quickest for the summer. When I bounced out Goochy and Atherton, I felt as good as I had all summer for a brief moment. Then I tweaked my right hamstring.

That night, I doubled as a bodyguard for the hometown hero, Greg Blewett. After his ton it was Blewymania, and I was keen to soak up the aura around him. He led us to various pubs, and I limped after him with an ultrasound device strapped to my leg. Not my most professional effort.

Although the ultrasound helped – my right hamstring felt pretty good the next day – unfortunately, I tore my left hamstring in my first over! Craig McDermott and I might be the most injury-prone opening bowling pair in the history of Test cricket. Apart from our opening spells on day one of each Test match of that summer, I don't think we were actually on the field together at the same time at any other stage.

For the second innings, Hooter strapped my hamstrings so tight that I could only run in like an Egyptian mummy, and I bowled at about the same pace.

On day five we were behind the eight ball, attempting to save the Test against the Poms on a wearing wicket. After being flogged all series, the Poms could smell a victory. Devon Malcolm and Chris Lewis – with a combined four Christian names between them – were leading the way. Malcolm was bowling at a pace few have managed before or since, and the side-on view from the Adelaide Oval dressing rooms only multiplied the pace.

Steve Waugh was a picture of balance as he played a forward defensive shot, his lower body still, his front elbow nice and high, showing the full face of his bat. Unfortunately, his middle stump had impaled Steve Rhodes in his stomach. We were in trouble.

Billy McDermott was then bounced out by Chris Lewis, and I was next in. Out in the middle, I said to myself, 'Back and across, no backlift, watch the ball. You could get hurt here.'

Heals and I batted for around two hours, trying desperately to save the Test. I started to believe that Heals and I could have been the new Ken McKay and Lindsay Kline, who famously saved a Test against the West Indies in Adelaide in 1960/61. But with six overs to go to the end of the game, I failed to pay my brain bill and attempted to pull a half-volley off Lewis – out lbw.

Now 'Aussie Mac' held the nation's hopes in his hands. He had to survive for just six overs to save the Test match and become a national hero. He walked out to the batting crease on a pair.

Well, it was duck season, and Macca duly acquired his pair. We lost with 35 balls to spare.

Many soul-searching questions went through my head after this devastating loss:

Why did we collapse so badly on day five?
Why did I attempt a pull shot on a wearing wicket?
Which pub was Blewy going to tonight?

❄ ❄ ❄

To finish off the summer, we played the controversial match between Australia (the old-school players, e.g. Taylor, Healy, Boon, the Waughs) and Australia A (the cool, young guys, e.g. Martyn, Blewett, Ponting) in the finals series of the ODI competition. Have a guess which team the Aussie public barracked for?

I was playing against the crowd favourite because I was playing for Australia! It's not often you get booed playing for Australia in Australia. but this was one of those occasions. I think our skipper, Mark Taylor, helped make sure this event never happened again.

In the first final I was fielding in front of the Doug Walters Stand, where only a month earlier I had been privileged to receive a standing ovation for my first over in the Test match. So I felt comfortable and at home, and I was fielding in a position where I was respected.

I bowled my first over to my mate Greg Blewett. I proceeded to bowl three lame half-volleys, which Blewy easily smashed for four, one after another. I then strolled down to fine leg in front of my mates in the Doug Walters Stand, where, with 0/12 off one over to my name, I received another standing ovation from the crowd.

Fickle bastards.

Chapter 14
Lara, Lara, Laraaa!!!!!

AT THE START of our 1995 tour of the West Indies, we got off the plane in Barbados. Waiting for us were a couple of huge Barbadian baggage guys, who pointed at us and said, 'You're going to get some licks, maaan,' flicking their hands to make a noise like a ball hitting skin. ('Licks', I found out, meant cricket balls flying at 90 miles per hour into your unprotected flesh, ribs, shoulders and head.)

'Amby, he coming to get you,' one of the guys said, pointing at me.

'If he don't get you, Courtney will be provide your licks, maaan,' said his mate.

They looked at each other, laughed and high-fived.

I was thinking, *Jesus, the intimidation has started and we haven't even got our baggage!*

The next day, I was on the beach with a few teammates, and we were approached by some Barbadian locals. Generally, I found the West Indian people to be very knowledgeable and passionate about their cricket.

'Where is Merv Huge?' one bloke asked. 'We want to meet Merv Huge.'

'He's not on this tour, mate,' we replied.

'Noooo! We scaaared of Merv Huge. He look like an *elephant* when he comin' in to bowl.'

'Where are the Wogs?' another bloke asked. 'Where are Steve and Mark Wog?'

'They're on the tour but they're not here right now,' I answered.

'Steve Wog! *Ferocious* cover driver and *deceptive* slower ball! And Mark Wog! Hits them *sweeeeet*, like a lady . . . but he got no brains, though.'

A pretty good assessment, we thought.

A couple of weeks later we were in Trinidad, the southernmost island in the Caribbean, for the third one-day international. Christopher Columbus, an adventurer with the power of precognition, had named it 'Lara de la Trinidad' – which didn't make a lot of sense until the birth of Trinidad's Prince Brian Lara in 1969. The left-hander with freakish batting skills was the most destructive of modern batsman. His ability to take down top attacks with his amazing eye and reflexes, often on his own, was truly amazing.

At home, he was god. Fresh off his world-record score of 400 against the Poms the year before, he was on billboards everywhere. There was even a song about him, which was cleverly titled 'Lara'. Basically, it went like this: 'Lara, Lara, Laraaa, Lara, Lara, Laraaaa . . .' for about three minutes. It was only slightly less annoying than Aqua's 'Barbie Girl', which was in Michael Slater's CD collection at the time.

Everywhere we went – in restaurants, pubs, etc. – this 'Lara' song would be blaring out. I soon found myself humming it. When I woke each morning, he was already in my head.

Game day in Trinidad. I was playing, we bowled first and my right shoulder was feeling pretty good. I dismissed Phil Simmons early. Out walked Brian Lara, and it was like the bounce of the ball at the AFL Grand Final. The atmosphere was electric, spine-chilling, as the diminutive figure walked past me to take block. The whole stadium was roaring.

LARA, LARA, LARAAA!!!!!

I charged in and released a beauty of a ball. It swung slightly in, on a good, full length, hit the pitch hard and then seamed away. It was almost Bowlology gold. Most left-handers would have looked to defend the inswinger, and then would have nicked the away-seamer to the keeper or slips. I couldn't have been happier with the delivery.

But Lara saw the ball swing in early, pressed forward with his front foot to protect off stump and simply left the ball.

I knew I was in trouble then. I had been left before, but this was the most confident, imposing leave I had ever seen a batsman play. Nothing could have crushed my confidence quite like this. I'd bowled almost the perfect ball, yet Lara played it without even a fluttering of his heartbeat.

Nevertheless, we actually managed to contain Lara pretty well early on.

A little later I was running in to bowl to Carl Hooper (one of the only international batsmen not to wear a thigh pad). I bowled a stock ball just outside his off stump, but my shoulder didn't give me a stock response. I got a jarring pain like an electric shock. I'd felt this before during our tour of Pakistan, but it hadn't been as bad. I knew my shoulder had fallen out slightly, and I was in trouble. I bowled the next ball probably 30 kilometres per hour slower, which luckily was the finish of my spell, and I didn't say a word about my shoulder, hoping for a miracle the next time I bowled.

When I came back on later, bowling to Jimmy Adams, I proceeded to send down three of the mildest medium-pacers ever bowled. Jimmy was feasting on them like Homer Simpson at an all-you-can-eat buffet. Even though I was holding back, I could feel my shoulder slipping more and more, and I was experiencing more intense electric shocks with each ball.

As I ran in for the fourth ball of the over and planted my back foot, a voice in my head questioned me without emotion, *You're not really going to bowl this ball, are you?* It's amazing what your inner voice can say at times, and in split-second detail. I was surprised that it had time to say all that but it did. I pulled out of delivering the ball.

After I had chatted to Tubby, I knew that my tour was over and that I'd soon be having shoulder surgery. Making matters worse, Lara went on to cut our attack to ribbons, scoring 139 off 123 balls.

The only highlight in our innings was when Greg Blewett was out off his first ball in bizarre circumstances. Carl Hooper threw the ball up outside off stump, and Blewy launched into a cover drive but missed it. For some reason, he thought the Windies' keeper, Junior Murray, had also missed the ball, so he took off for a bye. The bad news for Blewy was that Junior had gloved the ball just fine. I think he was momentarily stunned that Blewy began running, so it took him a second to compose himself before he stumped our skinny middle-order bat.

Despite this loss, the Test series was a watershed for Australian cricket, as we beat the West Indies, who had dominated world cricket since 1975 like AC/DC had dominated the music charts. The Waugh twins' runs in the last Test proved decisive, and the Fast Bowling Cartel – Glenn McGrath, Paul Reiffel and Brendon Julian – along with the Spin King, Warnie, were sensational.

And while that was happening, my surgeon, Greg Hoy, got to do what the West Indies quicks didn't, giving me some licks with a scalpel as he operated to stabilise my shoulder.

Chapter 15
The Roommates XI

THE CURRENT-DAY Australian cricketer doesn't know what having a roommate is like, as single rooms had been phased out by the late 1990s. Getting a good pairing was always a tender balance – sometimes there were disasters because the traits of the individuals weren't compatible. A good roommate was someone to have a chat with, share a joke with, and make a tea or a coffee for. Also, it was important to have common interests, such as movies, music and footy. At the other end of the spectrum, you could have some sleepless nights if your roommate came home late or woke up too early, or if he smoked too heavily or snored too loudly. Read on for some other insights into Australian cricketers' rooming habits . . .

GEOFF MARSH, aka MR NUDIST
Long-time roommate and friend of the legendary David Boon. 'Swampy' Marsh lived and breathed cricket – mostly batting, as anyone who saw his bowling action would testify. In fact, he was so passionate about his batting that Boony often woke very early in the morning to see Swampy in his birthday suit practising his forward defence in front of the mirror. Also, he loved a chat with his roomies as he wasn't great at entertaining himself with books, magazines or music. He would get annoyed when Boony was reading a novel and not talking to him. Once Boony left the room for 10 minutes, and when he returned he found his novel ripped to shreds by a smiling Swampy, who was holding some scissors.

JUSTIN LANGER, aka MR SLEEPWALKER

This nuggety left-hander has made thousands of runs for his country, and at times he looked like he could have scored runs in his sleep. Funnily enough, he was a noted sleepwalker, and he also tended to talk in his sleep. Now, this might not seem like such a big problem, but 'Alfie' Langer is a black belt in martial arts. It's not pleasant to be awoken by him screaming obscenities, and then to see him walking towards you throwing kicks and punches. This was one of the factors that led the Aussie team members to want single rooms – not so much for solitude but for our own protection.

STEVE WAUGH, aka MR MESSY

There was an old TV sitcom called *The Odd Couple*, about Felix, who was too neat, and Oscar, who was too messy. When I roomed with Steve, this brought together two Oscars, and that meant trouble. I only roomed with him once – in Brisbane in 1994/95 for the First Test against the Poms – and it was a disaster. We got along fine as blokes but we had a few problems with our domestic duties. Shirts, shoes, socks, cricket gear and chocolate wrappers were all sprawled around our room after our week-long stay. At the end of the Test, he left with half my gear and I left with half of his, although I didn't get his cherished baggy green cap. It took us the whole summer to sort out whose gear was whose . . . come to think of it, I never did get back my Motley Crue tour T-shirt.

THE ROOMMATES XI

MARK WAUGH, aka MR JULIO
I roomed a bit with Junior early in my career, which was before I really got to know him. We didn't really have a lot in common early on. I was a massive Hawthorn fan in the AFL, while his love was for the Canterbury Bankstown Bulldogs in the NRL. On a day off he loved nothing more than 18 holes of golf, while I was a non-golfer back then. He was a prominent member of the 'Julios' – the guys within the team who took a lot of pride in their personal grooming. I was in the 'Nerd' clan and was very fashionably challenged. To motivate myself for big games, I pumped up by listening to Metallica, AC/DC or Kiss, while he sipped a cup of tea and quietly listened to the Little River Band.

MICHAEL BEVAN, aka MR MISSION IMPOSSIBLE
Rooming with Bevo was a bigger challenge than Tom Cruise faced in any of his *Mission Impossible* movies. Bevo was a perfectionist who had to have the right amount of sleep (eight hours, three minutes and 32 seconds, to be precise), so he took objection to the following: smokers, snorers, early risers, late-to-bedders, tall blokes, small blokes, drinkers, etc. And Bevo is a man who has had the flu for 43 years now; he took his own pharmacy on tour with him to keep on top of his health. Another individual who pushed the possibility of single rooms to the forefront of our minds.

DARREN 'BOOF' LEHMANN, aka MR MCDONALD'S
Boof was Michael Bevan's nightmare roommate from hell. He smoked like a trooper, loved a beer and the odd late night, and when he did eventually get home he would snore like a herd of rioting elephants. We roomed together in 1996 in Sri Lanka, where we were playing in a one-day tournament. There was heavy security, and we were told we couldn't leave the hotel,

which sent us stir-crazy for the three weeks we were there. The highlight for me was when I quizzed Boof about the McDonald's menu. By this stage he had a McDonald's card and they gave him free food.

'How much is a Big Mac meal deal, six nuggets and a caramel sundae?' I would ask.

'Super-size or regular?' he'd say.

'Super-size.'

'Nine dollars and 55 cents,' he'd answer, quick as a flash.

We had hours of fun!

BRAD HOGG, aka MR FITNESS

Hoggy made his Aussie debut on our tour of India in 1996, and he was keen to set a good example. He was always the first to training and the last to finish, which would have earned him the awe of his teammates, except for the fact that the team bus couldn't leave until he had finished. Jeez, we watched him bowl a lot of balls in the nets.

Being from the country, he was always up early and ready for action. His roommates awoke to his grunting and sweating as he punched out push-ups and sit-ups at 5.30 a.m. He is still the only Australian cricketer to actually buy some barbells while on tour. I think he had a reasonable excess-baggage bill on the way home!

SHANE WARNE, aka MR ENTERTAINMENT

Warnie was always enjoyable, as he loved his gadgets – DVDs, Minidiscs, and of course mobile phones. He actually used to bring whole home-entertainment systems on tour. He'd lug around a subwoofer and speakers in its own suitcase, then he'd proceed to play his music and movies at maximum volume. That wasn't a problem when he played some Powderfinger, but

I think Geri Halliwell and Spice Girls should be listened to in the privacy of your own headphones.

I remember Warnie buying a mobile phone in Dubai in 1994, when they were only just new and the size of house bricks. He was disappointed with the low volume when he was speaking, but then he realised he was talking into the wrong side of it! He was a bit of a softy at heart. I once woke to see him crying at the movie *Notting Hill*.

MERV HUGHES, aka MR BODILY FUNCTIONS

I've already told you about what it was like to room with Big Merv. One time, I took the piss out of him during a stay in Perth. We were watching TV, and he grunted to me that the volume was too low and that I should turn it up for him, as he was the senior roommate. I usually responded straight away to the big fella's requests, but on this occasion I said, 'Do it yourself.'

He grunted something about my lack of respect for my elders, then he got out of bed and manually put up the volume. What he didn't know was that I had the remote control. Once he was back in bed, the volume mysteriously went down. With a bemused look on his face, Merv went back to the TV and turned it up again. We repeated this a couple more times, with Merv swearing like a trooper and getting more frustrated, before finally the penny dropped. He turned to me sheepishly and said, 'I walked right into that, didn't I!'

CRAIG MCDERMOTT, aka MR NEAT

Billy was the leader of our pace attack when I first came onto the Test scene, and going from Big Merv's laid-back attitude to Billy's intensity was quite a change. We really were the Odd Couple. Billy had to pack everything neatly, clothes were put into drawers and shirts hung up on their hangers. In my seven years touring with the Aussie team, I never packed any clothes in the drawers in a hotel room. Billy also picked up any rubbish I had thrown around and put it in the bin.

He was a massive snorer, though. The night before a Test in Adelaide against the Poms, I was in bed early, wanting a long and relaxing sleep. Just as I was dozing into a deep sleep, Billy started snoring. It was like a foghorn going off. Finally, after tossing for hours, I finally screamed out, 'Stop snoring, Billy!' It woke him up, and in a semiconscious state he said sorry – and then he didn't snore any more! I've no idea how that worked.

TROY 'RONNIE' CORBETT, aka MR FAST FOOD

Special mention to one of the great blokes of Victorian cricket. I was rooming with Ronnie and Laurie Harper in Darwin for pre-season one year. Our apartment had one bedroom with a double and one with two singles. As an Australian player, I pulled rank immediately and chose the double. I slept beautifully and woke to see Laurie camped with bed sheets in the kitchen, looking like he'd hardly had a wink of sleep. He told me he'd been forced to move out as he was too scared to sleep in the same room as Ronnie. It emerged that Ronnie, who was working at McDonald's at the time, was a sleepwalker, and Laurie had awoken to see his teammate looming above him flipping burgers in his sleep – naturally, in the nude!

Chapter 16
We're Not the Champions of the World

THE WORLD CUP is the most prized tournament in international one-day cricket. It's a long campaign, too, the closest thing cricket has to an Olympic Games or a football season, being a six- to eight-week tournament, and you have to peak at the pointy end. It's a competition every cricket team loves. The 1996 World Cup was hosted by three nations: India, Sri Lanka and Pakistan.

The involvement of Sri Lanka was very contentious, due to some aggro and simmering tensions between the Australians and Sri Lankans in the 1995/96 season. During the one-day series, Ian Healy had given one of the all-time great sledges to Sri Lanka's chubby captain, Arjuna Ranatunga – a man who looked like he preferred a bun to a run. Arjuna, who wasn't bad himself with the sledge, regularly called for a runner while he was batting, but when he requested one on a particularly hot night during a one-dayer in Sydney, Heals had said, 'You don't get a runner for being an overweight, unfit, fat bastard!' (Or words to that effect . . .) The relationship between the two teams had deteriorated so badly that there had been no handshakes after the finals.

As a team, we discussed forfeiting our first game in the World Cup, to be played in Colombo in February 1996, since some of our players had received death threats. We were as popular as dysentery over there. Then, tragically, a terrorist bomb attack near our intended hotel killed over 100 people. After consulting with the Australian government and the ACB, we decided to skip Sri Lanka and default a game. The West Indies did the same thing.

So we started the tournament behind the eight ball. And to make things even more difficult, we were playing most of our matches in India, which was not exactly home.

We arrived in the great city of Calcutta, which had a population of about four million people, a third of whom seemed to be crammed into the airport to greet us. I hadn't been to India before, and the crush of people blew my mind. Walking outside for the first time, I was hit by the intense heat and smell.

We were quickly rushed onto our team bus. Off we went, and I quickly worked out that the Indian road rules were that there were no rules. Our bus was going so fast that I checked to see if Keanu Reeves and Sandra Bullock hadn't jumped on board.

Drivers were moving their vehicles as if they were blindfolded, all the while ringing their bells and horns loudly and moving from lane to lane chaotically. Frogger from the arcade game would have had no chance of getting to the other side of the road. There was none of the Australian concept of giving way to pedestrians – it was more like Spain's running of the bulls.

Finally, we arrived at our hotel. Another third of Calcutta's population were camped in the foyer. Families were looking for photos, autographs or handshakes. *Wow, this is insane*, I thought – but that was only the start. Welcome to India!

※ ※ ※

I was expecting to be running the drinks for the whole tour, since Craig McDermott, Paul Reiffel and Glenn McGrath were our main quicks. But no sooner had we settled into the World

WE'RE NOT THE CHAMPIONS OF THE WORLD

Cup than our ginger-haired spearhead McDermott blew out his dodgy calf in our first game, against Kenya. He was soon flying business-class back to Bris Vegas.

So I was back in for our massive game against the home team, India, at Wankhede Stadium in Mumbai. It was my first game for Australia since my shoulder injury in Trinidad. I'd spent virtually a year out of the Aussie team after my shoulder reconstruction, which had tightened up all my ligaments to stop me sub-flexing. My shoulder felt strong, but somehow too strong – as if the doctor had turned the bolts too tight, or used too much glue. It was stiff, and I was worried about it.

We bowled first, and the atmosphere in the stadium was incredible – like being in a Metallica moshpit, only louder. There were more men with moustaches too. I'd seen cricket in India on TV, but being inside that noise, that constant frenzy, was impossible to understand without experiencing it. These people did not hold back. Cricket is the high for Indian fans, and they were intoxicated by the names of Tendulkar and Azharuddin, but they got almost as worked up over stars like Warnie and the Waughs – who, like in the West Indies, were known all over India as Steve and Mark Wog.

Well, Mark Wog got a good hundred at the top of the order and Tubby got a 50, but nobody else could get a sniff. I strolled out to bat at number 10. I'd like to see my run-out stats when I batted at 10 or 11, as opposed to at eight or nine. For some reason, when I batted at 10 or 11, I lost the basic ability to judge a run properly. Running singles looked as foreign to me as driving a space shuttle. Not surprisingly, then, I was run out for a duck at the bowler's end, attempting to run a bye.

Tendulkar began in ominous form, hitting three fours off one over by Pigeon. At training the night before, I had noticed that the new ball was swinging a long way, so I knew it was crucial to bowl full – and it was also crucial to try not to bowl to Sachin. I dismissed India's other opener, Ajay Jadeja, lbw with a ball that started on leg stump then swung late and was going to hit middle and off. It was my first Aussie wicket for 11 months, and it's fair to say I was pumped.

With my adrenaline up, I bowled my first ball to India's new whizkid, Vinod Kambli, a left-hander who had as much bling as I had swing. I released a beautiful inswinger that swung a mile and beat him for pace and movement, smashing him on the pad. He was an eye player whose technique was looser then Lindsay Lohan on a night out, and with my next ball I got my line right. The ball started outside off stump and swung sharply to hit his middle stump. Gone for a duck!

I then dismissed Azharuddin, the Indian captain, with my first-ever slow leg-cutter, a ball I'd been working on in the hope that it would work on the slow Indian pitches. I dragged the ball down short, and Azhar dragged the ball onto his stumps. Three wickets in my first spell back! My shoulder was feeling strong and we were on our way to beating the home team. Only Sachin was standing in our way.

Mark Waugh eventually tamed Tendulkar with some brilliant bowling. By now Junior was bowling off-spinners; Sachin charged him, and the instinctively smart younger Wog spun the ball wide. The Little Master couldn't reach it and was stumped by the reliable Ian Healy. Now, there is only one time you experience complete silence on the subcontinent: when Tendulkar is out. For a moment, after it happens, there is almost a suspension of life. The earth stops rotating – maybe it's something to do with a billion people not breathing – and then starts again.

Anyway, I ended up taking 5/36, which, after my rehabilitation from surgery and a tough summer with the Vics, was very satisfying. I was back – and what a place to have a good day. I

WE'RE NOT THE CHAMPIONS OF THE WORLD

was back on the international cricket rollercoaster and I just rode the emotion.

* * *

After defeating the tournament favourite like that, we partied hard. The next day we were all nursing hangovers as we dragged ourselves down to a recovery session in the hotel pool (although whether it was recovery from the game or the beer, I wasn't sure).

Michael Slater mentioned that he was speaking to the American actress Demi Moore in the hotel lift the night before. Now, if we'd held a drinking Olympics, Slats would not have been a superpower like the United States – he'd have been Nepal (29 million people, no medals). So most of us reckoned that he'd been so drunk that he *thought* he'd bumped into Demi Moore. It had probably been a pot plant.

All of a sudden, someone yelled out, 'Demi's in the foyer!'

Chaos erupted. Blokes were jumping out of the pool with a ferocity not seen since the infamous Polly Waffle swimming scene in *Caddy Shack*. It was every man for himself, and guys were pushing teammates out of the way to run to the foyer. Demi was the hottest woman in the world at that time, and particularly so for a bunch of blokes who had spent, well, whole days on a cricket tour in a country where women were not exactly as welcoming as the lasses at home. Or as visible.

Warnie and I took the time to punch out 20 push-ups, just to get our upper bodies as puffed as possible. We were looking pretty good in our World Cup 1996 team singlets. He and I then sprinted into the foyer, where we spotted Demi about 30 metres away. She was much smaller than I expected – except for in one rather important area. I don't mean to be coarse or anything, but let's just say that her plastic surgeon had probably paid for his home extension that year with one patient.

As she approached us, Warnie nudged me and said, 'We have to talk to her.'

'What can we say?' I replied, feeling just like a teenager again.

'Well, you've just got to say something to her!'

'How about, "Hey, *St. Elmo's Fire* rocked"?'

Suddenly, she was only a couple of metres away. We stared like star-struck schoolboys, completely dumb. Never before or since was Warnie tongue-tied in front of a woman, but Demi had us. Then she said, in her thick American accent, 'Nice win the other night, guys. Good stuff,' and she kept walking. Warnie and I were stunned, as if we had seen a *Ghost* . . .

For our next match we travelled to Nagpur to play against Zimbabwe. Once again, we were subjected to India's great contradictions. Nagpur is the city of marriages and oranges, but I have never seen a marriage or an orange on any of my visits there. Nagpur is also the second-greenest city in India, but it probably has the 48th-driest cricket pitch.

My main memories of the match are of the group of Aussie tourists later known as 'the Fanatics'. They were singing Aussie songs like 'Throw Your Arms Around Me' by Hunters and Collectors, and Men at Work's 'Down Under'. When you're down at fine leg with no one to talk to, a little singalong goes a long way.

The Hoodoo Gurus' classic anthem 'Like Wow – Wipeout!' would have been more appropriate, as we smashed the Zimbabwean team by eight wickets with 14 overs to spare.

WE'RE NOT THE CHAMPIONS OF THE WORLD

※ ※ ※

Having made it through the group stage, Australia was up against the dangerous New Zealand in a quarter-final in Madras (since renamed Chennai). In our team meeting the night before the game, Bob Simpson led a discussion of how we should handle the various Kiwi players.

'Nathan Astle's an explosive opening batsmen who has already scored a dynamic hundred in this tournament,' he began. 'Don't give him too much room outside off stump, and look to move the ball away from him, as he's a knocker early on. If he settles early, look to change your pace with slower balls. Then there's Stephen Fleming, an elegant left-hander who's very vulnerable early to the inswinger. So get the ball moving in to him, or use bounce angled across him. If he gets set, look to change your pace.'

The next batsman was Chris Harris, but before Simmo could say a word, Steve Waugh chipped in. 'I'm sick of talking about this bloke,' he said. 'We've played him 20 times and he has never scored 20 runs against us! Bowl straight and just knock him over.'

After these comments from the Iceman, we moved on, going through the rest of the Kiwi batting order pretty quickly.

Madras was an oppressively hot place, which was only just tolerable if you were well hydrated and fed. I didn't have that luxury. After a couple of weeks on tour, I had gremlins living in my stomach. For fans of the movie *Gremlins*, they were more like Stripe gremlins than cute little Gizmos. Anyway, I was like a leaky spout – everything was passing through me. I'm sure you get the picture, but if you don't, you soon will. (Sorry in advance.)

On the day of the match it was 40 degrees and close to 100 per cent humidity. Not even the fit players were looking forward to it. We weren't even finished our warm-up when I did the dreaded but very common in the subcontinent 'shart' (which, as the Urban Dictionary website notes, is 'a small, unintended defecation that occurs when one relaxes the anal sphincter to fart'). It was going to be a very long day.

We bowled first. I knocked over the dangerous Astle early with an outswinger, and Pistol snagged Craig Spearman. Then Glenn McGrath had the lesser-known Fleming (Stephen) caught by Steve Wog. *Everything is going to plan*, I thought, clenching my butt cheeks together to prevent any more sharting.

Out walked Kiwi left-hander Chris Harris at 3/44. He couldn't have been feeling too confident, as his career record against Australia at this stage was nine innings for a paltry 85 runs, with a highest score of just 18. I could see Steve Waugh shaking his head in disgust as Harris walked past him to take centre.

Well, what do you know, if he didn't go on to make the greatest 130 ever scored in cricket history. Harris channelled every great left-hander, from Gary Sobers to Brian Lara. He smoked our bowling attack to every centimetre of the Madras stadium. One pull shot off McGrath hit the roof of the grandstand. With each boundary, I could see Tugga staring at his feet, scratching in the dirt, just wanting to dig a bigger hole for himself.

By the end of the innings New Zealand had scored a massive 286.

No problems here, though, as Mark sensed the opportunity to help out his older brother, scoring his third hundred of the tournament. Contributions from Tugga and Stuart Law got us home and into the semi-finals.

And I can't remember Chris Harris scoring over 20 against us again. Go figure!

WE'RE NOT THE CHAMPIONS OF THE WORLD

❋ ❋ ❋

Our semi-final, against the West Indies, was in Chandigarh, which was another city of contradictions. It was a planned town, like Canberra, although it was better than Canberra because it didn't have politicians. Just Sikhs – lots of them. In fact, it was so well planned that it was the capital city of two states, the Punjab and Haryana.

Apparently, the name 'Chandigarh' means 'the Fort of Chandi' but it was our fort under siege against the West Indian quicks. Curtly Ambrose and Ian Bishop tore through our top order, and very quickly we were 4/15 and looked gone. Our match against the Windies in the early rounds had been close, but this was looking ugly.

Ambrose was the most physically intimidating bowler I ever played against. He was tall, quick and bouncy, and he didn't socialise with the opposition, always keeping up an aura of hostility. It worked – everybody crapped themselves around him (and I'm not talking 'sharts' here). Mentally I thought we gave up too, at times, as he never bowled a bad ball.

Then 'Mr One-Day Cricket', Michael Bevan, teamed up with Stuart 'Judge' Law and Ian Healy and got us to a total of 207, which felt about 20 runs too short. Bevo was a freak one-day player. Like a cricketing Rain Man, he continually calculated the game situation in his head. He was always building a game plan, thinking about which opposition bowlers he would defend against and which he would take risks against. He was so precise that he would aim to finish the game with a certain number of runs off the last over, calculating it down to the last ball.

The Windies started their innings well, with Lara, Shiv Chanderpaul and then Richie Richardson batting well. Steve Waugh bowled Lara with a beauty from around the wicket, but they kept going, moving on to 2/165. I remember Steve saying that if we could get a couple of wickets, the Windies, who were known to lose wickets in clumps, might panic and gas it.

Our two superpowers, Warne and McGrath, stepped up, with the latter getting Chanderpaul. Everyone lifted in the field. The West Indies lost 6/33 but the game still wasn't over. When the last over started they needed 10 runs to win, with two wickets in hand.

The Aussies gathered in a huddle, and I could sense Tubby looking around the group and trying to decide who should bowl the last over. From instinct, he looked first to his two best bowlers. Warnie had bowled us back into the game, and Tubby's gaze moved from the blond leg-spinner to the scoreboard. 'Warne, 10 overs, 4/36' – there goes that idea. Next he fixed his gaze on 'Pigeon' McGrath. Scoreboard: '10 overs, 2/30'. Tubby was in the shit.

'Fuck it!' he said. 'Good luck, Flem.' And he threw the 49-overs-old white ball to me. Our World Cup campaign was on the line. Thanks, skipper.

We quickly decided on our bowling plan: yorkers in the blockhole to the set batsman, Richie Richardson, and short of a length to the tailender, Curtly Ambrose – and to the next man, Courtney Walsh, if I could get a pole. I went back to my mark excited and nervous.

Tubby ran up to me. 'Just do your best, Flem. Bowl it in the blockhole. We're all behind you.'

What a great captain, I remember thinking. *Cool under pressure, and he gives you plenty of support.*

I ran in and bowled the first ball – a half-volley, which Richardson dispatched through mid-wicket for four. Shit. That hadn't gone to plan.

WE'RE NOT THE CHAMPIONS OF THE WORLD

The West Indies now needed six runs off five balls with two wickets in hand. Up ran Tubby again to give me another reassuring word. I was glad to see him coming, as I'd been a bit put off by that start.

'Hey, Flem,' he began, 'you know all that shit I said last ball about "we won't care as long as you do your best"?'

'Yeah,' I replied.

'Well, fuck that – if we don't win, you won't ever play for Australia again.' And with that he ran off.

At times like this, I felt I could relate to Tom Hanks' character in the movie *Castaway*. I was alone with a ball, although it wasn't a volleyball named Wilson. 'Please transport yourself to a yorker length,' I said to it, but got no response.

I charged in and bowled a good yorker to Richardson about 15 centimetres outside off stump, and he could only chop it through to Heals. I thought all the Aussies were tense, but Ambrose then had a brain explosion and called for a risky single. Heals got his glove off and hit the stumps to run Curtly out by two centimetres.

Heals was a meticulous planner and trainer – and his preparation was always perfect. He had a habit of taking our bowling in the middle of the ground when we were warming up, and every few deliveries he would underarm the ball back at the stumps. I remember being a bit annoyed whenever he hit the stumps as it meant walking further to fetch the ball. Bloody selfish keepers! Well, after that I never complained again.

I ran in for the next ball visualising a yorker, and I tried to bowl it as fast as I could. Courtney Walsh must have been as surprised as I was when I sent down another half-volley, as he tried to hit me out of the ground and was bowled.

Everything went in slow motion, then sped up. For some reason, I decided to run flat-out, stopping no stations, to Ian

Healy. Steve Waugh later wrote that I 'took off like a looter who had just stolen a TV in a riot'.

I could feel teammates flying past me on both sides, but I was determined to get to Heals. When I got there I bear-hugged him, then Mark Taylor, then Shane Lee. Hang on . . . What the hell? Shane wasn't even playing, but he was the third man in the huddle. Good effort, that. I reckon he might have been running even faster than me.

Curtly Ambrose, a man who could count his conversations with our team members on one hand, suddenly found his tongue. 'Go all the way now, maaaaan,' he said. 'You can do it. Dooo it!'

I don't know what was more surprising for us – taking 8/37 to win the match, or hearing Curtly not only speak to us but encourage us! It was the longest conversation I ever had with him, but I remember it well.

We felt like we had got out of jail, and – to quote the great singer Prince – we partied like it was 1999. Unfortunately, it was 1996 and we were three days away from a final.

World Cup semi-final – 'I'm coming, Heals.'

WE'RE NOT THE CHAMPIONS OF THE WORLD

* * *

Strangely, the final of the World Cup – against Sri Lanka – was played in the Gaddafi Stadium in Lahore, Pakistan, a country we hadn't visited all tour. It was named in honour of the Libyan leader Colonel Muammar Gaddafi in 1974, following a speech he gave in the city, in which he supported Pakistan's right to pursue nuclear weapons. Apparently, he promised to pass on his country's nuclear know-how – and also, allegedly, his secrets to reverse swing. (Sarfraz Nawaz and Imran Khan were rumoured to be in attendance.)

We had two long and hard daytime training sessions in the build-up to the final, so we could get used to the conditions. We batted first and scored 241. In the tea interval there was a power blackout, and it looked like we would have to come back the next day to finish the game. I was all for battling on and bowling in the dark – I was thinking only of the crowd, of course.

We did get back on the field that evening, and we started well, running out the dangerous Sanath Jayasuriya. When I dismissed Romesh Kaluwitharana, Sri Lanka was 2/23 and things were definitely going our way. Then, with my first ball to Asanka Gurusinha, I bowled a big inswinger that he nicked behind, just evading Ian Healy's glove and going for four. In hindsight, that was a match-turning moment.

From that time, the dew started to set in over Lahore, making it increasingly hard for us to grip the ball. No one was more hindered by the wet conditions than Warnie, who would have had better luck gripping a piece of soap. We dropped catches. Aravinda 'I Hook Half-Volleys' de Silva and Asanka Gurusinha batted beautifully to get Sri Lanka home in a historic victory. Like a few of his countrymen, 'the Guru' (who scored 65) now lives in Melbourne. He was one of my favourite Sri Lankan players, a wonderful left-hand bat – and he looks exactly like Rodney Rude!

To this day, I still ask myself why we only trained in the daytime before the match. The dew took us right out of the game, and it was something we should have been prepared for. It might not have changed the result as the Sri Lankans were superb – Ranatunga had galvanised them beautifully – but we had lingering questions in our heads and our hearts, and the loss really hurt. I hadn't been that devastated after a sporting contest since my beloved Hawthorn Football Club lost the 1984 Grand Final to Essendon after leading at three-quarter time.

Damn you, Aravinda de Silva, and damn you, Tim Watson!

I'm not sure what Arjuna Ranatunga would find funnier these days – the way that Sri Lanka thrashed us in the final, or that 20 years *after* he retired, the ICC changed the rule so that a batsman can't use a runner any more.

One small consolation after the match came when we were told that, since we were in a dry state, even if we had won the final we couldn't have drunk any alcohol in celebration. Now, that would have really hurt.

Chapter 17
Sympathy for Gilly

SUPER 8s WAS a precursor to Twenty20 cricket, and it came as the cricket authorities were looking for a shorter version of the game. It was a 16-over match in which everyone had to bowl at least one over. The ACB ran a Super 8 cricket tournament involving all six Australian states, held in Queensland over three weeks in midwinter of the 1996 off-season. Centred in Cairns, Townsville and Brisbane, the tournament incurred a loss of over a million dollars, but it was the greatest cricket junket that the cricketers involved would ever have. It was short on game time and long on partying time.

Adam Gilchrist, Paul Reiffel and I were sent up to Cairns to promote the tournament up in the top end. Gilly has since become a very polished media performer. These days, anyone listening to him miked up in the T20 games would see what appears to be a natural media talent, although that wasn't always the case.

We were sent to a Townsville school to have a chat to the kids about Super 8 cricket and to drum up some interest in the series. Gilly was volunteered by his two Victorian mates to do the speaking honours. He wasn't yet the superstar cricketer he later became, having played only a couple of one-day internationals.

When we arrived, the kids were in the middle of a very competitive, loud and intense basketball game. A teacher blew a whistle to get their attention but it was pretty tough as they

BOWLOLOGY

were so into their game. Finally, after about a hundred whistles, there was some calm. 'We have a very special cricketing guest,' said the teacher, 'and his name is Adam Gilchurch.'

There was dead silence for a minute, as the kids racked their brains to recall an Adam Gilchurch. I knew he was in trouble.

Unperturbed, Gilly started talking about the Super 8 series, and pretty soon the kids were getting restless. They began talking at an ever-increasing volume, and some kids started to get their basketball out again. Most of them just turned their back on Gilly and started chatting or playing cards. The noise was getting deafening.

But Gilly was a fighter, and he kept going with his speech – which by now was not even audible to those of us closest to him. Eventually he faltered a bit. 'Is anyone listening to me?' he asked. 'Anyone . . . anyone . . . Hello?' Finally, he looked over to Pistol and me and shrugged his shoulders in surrender.

The kids had done something that numerous future international bowling attacks would be unable to accomplish: total defeat of Adam Gilchrist.

At that moment, a little kid, no more than nine years of age but mature beyond his years, turned to me and said, 'Jeez, he's really dying out there, isn't he?'

'I know,' I said, a big grin on my face. 'Isn't it great?'

Chapter 18
Stuck in a Rut, and Freddy Krueger vs Predator

CAREER DRY SPELLS or slumps are as inevitable as petrol price hikes at Christmas time. All the greats, from Sir Donald Bradman to McGrath, Warne and Ponting, have felt the selectors' axe because of poor form or (in the selectors' cliché) 'team balance'. It seems to be a natural sporting evolution, culling the weak, who drop away and are not heard of again, or inspiring those left, who are strengthened with a new determination to make the most of their next chance.

As we approached the 1996/97 Australian summer of cricket, I began the season on tour in India with the Australian team. Back home in my first Shield game, against New South Wales, I started well, taking three top-order wickets – Taylor, Slater and Bevan – and made a nicely compiled 34 with the bat. I was booked in for the First Test against the touring West Indies. Well for a brief moment as I cancelled my Test match booking when I tore my quad muscle bowling in the second innings.

Okay it's a slight hiccup I thought and then rehabbed well over the next month determined to get my Test spot back. Big Hiccup in my first game back against England A as I tore my quad again after bowling 32 overs so playing Test cricket this summer seemed as likely as a Milli Vanilli comeback album. By the time I got back again after two torn quad muscles, half the season was gone. Because I had rehabbed well after a hard run with the quad injuries, I figured that I deserved some success straight away.

But the cricketing gods don't work that way, and all I'd done was get myself back to a level playing field. My impatience to make up for lost time quickly from my injuries would come back to bite me like a rabid dog. After a disastrous season I had to reassess my total approach to the game.

TECHNICAL

On the Indian tour (a Test match and five one-dayers across a six-week trip!) we had trained for hours. I had thought I was bowling close to the stumps but in reality I was jumping into the stumps, with my momentum going towards leg slip. So then I had to switch my top half back towards the stumps, which meant I was bowling around myself and running along the wicket. I was losing pace and bounce, and swinging the ball straight out of the hand. I'd gained a bad habit and it wasn't going to disappear overnight.

No, we don't. We reward patience, skill and execution.

PHYSICAL

I tore my quad twice and my hamstring once, and had constant shoulder stiffness.

MENTAL

My confidence was at an all-time low due to the above issues. I didn't have any vision or process goals. I was simply trying to get through games uninjured. I'd lost all the enjoyment and fun of cricket, and I was mentally shot.

STUCK IN A RUT, AND FREDDY KRUEGER VS PREDATOR

* * *

All in all, then, I was bringing my Z game to the field. I was a fighting umpires over whether I was running in the danger area, and I was getting tweaks in my hamstrings and quads, which made me question whether I had tears or whether it was just scar tissue. Patiently planning to get the batsman out was the last of my thoughts.

My body language was like that of a zombie cast member of *Shaun of the Dead*. But really it was *Nightmare on Flem Street*, since Freddy Krueger was well and truly in my head.

I finished the season with non-selection for the 1997 Ashes tour. In truth, I was even struggling for Victoria.

In reviewing the season, I had to answer this question: Was I prepared to take responsibility and change my approach to cricket? Because what I was doing clearly wasn't working. I had to find a way to strengthen my physical and mental presence on and off the field.

I knew I wasn't an expert in all areas, so I had to outsource the job to people who were experts in their fields. Luckily, I had some top blokes to call on.

TECHNICAL

Ashley Ross, who was then at Cricket Victoria and is now at the South Australian Cricket Association, helped me to straighten up my action, particularly my hips and feet, so that I was more aligned to off stump. I benefited from staying more upright at the release point, and a higher release point gave me more bounce, more pace and later swing.

PHYSICAL

I was still worried that my shoulder might fall out again, so I decided to put on as much muscle as possible around my body, and in particular my shoulders. I spent a lot of time at the King Club Gym, thanks to the late, great Trevor Barker – what a great man. I set up a better balanced program with (fitness guru and net half volley bowler) Steve Laussen.

MENTAL

Working with Anthony Stewart (who had worked at the successful Hawthorn Football Club for years and with the 1995 Carlton premiership team, and was then working with the Victorian cricket team), I established a clear plan for where I wanted my career to go. Stewy and I settled on the *Predator* theme. A predator knows his mission, stalks his opposition and is relentless in his pursuit of his goals. And it was my favourite Arnie movie.

THE PREDATOR: 'IF IT BLEEDS, YOU CAN KILL IT . . .'

1. Use my *skills* to *dominate* my opponents.
2. *Expect* to do well, every ball.
3. Always show the team that I *want* the ball in my hands.
4. Whether the opposition is 5/50 or 0/200, *act* or *be* energetic and positive.
5. Even if I'm a bit down, don't show my teammates. Think and act *tough*.
6. If things are slipping, *fight* hard. Turn it my way.
7. *Love* the competition.

STUCK IN A RUT, AND FREDDY KRUEGER VS PREDATOR

❋ ❋ ❋

My goal was 'to be a good Australian player by the end of the summer' – which was miles away from where I was at that stage, but I needed a clear goal to work towards. And I didn't just want to make it back, I wanted to be considered a *good* international player.

Preparation was the key to my confidence going into games, so I committed myself to preparing so that I could let things happen in game time. I wanted to go into games knowing that there was nothing more I could have done – physically, mentally, technically and tactically – to prepare for that game.

- My aim was for *planned* training, as close to game intensity as possible.
- I strove to minimise the likelihood of fluctuations in my performance, because I knew that *consistency was the key*.
- I wanted to be seen as a *low-maintenance, professional* player, who worked hard on all aspects of his game and gave himself the best chance of success. I wanted to build a reputation as 'Mr Reliable'.

After some testing times early in the season, the Predator gradually subdued Freddy Krueger and my confidence returned. My pace and late swing also returned. Significantly, I drastically changed my run-up, cutting it in half to just 15 steps, which clicked straight away when I took five wickets against Queensland.

With a shorter run-up, I felt there was less chance that I would overstride and lose my rhythm. I also felt more balanced at my take-off step, which gave me more momentum and power through the bowling crease. I could keep my pace and bounce for longer, and I got through my overs quicker.

BOWLOLOGY

And, after leading the domestic bowling averages with 40 wickets at an average of 18, I was picked in the Australian team as a replacement on the 1998 tour of India. In Bangalore, I had a quick chat to our skipper, Mark Taylor, who asked, 'Where have you been?'

'I was starring in *Predator vs Nightmare on Flem Street,*' I said, 'and Freddy's dead.'

Chapter 19
Cochin – Our Papillon

THE NAME 'COCHIN' still sends a shiver down the spine of all the Australians who played there in a one-day international on 1 April 1998. Cochin is on the south-west coast of the Indian peninsula, and the match conditions were the hottest and most oppressively humid that I and many of my teammates ever experienced. Players were tested both mentally and physically in conditions that made a sweaty day in Brisbane seem like a cool winter's day in Melbourne. It was our *Papillon*!

We arrived in Cochin for the first one-day match of a tri-series between India, Zimbabwe and us. Immediately, we were hit by the heat and the sweaty, humid conditions. The day before the match, as per our coach, Geoff 'Swampy' Marsh's regime, we trained for a lazy five hours or so – a fielding session, followed by a net session, followed by another fielding session. As I was struggling for breath, I remember thinking that I'd become very unfit all of a sudden.

The next day we arrived for the game full of enthusiasm about another chance to wear our Aussies colours with pride. We quickly changed into our training gear and bounded out on the ground for a 'warm-up'. I use the term loosely, as there really was no such thing as a warm-up under Swampy's leadership. We started off like commandos, doing run-throughs and diving for catches, then I bowled numerous overs in the nets.

Meanwhile, the Indian players were sipping cold water in the shade. The odd guy would come out and have a couple of throw-downs, then he'd shake his head at the heat and go back undercover. 'Soft!' was the general call from our group in response. Soon our warm-up entered its second hour; it had now officially become a top-up training session!

India won the toss and decided to bat. We had immediate rewards, as the big banana-bender Michael Kasprowicz dismissed Sachin Tendulkar, who had scored 650 runs in six innings against us so far on the tour, for just six runs. We were pumped. Someone said, 'Well, at least the Little Master has shown that he's human and can have a bad day!' We all had a giggle at that one as we watched the downcast figure of Tendulkar leaving the field.

Gradually, the 40 degree heat and 100 per cent humidity sank in. The lionhearted Kasper had been the sole quick to survive to this stage of the tour, having bowled his heart out in the three Test matches. Heartened by dismissing Tendulkar, he charged in repeatedly but the horrific conditions were taking their toll.

After a while, he got halfway though his run-up and just collapsed. We looked around for the grassy knoll! Once we realised we were safe, we ran over to our big quick, who was a real mess. He was mumbling something we couldn't comprehend, but amazingly the locals understood him. It turned out he was so delirious that he was speaking Cochinese. We gave him a wave as they stretchered him off. Meanwhile, the Indian captain, Mohammed Azharuddin, and Ajay Jadeja were belting us everywhere, putting on a hundred in no time.

Like Lazarus, Kasper reappeared, determined to get through his overs. All was not well, though, and after a couple of balls it was clear he had forgotten the basics of running. As a right-hander, he generally pushed off with his left foot, but he was so disoriented that he tried to start on his right foot and just fell down.

COCHIN – OUR PAPILLON

He rose again and bravely started belting his behind, like a jockey might hit his feeble horse in an effort to get him going. He started his run-up, then pulled up and wobbled like a bowling pin that has been nudged by the ball. For a brief moment he proudly stabilised, then the wobble started again and he collapsed onto the ground. It's a strike! We quickly carted Kasper off the ground, just as some vultures were starting to circle overhead.

Damien Martyn took the ball to complete Kasper's ninth over. If anyone could tolerate the heat, it was our man Marto, who was born in the humidity of Darwin and bred under the harsh sun of Perth.

Being a glutton for punishment, I waved my right to bowl a minimum 60 balls in my 10-over spell – and gave the umpires plenty of exercise – with three no-balls and three wides. Umpire Shyam Bansel was particularly keen on my bowling and allowed me to bowl seven balls in my last over, even though I'd failed to bowl a wide or no-ball. Nice gesture.

I remember being totally disoriented in my last over, My only goal was to run in and bowl the ball as quickly as possible, so I could finish the innings and get off the ground. The possibility of a wicket was the last thing on my mind. By the time we had finished – at last – India had scored 5/309.

The scene in our dressing room was chaotic. Kasper was lying on the table, moaning about aliens, and we warned him to stay away from the light. Our Darwin man, Damien Martyn, had collapsed from heat exhaustion after his three-over stint and was put in a chair under a cool shower. He didn't look like batting; everyone else was either vomiting or comatose. The comforts of home seemed a long way away.

Unsurprisingly, not much was said. As I walked, my boots were squelching in sweat. I felt like I'd jumped into a very hot steam bath and dog-paddled for a few hours. I planted myself on

State of the art: Cochin Stadium.

the first chair I could find. I tried a couple of times to bend down and untie my boots but I didn't have the energy, so I just sat back and watched the group.

Just then, Adam Gilchrist, after keeping for 50 overs, received some great news. Because we took so long to bowl our overs, he was told, the match referee had called for a 10-minute changeover – and we'd been fined for the slow over rate.

But the cricketing gods looked kindly on us, as Gilly and Mark Waugh got us off to a flyer, thrashing the Indians' quicks everywhere. When in the 11th over Javagal Srinath dismissed Junior, we were already 102.

Next, Tendulkar was introduced to the bowling crease after failing with the bat for the first time on the tour. Things seemed to be looking up for us. But, capping off his 'bad day', the Little Master proceeded to take five wickets – four with leg-breaks

COCHIN – OUR PAPILLON

and one with an off-break, which had Steve Waugh caught and bowled.

I was the last out, and we'd managed a reply of 268, a brave effort. We stumbled out for the match presentation to watch Tendulkar get another man-of-the-match award. There were a few rumours that he'd hired a Hollywood scriptwriter to spice up his inevitable match-winning performance. As we walked off at the completion of proceedings, the crowd showed their appreciation of our efforts by showering us with bottles, cans and fruit – including a watermelon. (Which was ironic, as the Indian batsman had treated me as if I was bowling one to them . . .)

When the Aussies played at Cochin during their 2007 tour of India, I was working as a commentator. Gilly and I reminisced about our first experience of the place and had a laugh. I remember him saying that it was one of the proudest displays by an Australian team in his time.

Looking back at the scorecard, I see that we actually played the match on April Fool's Day. If that was someone's idea of a joke, please step forward now!

Chapter 20
Tendulkar and Our Sharjah Birthday Bash

I'M ALL FOR birthday bashes – a way to celebrate each of life's milestones with a bit of fun and panache. What I wasn't up for on my 28th birthday was a bash in front of 30000 screaming Indian fans, and, in particular, getting bashed to all parts of the Sharjah ground by a fellow birthday boy, the Little Master, Sachin Tendulkar.

It was 24 April 1998, and the final of the Coca-Cola Cup in Sharjah. This match was the culmination of a long tour for most of the Aussie party. We had been crushed 2–1 in the Tests in India, and comprehensively beaten in all the lead-up games in the one-day series, although we had pulled off a memorable win over India in the final in Delhi.

Subcontinental pitches are generally low, slow and turning, which is not great when you are a fast-medium bowler who relies on pace, swing, seam and bounce. But you have to adjust to survive – and even, on the odd occasion, to thrive.

First off, I had to forget the Cricket Victoria coaching manual, which was quickly thrown out the door. It was practical in Australian conditions but not in the subcontinent. 'Stock ball just outside off stump to encourage batsman to cover drive, which will lead to nicks behind to the awaiting slips cordon,' it instructed. I don't think the Indian batsmen had read it, however, as my stock ball outswinger was either smashed straight down the ground or whipped behind square leg for four.

Azharuddin and V. V. S. Laxman were extremely puzzling. The wider I bowled outside off stump, the more they whipped me through the leg side. When I pitched even wider to force them to play with a straight bat, they would open the face and caress the ball through point for four. Playing 'in the V' between mid-on and mid-off was obviously not part of their cricket education.

Bowling to Tendulkar was a different proposition altogether. He was – and still is – a freak, possessing a great all-round game. Sir Donald Bradman once said he was the modern batsman closest to himself in stature and technique. Bowling to him over the years taught me a lot about Bowlology.

He always seemed brim-full of confidence, and he had that ability to knock a bowler off his length and hit him to different zones of the ground. Whether through his exquisite square drive, his lofted drive back over your head, his on drive, which went off like a gun, or his delicate leg glance, his scoring zones were as fully stocked as Pamela Anderson's bikini.

Actually, it was real buzz bowling to him, particularly in one-day games in India. The ground would always be packed – people would be hanging off the rafters. The noise would be deafening, so much so that unless you waved to a teammate before you said something, chances were that he wouldn't hear you.

Running in to bowl the first ball was exhilarating but also deafening, like the bounce-down to start a footy grand final. If you happened to bowl a couple of dot balls, the crowd got impatient and started handclapping – they wanted Sachin runs, not dot balls. Tendulkar gripped his bat a bit tighter – he was going to hit the ball hard. You couldn't give any width to Tendulkar; it would be like serving up a cold beer to Bob Hawke. They would both smash them.

TENDULKAR AND OUR SHARJAH BIRTHDAY BASH

Best way to bowl to Sachin: Get him down the non-strikers' end.

Despairingly, you would look for some support from your field . . . Damn, you're only allowed two men out in the first 15 overs. So you didn't have a lot of options. Too much width and it was four or wide. You had to bowl short of a length, with the odd bouncer; unless it was swinging a great deal, anything full was a big no-no against Sachin. All in all, I often felt as useless as a McDonald's gherkin when I was bowling to him.

In the final of the one-day series of our 1998 tour, played in Delhi, we decided to bowl more short balls to all the Indians, including Sachin. Kasper and I contained Sourav Ganguly and Sachin early with shortish balls, then I decided that the first ball of my sixth over was a good time to bowl my first real bouncer to Sachin. I went over my checklist:

PRE-BALL:
- *'Win the ball'*: I felt this was a great phrase for keeping me in the present, focusing on bowling the best ball I could.

Once I had *won* a few consecutive balls, my confidence would be up.
- *Deep breaths*: I had to play the game at my pace; I knew I tended to get into trouble when I rushed things.
- *Off stump*: This was the line I wanted to run in on, and the line I wanted to bowl.

The Bowlologist

- *Rhythm*: All bowlers say after bowling, 'Well, I had great rhythm today.' You can't see rhythm, so I had to define it. For me, it meant not overstriding too early in my run-up. Short and strong to start.
- *Power*: I tried to maximise my momentum through the bowling crease by pushing quickly and hard off my back leg, with a powerful pull-in to my body with my left arm.

POST-BALL:
- Aggressive stare, review the last ball, plan the next one.

I then sent down a beauty. The ball lifted steeply off a short length to around head height, and Sachin fended it away. The ball caught his bat and glove and Gilly took an amazing catch diving to his right.

It was the first time I'd scored the prize scalp of Tendulkar, and we went on to win the final. During our batting innings, we got a sneak preview of Steve Waugh's slog-sweep, which would become influential in his batting for the rest of his career.

TENDULKAR AND OUR SHARJAH BIRTHDAY BASH

After a surprise win in the one-day final, Big Kaspar and I had a celebratory beer. Kasper, ever the prankster, is wearing a fan on his head.

The only negative came when our team manager, Steve Bernard, was informed by the Indian officials as we were on the threshold of victory that there was no prize money for the tournament. Hmm...

* * *

In the Coca-Cola Cup in Sharjah we had India's measure before the final, although Tendulkar was the big thorn in our side. He batted at a level previously unseen in my time in cricket, but in a losing team. After being bounced out in the final in Delhi, Sachin changed his footwork slightly against us, looking to move back rather than forward, and then he started to pull and hook Kasper and me quite comfortably.

His scores warmed up through the short tournament. He made 80 out of India's score of 206 in our first match, then backed up with a dazzling 143 out of 250. Sachin was presented with a special award after that knock, even though he was on the losing team. That 'special award' looked pretty similar to our vanished prize money from the recent Indian one-day series.

Anyway, in the final – played on my birthday (and Sachin's) – we lost the toss and were sent in. We scored 272, thanks mainly to our determined captain, Steve Waugh, and a bludgeoning 70 from the gifted Darren Lehmann.

When we took the field, I was given the first over to set the tempo and get us off to a brilliant wicket-taking start. Well, India needed 11 fewer runs after my first over, which probably wasn't the start Tugga and my teammates were looking for. But the match then settled into an arm wrestle between Kasprowicz, Tom Moody, Warnie, me and the Indian top order. We finally dismissed Ganguly and Nayan Mongia, but Sachin stood strong, as he had all series.

One of the greatest sights in world cricket is a battle between legends, and you always get the best view from on the field. Tendulkar vs Warne was a promoter's dream – a colossal clash between the world's best batsman and bowler. On this day it was victory for the Little Master, as he hit our peroxided leg-spinner back over his head for six.

I heard a huge roar from the crowd at one point, and I looked up at the video scoreboard. The ground announcer was wishing Sachin a happy 25th birthday. He was probably enjoying his milestone, I thought, but he was ruining mine.

Tendulkar then started to take control. It was hard to think that he could have played better than he had in the last couple of months, especially since he wasn't getting a lot of batting support from his teammates. There was no 'corridor of uncertainty' or 'avenue of apprehension' when he was in full flight. Full balls were driven with class and power, while pulls and cuts were smashed square of the wicket as he brought up another century.

TENDULKAR AND OUR SHARJAH BIRTHDAY BASH

I was brought back on to try to break the partnership that had developed between Tendulkar and Azharuddin. In my first over, two huge lbw shouts against Sachin were turned down by Steve Bucknor, who showed about as much interest in them as I do in Mozart's five-hour opera *Così fan tutte*. It was obvious he wasn't keen to give me a late birthday present.

The game drifted away from us, and it was small consolation when Sachin was finally given out lbw to Kasper – to a ball that was pitched in Dubai and hit Sachin in Sharjah about a metre outside leg stump. He had scored an amazing 134 out of 275 Indian runs.

Suddenly, while I was drifting around the outfield, preparing myself for the loss, I heard the ground announcer wish me a happy birthday. There it was on the video screen – and it was greeted by Bronx cheers from the passionately Indian-supporting crowd. I'd turned 28 years of age, I'd just lost a final and I'd been booed by 30 000 people. *I've probably had happier birthdays*, I reflected by myself down at fine leg.

Chapter 21
Haggle Up

MONTY PYTHON'S LIFE *of Brian* is one of my all-time favourite films. I didn't find the 'big nose' scene that funny, for obvious reasons, but I loved the 'haggle' scene. In fact, it inspired me during our cricket tour of Dubai in 1998.

Bargaining is considered an artform in Dubai. The shop-owners expect you to haggle the price with them, and they're used to taking down soft western cricketers who have too much money and very little experience of the ancient shopping tradition. A lot of visitors don't have the stomach for it. But not me, baby! I couldn't wait for the duels to begin.

We were playing some one-dayers – or Tendulkar testimonial games, as I called them, since he averaged something like 545 on the lifeless decks. It was so hot and humid that bowlers dehydrated just while walking from the bus to the change rooms. All the matches were held in Sharjah but we were staying in Dubai, and I had come up with a plan that was going to destroy the 1000-year-old Middle Eastern haggling culture.

In between games, Adam Gilchrist, Michael Kasprowicz and I entered a watch shop in the Dubai markets. Gilly and Kasper were looking at some expensive watches for their partners, Lindsay and Mel. I was only looking at some cheap watches for my dad, Ian, and my brother, Justin, as I'd already purchased an expensive Tag Heuer watch for my future wife, Wendy.

The small shop-owner had probably been in the business since childhood, and the shop had almost certainly been in his family for generations. He could sniff out a tightarse like me from miles away, so he immediately worked out that I was the one to ignore. I didn't mind, I had got used to the same treatment from autograph-hunters, selectors, women and teammates. My kids have continued the tradition.

So he quite rightly focused his attention on the potentially more lucrative Gilly and Kasper, who were looking to spend hundreds, if not thousands, of dollars. Despite this, I called him over, insisting that he give me some attention too.

'How much for these two watches?' I enquired.

'$100 for both,' he said impatiently.

I paused, looked at the watches, then looked up at him and said, 'No, I'll give you $150.' I had started haggling up!

Gilly and Kasper looked at me as if I'd been out in the sun too long (I had), but the bloke was completely thrown. I could see his business mind trying to process my answer. Never in his life had anyone offered him *more* for an item. His genes were telling him that it had never happened in the thousand years since his great-great-great-great-grandfather threw open the doors and sold the first sundial on this very spot.

'No, sir, $100 for both,' he quite correctly corrected me.

'Okay, you sound serious,' I replied. 'I'll pay $175, no less.'

I was now in my IHS (Ideal Haggling State) and in complete control of the situation. My reverse haggling was short-circuiting his mercantile mind, logic was turned on its head and he couldn't for the life of him work out what this lunatic was doing. He looked at me and across at Gilly and Kasper – he didn't want to lose their business but he didn't know what was going on.

I went in for the kill. 'Mate, $180, last offer.'

He was reeling, knocked out on his feet.

I reached into my wallet and pulled out a single $50 note.

HAGGLE UP

Dazed, he looked at it, and then over to Gilly and Kasper. He took my $50, gave me the watches, then ran back to the others. But it was too late, and my teammates had turned and headed for the exit, waving their hands at his desperate attempts to get them to buy something. Anything.

I was very pleased with my theory of haggling up, but the poor shop-owner just shook his head. He was a broken man and I was the proud owner of two $10 watches, which I gave to my dad and brother. They worked brilliantly for the next seven days or so.

There's one born every minute.

Chapter 22
Reverse Swing

IN THE EARLY 1990s, reverse swing gave fast bowling a shot in the arm – a bit like what the grunge movement led by Seattle's Nirvana, Pearl Jam and Soundgarden did for the music industry. Pakistani pace pair Wasim Akram and Waqar Younis were its greatest exponents. They didn't look anything like Kurt Cobain or Eddy Vedder – instead of ripped jeans, they ripped through batting orders with their sandshoe-crushing reverse-swinging yorkers.

Reverse swing had already been around for years. In the 1970s, funnily enough around the time of another music explosion, 'the Sex Pistols inspired Punk era', Sarfraz Nawaz mastered the skill of making the ball swing in a 'non-traditional' fashion. This created 'anarchy' on flat, low, abrasive wickets in his native Pakistan. In the summer of 1978/79, he brought his boomerang old ball swinging skills to Australia, taking nine wickets in one Test innings, including a spell of seven wickets for one run (Australia was 3/305 chasing 382 to win) which left the Australian batsman as confused as I was at the end of the movie *Donnie Darko*. Eventually, he passed on his knowledge to Imran Khan, who in turn passed it to Wasim and Waqar.

Swing bowling is about integrating the *uncontrollable* factors, such as the weather, pitch and outfield conditions plus your captain's mood, with the *controllable* factors of wrist position, seam position, the condition of the ball and possibly ... bottle tops! And, of course, bowling the ball into a *snick street* line is crucial. The theory is to get the texture of the leather on the two sides of the ball as different as possible, one side like George Clooney (smooth) and the other like *Entourage*'s Ari Gold (abrasive), which creates more airflow over one side and thus makes the ball move.

With a new ball, it is the seam that dictates the swing. It acts like a rudder: get it angled the right way, with enough backspin to give the seam stability in flight, and the ball will swing. After a few overs, the deterioration of the leather comes into play, and players shine one side and leave the other to rough up with cuts, dimples and so on. The air fills in the cuts, dimples etc. on the rough side, and the ball moves to that side.

After 50 overs or so – sometimes even earlier, if the pitch or outfield has an abrasive surface – the rough side of the ball starts to get too rough and the shiny side starts to get duller, with cuts and little divots in it. The air starts to prefer this side, and it fills in the gaps and sucks the ball to that side – the opposite from normal swing.

Pakistani teams talk about the need to keep the ball as dry as possible – like their country's alcohol policy – and prohibit sweaty players from touching the ball. They have as few players as possible handling it before it gets back to the bowler, who must hold the ball on the seam.

Late swing is the key to reverse swing's destructive power, as demonstrated by Freddy Flintoff and co. in the thrilling 2005 Ashes series. A batsman makes his decision on what shot to play when the ball is about two-thirds of the way down the pitch. If you can swing it in the last third of the pitch, you've struck Bowlology gold.

REVERSE SWING

※ ※ ※

When I think of some of the fun moments throughout my cricket career, facing 95 mile per hour, reverse-swinging toe-crushers from Pakistani paceman isn't at the top of the list.

My introduction to the world of reverse swing was for Victoria against Pakistan in the 1989/90 season at the MCG. I walked out to bat on a hat-trick, and to be fair I hadn't taken much notice of the bowling from our dressing rooms. I took centre and looked past the umpire to the bowler, who looked a Bernie Quinlan torpedo punt away. He was so far away that he looked like an ant, although a quirky ant who wore a headband and a 1970s-style moustache. He didn't look dissimilar to the guy who played guitar in Hall and Oates. He charged in to bowl, like a bloke at the running of the bulls. Dennis Lillee used to say you should build your run-up like a train leaving the station – a slow start to long steps. This bloke looked like he had been inspired by the Chinese bullet train.

Now, I'd faced plenty of blokes who charged in like Tarzan but bowled like Jane. So I knew there was still a chance he wouldn't be as quick as he looked. He released his 95 mile per hour thunderbolt, and my self-talk went something like this:

1. *Fuck! This guy is quick!*
2. *Beauty, it's wide...*
3. *Shit! It hit my pad!*
4. *Fuck!* (Searing pain engulfed my tender shin area.)

There was a massive appeal but I was given not out. It was one of those 'What the fuck?!' moments. I looked at the scoreboard and the ball was 120 overs old – no new ball had been taken. This was my first introduction to Waqar Younis and reverse swing.

I looked to my batting partner, Paul Reiffel, for some support. He needed some support himself as he was doubled over in laughter.

One of Pistol's favourite bands was the Australian rock legends AC/DC, and in some ways the way he played his cricket was similar to this great hard-rock band. Both Reiffel and AC/DC rarely sprang any surprises: their style was based on consistency and tightness, with no frills. But they were both professionals and always got the job done. Most importantly, they delivered the goods when it was needed.

As a player, Pistol was a model of consistency over a long period of time for both Victoria and Australia. With the ball, his main assets were pace, bounce and accuracy; he was more a seamer than a swinger of the ball. However, if conditions suited him, he could shape the ball away from right-hand batsmen, and had a beautiful off-cutter to left-hand batsmen. Patience and a smart cricket brain were key factors to his success. Very rarely did he lose his cool, and he was one player who could keep his emotions in check and deal clinically with any situation.

He would probably have been voted the least likely of our teammates to become a Test umpire, but he has actually taken his low-fuss, highly competitive nature to the umpiring fraternity.

So for the next hour, I was in armed conflict, dodging and weaving Waqar's fully loaded banana-bending thunderbolts. I was underarmed and vulnerable with my spindly Kookaburra bat.

Meanwhile, Pistol was blocking every subsequent over from the other end, where a Lionel Richie lookalike wasn't 'Dancing on the Ceiling' but rather bowling innocuous non-spinning left-arm orthodox balls. Whenever I tried to nudge a single to get away from my nightmare, Pistol would be leaning on his bat and not backing up an inch – but with a big smile on his face. There would be no singles from Pistol this day.

※ ※ ※

Waqar was a very good exponent of reverse swing, but the master was Wasim Akram. I came up against him in the First Test of our 1998 tour, when we played at Rawalpindi. I had not batted in a Test match for three years.

I walked out at number eight, feeling very nervous. Not only was I going out to face a hostile Pakistani pace attack, but the batting advice from the top order was that the ball was reverse-swinging very late. They suggested I negate the swinging ball by
1. getting a full stride forward
2. using a short backlift to negate the swing.

This didn't tally with my natural instinct to
1. go back as far as I could to maximise time to see the ball
2. stuff the swing – I didn't want to get killed.

I asked the umpire for centre and looked up to see Wasim with the ball in hand. He was my favourite bowler in the world, the bowler I'd love to be most, so I was looking forward to the challenge. First ball, Wasim bounced me with a 'perfume ball' that I swear spilt two of my nose hairs.

He followed through deep, swearing in Urdu at me. Then some other Pakistani players behind the wicket joined in. I really couldn't take offence as I couldn't understand a word. Then, out of nowhere, I heard an English sledge. Someone in the slips said, 'C'mon, Wasim . . . he poo-pooing his pants!'

Bloody oath I was.

Wasim's next ball started outside off stump at pace and, before I could react, swung sharply in and cannoned into my pads. That brought a mighty appeal from the Pakistani team.

The umpire said it was going down the leg side. That was lucky, as I would have needed a stretcher to get me off, such was the dead feeling in my leg. I looked at the scoreboard, which showed the ball was 110 overs old.

The next ball pitched in the same area. I kept a short backlift and got bat and pad together, but this time the ball moved away. I missed it, embarrassingly, by a metre. This was compounded by laughter from behind the wicket from the Pakistani fielders. End of the over.

The next over I faced, Wasim ran in with both hands on the ball to cleverly disguise the shiny side, so I couldn't predict the direction of the swing. But the joke was on him, as I was not even looking at the ball as he ran in. I was thinking more about self-preservation than wicket-preservation. The ball started on off stump and I threw my bat at it. Luckily, it was the away-swinger and I accidentally hit the ball off the back foot through the covers for four.

Wasim was seriously pissed now and decided to bowl around the wicket. I posed a question to myself: *Is he going to bounce me or york me?* I predicted the former, and unfortunately he did the latter.

Batting is about split-second decision-making. Just as I was deciding to block his inswinger, delivered very wide of the crease, the ball swung away from my bat, first subtly, then acutely. It hit the crease and then off stump. I walked off, thinking to myself, *Thanks for the master class in reverse swing, Wasim, but that ball was totally wasted on me.*

REVERSE SWING

1998 Commonwealth Games Australian Squad.
Okay, who can pick me out?
We lost the final to South Africa to take the silver medal.
Now I would take a silver medal any day of the week, but a little voice in my head questions whether Steve Waugh (leading run-scorer) and I (leading wicket-taker) surely deserve an individual gold medal.
I'm also comfortable with retrospective medals.

* * *

With no Shane Warne, due to injury, we were underdogs against a strong Pakistani team in 1998. We had the experienced Glenn McGrath, but with Fleming (fifth Test), MacGill (second Test) and Colin 'Funky' Miller (debut Test), I don't think the strong Pakistani batting line-up of Saeed Anwar, Inzamam-ul-Haq and co. were quivering in their boots. But we worked beautifully as a bowling unit, with Stu MacGill as our trump card – he took 15 wickets in the series at an average of 27.

Was Stuart MacGill the Rodney Dangerfield of Australian cricket – with no respect? He was a bit like boxer Larry Holmes, who took over from the extraordinary Muhammad Ali; Craig McDermott, who replaced Dennis Lillee; and even AC/DC's Brian Johnson, who followed the late, great Bon Scott, in that, regardless of how well he performed, he would always be compared with and live in the shadows of the King of Spin, Shane Warne. But with 208 Test wickets in just 44 Tests, MacGill was a match-winner in spinning conditions.

He was a wine connoisseur who demolished novels on tour as ferociously as Homer Simpson consumes donuts. Socially, he was one of the most interesting people to wine and dine with, being intelligent and passionate and having a good sense of humour. People are often surprised that his on-field persona image was replaced off-field by that of a man generous with his time and engaging.

Some say it's white-line fever or just a competitive edge, but I think all elite sportsman change their demeanour once they step onto the sporting field. Some are just better at hiding it.

Stu's on-field presence included a stern, Dirty Harry–like intensity and a dramatic battle cry when an lbw appeal was turned down. With him, a wicket wasn't cause for party time, it was expected. Bowling was as much a mental battle with himself as with the batsman.

When you field at mid-on or mid-off, you usually encourage your fellow bowler with a 'Good luck' or 'Keep going, mate'. This is generally acknowledged with a nod from the bowler. Not so with Stu, who would acknowledge your support with a dead-serious 'Don't talk to me'. Then his intense stare would be back.

His on-field intensity could translate to training as well, much to the amusement (and sometimes the bemusement) of his teammates. On tour in Pakistan in 1998, Stu was batting in the nets. There was always a heap of bowlers in the nets who were keen to run in and send a few down, and so things weren't always in control. Sometimes you looked up to find the ball already halfway down the pitch.

Stu was batting one day, and his stumps were knocked over just as he looked up. He picked the ball up and threw it back at the bowler with a warning: 'Mate, wait till I'm fucking ready before you bowl.'

A couple of balls later, same bowler, same result.

MacGill started screaming at the bowler, 'Mate, I fucking warned you . . .'

He picked up the ball, lobbed it in the air and smashed it into a grandstand. With a few more expletives, he added, 'Go fetch that.'

Geoff Marsh, our coach, was never that keen on a confrontation. I walked past him and said, 'Swamp, what about MacGill?' I was interested to see what tack our coach would take.

Swampy just looked at me and said, 'MacGill – pyscho!' He shook his head and headed off to the dressing room.

* * *

Anyway, we won the First Test – a crushing victory by an innings and 99 runs. It was the first time we had won a Test match in Pakistan for 40 years. Since we took the last wicket at the sprightly time of 9.43 a.m. on day five, it seemed a bit early for a beer. So we waited until 10 a.m. to start the celebrations, which were always going to be rather large.

After singing 'Underneath the Southern Cross I Stand', we progressed from the dressing rooms to the American Club so we could have a few more beers. As always, the jukebox was getting a fair workout – one song in particular, the glam-rock band Sweet's 'Ballroom Blitz'. All the New South Welshman (or 'Bluebaggers', as they called themselves) kept requesting the song and changing the lyrics from 'ballroom blitz' to 'Bluebag blitz'.

That was starting to rankle a few of the boys, and none more so than big Kasper. I was adding fuel to the fire by noting how arrogant these New South Wales blokes were. Charged up with beer, and pretty miffed, Kasper started to prance around like a caged lion. Then he suddenly came off his full run and, channelling his inner Bruce Lee, launched a high kick, which split the Bluebaggers into a crumbling mess.

Like a scene out of *Rambo*, Kasper left Bluebagger bodies all over the dance floor. Gradually, they pulled themselves up and staggered from the dance floor. Suprisingly there were no requests for an encore of 'Ballroom Blitz' for the rest of the afternoon.

HIGHLIGHTS OF OUR 1998 TOUR OF PAKISTAN

1. We won a Test series in Pakistan for the first time in 40 years.
2. Heals broke Rod Marsh's Test wicketkeeping world record in the First Test, with a dismissal from 'Swiller, Killer, Chiller' Col Miller's bowling.
3. Tubby's 334 not out in the Second Test equalled Sir Donald Bradman's highest Test score by an Australian. Tubby even scored a hundred in a session, which I nearly repeated when we were bowling.
4. Magilla read 48 books on the tour, beating Bill O'Reilly's 47 books on the ship over to the United Kingdom in 1938.
5. Thanks to Kasper, 'BlueBag Blitz' was never sung again on any tour.

Chapter 23
Nerds and Julios

I REMEMBER BEING shocked to read that gear belonging to Michael Clarke and Michael Kasprowicz was stolen from the Australian dressing rooms during the 2005 Ashes series. Fortunately, I was able to see the relevant insurance claims, which revealed two drastically different individuals.

Clarkey's claims were for hair dye, wax, gel and mousse, Calvin Klein aftershave, moisturiser, lipbalm, facial scrub, a personal mirror, three Diesel shirts, a hairdryer and an iPod with Bose speakers. Kasprowicz's claims were simpler: a couple of AC/DC tapes, flannel shirts, ugg boots and his Teac cassette player. He lost some shavers, but no problems – he just grew a beard.

The difference this revealed was that Clarkey is a Julio and Kasper is a Nerd. Julios are named after Julio Iglesias; just like the great Latin singer, these players take too much pride in their personal appearance. Nerds – who take their name from Louis and Gilbert from the 1983 college comedy *Revenge of the Nerds* – are people who are fashionably challenged.

Much has been written about losing the 2005 Ashes series, and various reasons for our loss have been given. But no one has considered the possibility that the team was unbalanced, being weighted too heavily towards the Julio-type players. Less hair product and teeth whitener and more bowl cuts and outdated facial hair could be the key to an Australian resurgence.

The concept of Julios and Nerds in the Australian team was created on the 1993 Ashes tour. The first contest between the two camps was the decidedly nerdish game of ten-pin bowling, which surprisingly the Julios won. From that day, training session games were no longer a leisurely warm-up for the nets. No, this was warfare; each game of soccer, touch footy, Aussie Rules or foccor (which I'll explain later) was a battlefield of *Gladiator* proportions.

The Nerds generally had the better of the two teams on the sporting field, due to some superficial injuries that hurt the Julios. Split fingernails, ruffled hair and creased shirts were the main injury concerns.

With the help of some former teammates, I have selected a dream team of Julios vs Nerds.

JULIOS

Michael Slater: Opening batsman who set up Test matches early with his daring strokeplay, particularly square of the wicket. A pocket dynamo with the bat; a real match-winner who preferred hitting boundaries to running singles. Probably Australian crickets first 'manscaper' – he once shaved off every single hair on his body in India in 2001. Had a mancrush on Jon Bon Jovi and also owned a smorgasbord of bubblegum-pop records that any 15-year-old girl would be proud of, including Britney Spears, Aqua and the Backstreet Boys.

Greg Blewett: Classy performer who smashed hundreds against England in his first two Tests. Always on the cutting edge of fashion, but at 41 does he have to dress like an 18-year-old? Had an eagle eye for any fashion mistake or any embarrassing physical fault in a teammate. For example, at the bar he would ask if you wanted a beer and also one for your mate, pointing at a pimple on your face. Not scared of a mirror, often seizing the opportunity for a quick lip pout or bicep flex on the way to the crease. Frustrated by his inability to put on muscle bulk throughout his career, he went on a bodybuilding and drinking regime one pre-season. It didn't result in any biceps or calves but he did acquire a taste for stout.

Justin Langer: One of Australia's toughest batsman of all time. For the most part of his career, he always seemed the batsman under the most pressure to keep his spot, until an opening batting 'bromance' with Matty Hayden blossomed on and off the field. What he lacked in stature (who cares if he needs a booster seat when driving his car?), he made up for in character. A black belt in martial arts, including origami, so therefore could join any group he wanted to. Went through a Jean-Claude Van Damme stage in the late 1990s, with an open vest shirt with no sleeves and white linen trousers . . . Nobody questioned it.

Mark Waugh: Classy, laid-back cricketer – what a classical batsman. His caressing through the leg side was a purist's delight. Very handy quicker bowler in his youth, rarely pitching the ball in the batsman's half. Good enough to impress the great Bishen Bedi with his off-spinners. Top-class fieldsman. I had probably my only deep conversation with Junior during the 2001 Ashes tour, when we got a free bag of Nivea products. He caringly and selflessly talked me through the need to moisturise thoroughly after facial scrubbing, etc. Owner of one of the most lovingly cared for buffonts the world has ever seen – a big Billy Ray Cyrus and Richard Marx fan. Collar always up, on and off the field.

Damien Martyn: Beautiful off-side player. Came back from an unfair six-year hibernation to become one of Australia's great middle-order players. A very smooth batsman, and a too-cool-for-school type who values street credibility. May have based his image on Maverick (Tom Cruise) from *Top Gun*. Was never a big conversationalist but instead used lingo like 'What's up?' and 'Bro' and 'Giddy up'. Plans to eventually open up a coffee shop specialising in skinny mocha café au lait for his brothers in the hood in the Bronx, New York.

Michael Bevan: One-day run machine. A methodical and calculated batsman who worked out game scenarios and field placement and built a plan to win on the last ball of the game. Not afraid to get his top off in photo shoots to show off his sixpack and his full-toothed smile. Julio gold. One chink was his fashion sense, which trailed at times – bandanas, leather pants and vests with nothing underneath. Kindly donated these clothes to Captain Feathersword from the Wiggles.

Shane Watson: I didn't play with Watto but I have admired his Julio tendencies from afar. What a cricketer! A hard hitter when opening the batting, and a clever medium-pacer with great swinging skills. Robust, with the build of an Adonis. Loves a battle but has been haunted by back stress fractures (and ghosts, during the 2005 Ashes tour). Once listed his hobbies as clothing and shopping – two things that make Nerds cringe. Prides himself on his personal grooming. It must be tough to get in front of the mirror at lunch or tea with so many Julios in the team.

Ian Healy: Australian wicketkeeper in the team of the century. A passionate team man, good leadership skills and the worst kick of an AFL ball ever. Ex-schoolteacher, which would come out every now again as he always wanted a lot of holidays. Once when I dropped a catch he told me to stand in the corner for the rest of the session. Actually a massive nerd, but I needed a

NERDS AND JULIOS

Julio keeper and he was voted third-best-dressed sportsman in Queensland (losing to Steve Irwin and Wally Lewis). He got the nod over Gilly.

Brendon Julian: Known in Julio folklore as 'the Natural'. Tall and tanned, six foot seven, good-looking, with a body any NBA basketballer would kill for – which begs the question why he wasn't cast in the critically acclaimed *Baywatch Down Under* TV series. One chink in his Julio armour is that although he often buys the most expensive designer clothes, he selects and wears the worst items. Uses enough hairspray to create his own ozone layer.

Shane Warne: A Julio hall-of-famer. Has all the natural attributes of a media headliner: vanity, a good fashion sense, money and fast cars. Nicknamed 'Showbags' by his St Kilda teammates early in his career because he looked good on the outside but had crap in the middle – surely a Julio motto. Bagged 1000 international wickets on a diet of cheese sandwiches, pizzas and salt-and-vinegar chips. Still bowling maidens over, having become engaged to Liz Hurley.

Brett Lee: No one bowled express pace for longer than Binga. His first two Tests against India were the quickest bowling I ever saw. If Warnie was the original Julio prototype, Lee has taken it into a new era. Some very strong Julio attributes. Fastest bowler in the world, good looking, blond hair, owns his own clothing line and plays bass in a rock band (Six and Out), along with his brother, Shane, Richard Chee Quee, Brad McNamara and Gavin Robertson – but don't let him sing! Was a presenter at the Indian Bollywood awards and had a number 2 Indian single. Could be the Brad Pitt of Bollywood in years to come.

James Pattinson – or NJOTB 'New Julio On The Block': Following in Bingas footsteps with classic Julio attributes: good looking, killer smile and a hit with the ladies. A solarium pro, which has teammates worried he could end up looking like Magda from *There's Something About Mary*. Like Slats, has a music collection most 15-year-old girls would own and is rumoured to be in the Justin Bieber fan club. Likes to set dress trends in the team and is known for shopping in the trendy Chapel Street, Prahan precinct and spending his whole Test match fee before his two-hour parking limit is up. Single-handedly tried to bring the 'Vanilla Ice' haircut back last summer but luckily for Australian cricket we had no takers.

Glenn McGrath: Wicket-taking machine. Former Nerd hall-of-famer, thanks to his haircuts, pig-shooting magazines and time spent squatting in caravans. Has tainted his image more recently, with an early midlife Julio-influenced fashion crisis. In years gone by, his bowling was like his haircuts: straight, slightly short of a length, predictable but very effective and nerdish. Now, we see a new McGrath, his latest haircuts probably from a stylist, resulting in more options: a bit of flair, colouring, a part and even a fuller length. He committed Julio suicide. Sad to see the decline of a once-proud Nerd.

Errol Alcott: Was the Aussie team physiotherapist under five Australian captains since 1984. Alcott was also a trainer, throw-down partner, strength and conditioning guru, manager, father figure, psychologist and mate to a couple of generations of Australian cricketers. He was bestowed with the nickname 'Hooter' on his first tour to the West Indies, 22 years ago, when he was a novice to the game of cricket. During the first tour game he was getting a bit bored as the hours crawled by, and

NERDS AND JULIOS

Potential sitcom: 'Two Nerds and a Julio'.

when it became too much, he finally asked someone when they blow the hooter to signal the end of the day's play. Immediately, his nickname was set in concrete. Hooter's Julio tendencies were captured in the way he would run out to check on players who needed medical attention on the field. After checking that Channel Nine hadn't gone to an ad break, Hooter would give his well-waxed hair a flick, adjust his black Oakleys and make sure every part of his clothing was neat and tidy. He would start with small steps, pushing out his massive chest, with his well-muscled arms on show in a shirt that was slightly too small. You can just picture him running out to the music from *Chariots of Fire*.

NERDS

Mark Taylor: Tubby opening batsman and one of Australian cricket's greatest captains and gum-chewers. I loved playing under Mark Taylor. He could have just survived a plane crash and hitchhiked to the ground on a Harley-Davidson, and you wouldn't have known. Just give him his floppy cricket hat, his sunglasses and his chewing gum, and this man had the coolness of James Bond. It gave the troops a lot of confidence. He handled controversy and form slumps with a great deal of class. Made 334 not out against Pakistan in 1998, and won overwhelming support for declaring while he was equal with Sir Don's highest Test score. There was less support for his dress sense which was very nerdish and classless. Was noted for wearing tea towels with buttons on them for shirts and thinking they were cool. The death knell for any Australian cricketer of that era was if Tubby commented on your shirt in a positive fashion. That shirt would be stamped 'never to be worn again' and duly burned.

Matthew Hayden: A dominating and technically correct opening batsman who once held the record for the highest score in Test match cricket. Came of age on the 2001 Indian tour: his hundred in the First Test, in Mumbai, was a classic. He was the only batsman to dominate 'the Turbanator', Harbhajan Singh, on that tour, sweeping him or hitting him back over his head for six. Was nearly history when his and fellow Nerd Andrew Symonds' fishing boat sank, leaving them to swim a few hundred metres to shore (a scene that will be re-enacted for the movie *Dumb and Dumber 3*). Obsessive about fishing and cooking, two very Nerdish pastimes, he took his own kitchen on tour with him.

NERDS AND JULIOS

Ricky Ponting: Best Aussie batsman of the modern era. Explosive, attacking batsman who took the game away from the opposition bowlers, regularly driving balls on the up from short of a length and could pull quicker bowlers off full lengths. His 'corridor of uncertainty' was the width of a 20-cent coin when he was in full flight. Probably the best all-round sportsman of my era (even though I did beat him in an AFL goalkicking competition in Punjab in 2001, and thrashed him in the Big Dipper's footy quiz game in Colombo in 1999). Since his marriage to Rhianna, he has attempted to spruce up his image, including white Diesel shoes and jeans that are new but are made to look old. His Rexona and Swisse vitamin ads go against his Nerd tendencies. But try as he might, he has the classic Nerd trifecta: born in Tasmania; owns and races greyhounds; and is a North Melbourne supporter.

Steve Waugh: The Iceman. Cool under pressure, whether bowling at the death in a one-day international or playing a match-winning innings in a Test. Mensland clothing promoter and pin-up boy. His three ultimate dinner companions would be John Williamson, John Denver and Kenny Rogers. A talented but slightly obsessive photographer, he out-shot a Japanese tourist three to one at the Taj Mahal in India in 1996.

Andrew Symonds: Explosive all-rounder, with hard-hitting batting, clever medium pace or spin, and scintillating fielding. Loves fishing and hunting. Doesn't throw out old hooks, just puts them on his Akubra and his training hats. When out on the town, wears an R. M. Williams T-shirt that has turned from white to cream. On tour, his only dress shoes were for his team uniform; he's always much more comfortable in thongs. A genuine Nerd pin-up boy.

BOWLOLOGY

Darren Lehmann: Much-loved and punishing left-hand middle-order batsman. A Nerd prototype. A chubby, balding, smoker who requires constant beer. One of the most naturally talented Nerds of all time. He thought he looked like Bruce Willis, but we all thought he looked more like Shrek, especially since he did actually turn green when he heard the words 'fitness test' or 'drinking ban'.

Adam Gilchrist: Batting genius and good wicketkeeper. Was continually at the crossroads with his Nerd reputation throughout his career. A Nerd early in his career, he has since walked a fine line. Could be a guy who switches in order to even up the teams – not a reputation you want to have. Needs some facial hair or a badhaircut to consolidate his Nerd status.

Merv Hughes: Big-hearted fast bowler and now media superstar. Visually, the opposite of Brett Lee, so therefore is a Nerd. Does not possess a single Julio bone in his body. Probably the greatest dressing-room pest of all time. When he was a national selector, he showed some Nerdish leadership by selecting players with some of his traits, such as bad Hawaiian shirts, facial hair and uncontrollable bodily functions.

Jason Gillespie: Prominent-nosed aggressive fast bowler with over 250 Test wickets. The great man single-handedly held the Nerd mantle in his last couple of years in the Aussie team. If he had played in the 1970s, he'd have been a Julio icon with his mullet and sideburns. Released his own fashion label, DZ9, in 2005, advertising free radio hats as a promotional gimmick. Can be proud of the fact that he introduced individual stubby holders to the Australians' post-match drinks.

NERDS AND JULIOS

Tim May: Big-turning off-spinner with a deceptive arm ball. Played the occasional heroic late-order innings with his left elbow dominating his batting. Was an intellectual genius but a physically challenged individual, unless he had a cricket ball in his hand. Broke his arm five times as a youngster. Once, when he won a junior tennis tournament in Adelaide, he thought it would be cool to jump the net. His right leg didn't join the party and caught the net, and his arm broke on the hard bitumen. Not in the slightest bit interested in fashion. Some people have bad hair *days*, but Maysy has had a bad hair *life*.

Jo Angel: Giant-hearted fast bowler. Loved wearing band tour T-shirts to pubs and nightclubs. Nothing like the sight of his Angels, Rose Tattoo, Screaming Jets or Spy vs Spy T-shirts in between all those Diesel and Country Road shirts. Brought a Trivial Pursuit board game on the Pakistan tour of 1994, much to the amusement of some of his teammates (me and Tim May) who thought it wasn't cool. After a week of boring Pakistan touring life, those two teammates broke into Jo's room and stole his game, and then proceeded to play Trivial Pursuit every night for the rest of the eight-week trip. Thanks, Jo.

Chapter 24
Devil Worship

CAPTAIN JAMES COOK reckoned he clocked up some miles in his career. Well, from a 3 September 1998 Brisbane training camp I was off to Malaysia for the Commonwealth Games and then on to a Pakistan Test series before off to Bangladesh for Champion's Trophy (we played India – Tendulkar made 100, for a change) and back to Pakistan for three one-dayers. I was then told by Chairman of Selectors Trevor Hohns that I had to do the Willie Nelson and get back on the road again to play for Victoria in their Shield game in Perth on 12 November. By the time I arrived home in Melbourne after the Second Test match in Perth on 1 December I'd been away for three months.

In the Shield game in Perth, I seriously thought I'd broken my back while bowling, which was strange as I'd had nothing more than back stiffness up until this moment in my career; my shoulder seemed to be taking all the stress in my upper body with my side-on action.

Four days later my back had recovered enough to play the First Ashes Test at the Gabba, vs England. We batted all of day one and then, later on day two, I surprisingly smashed what was to be my highest Test score – 71, with a non-stickered/sponsored bat. Thanks to a Tony Greig tea-time interview, I quickly signed up with Gray Nicholls bat company for the Second Test match in Perth. On day two at the WACA, I strode out confidently with my new Gray Nicholls Calypso bat and proceeded to back up my slashing 71 with a first ball duck! This proved that for me, form and class with the bat really was temporary

I failed to take a wicket in Brisbane because I was probably still fatigued from the unaccustomed time spent at the batting crease. I felt this was a do-or-die Test for me and I needed a big game to continue my Aussie career. Before the Perth Test, for the only time in my career, I actually wrote down my match goal (apart from the usual to 1. sing the song, and 2. be the best bowler in the Test), which was to be Man of the Match. Now, superstars like Steve Waugh and Adam Gilchrist probably had their Man of the Match speeches written out pre-Test, but I was generally happy just to get a game. Well, didn't I have to knock a MOM speech out quickly when I took 9/92 in perfect swinging conditions! Luckily, I remembered to thank my parents.

I also introduced the Ronnie James Dio heavy metal sign to the team in post-match celebrations. (The origins of the 'raising the horns' sign are much debated. Some believe they first saw it used by Dio on Black Sabbath's *Heaven and Hell* album, while others feel Gene Simmons was the first to show the sign on the cover of Kiss's album *Love Gun*.)

Ronnie Dio's heavy metal sign lasted exactly two Test match wins. It was banned from our 'Beneath the Southern Cross' celebrations when our skipper Mark Taylor received a letter from a Christian cricket fan worried that our Dio sign was in fact a devil worshipping sign. I argued it was actually used to *ward off* the devil in medieval times. Regardless, Tubby got 'Paranoid' (title of Black Sabbath's only top 10 single) and banned the Dio sign, which was never seen again in Aussie dressing rooms.

After a solid Ashes series where we won 3–1 and I took 16 wickets, I hurt my shoulder in our loss in the Melbourne Test match. I was 12th man in the Sydney Test. I played a couple of one-day games but that electric shock tenderness was

DEVIL WORSHIP

Me, Funky and Pigeon, and the ill-fated Dio sign. We were feeling pretty happy after warding off all 10 Pommy wickets in the second innings of our win in the Adelaide Test.

unbearable and I had scans that showed tears in my shoulder ligaments. So the West Indies tour Tests were off my agenda, but I was desperate to be fit for the 1999 World Cup. I was told to have two months off and if there were no signs of repair, I would have to have surgery again – which would mean the end of my World Cup campaign.

It wasn't the most relaxing two months of my life. I trained as hard as I could with weights and running, evoking memories of Rocky Balboa in *Rocky IV*, although the soundtrack on my CD player was more tasteful than the band Survivor (I did like 'Eye of the Tiger' though). Soon my shoulder had shown signs of repair so, hesitantly, I started bowling again. My first game back for Victoria happened to be a one-day final, in which we soundly beat New South Wales, making it especially satisfying.

You beauty! On a one-day title for the Bushrangers at the MCG.

My shoulder was still a bit tender but I bowled through some games for Victoria and was picked for the West Indies one-day series, where we drew the series. The ball came out pretty well and I snared the second most wickets in the series, behind Warnie – who was coming back into form after being dropped for the last Test in the West Indies.

We also survived two riots – one in Guyana and another in Barbados. The Barbadian locals for some reason took exception when our 196 centimetre tall, and future *Getaway* host (who was later denied access to Barbados for a story), Brendon Julian hip-and-shouldered AFL-style the 150 centimetre 60 kilogram Barbadian opener Sherwin Campbell, and then ran him out as Sherwin was lying limp on the pitch, doing his best *Weekend at Bernie's* impression!

Once Sherwin was revived and stretchered off the ground, the locals started booing. Suddenly, we were getting showered with beer bottles and bricks and anything the locals could get their hands on. It was chaos.

To be fair, there were some terrific throwing arms in this hostile crowd. One beer bottle nearly flattened our skipper Steve Waugh's face. We checked immediately to see it wasn't Warnie doing the throwing, as he was still a bit upset at being dropped for the last Test, but, no, it was from a spectator – and it was half full, which was disgraceful as you don't waste half a beer like that. We reluctantly went back on the field, and Sherwin was recalled. The Windies won, and we were allowed to leave the ground alive.

By the end of the series we were all rioted out and ready to make our way to England for the 1999 World Cup.

Chapter 25
World Cup, Cardiff, No Regrets

THE AUSTRALIAN SELECTORS chose an experienced squad for our 1999 World Cup campaign. Eight of the squad had played in our losing 1996 campaign, Geoff 'Swampy' Marsh remained our coach and Steve 'Tugga' Waugh was captain. In Cardiff for our pre-series camp, they called a meeting to spell out their 'Vision and Standards'.

Keen to stamp their authority, they discussed our team plans. One element of our approach was going to be that our swing bowlers, Adam Dale and I, would open the bowling with the Duke balls (which went like boomerangs . . . English boomerangs). Then McGrath would bowl first change, in a role similar to that of South Africa's Alan Donald, containing the batsmen and getting wickets.

Tugga proposed a 'No Regrets' theme, which, he said, would give us every opportunity to win the World Cup. Another great initiative from Tugga was to put our numbers on our caps, which signified the importance of one-day cricket and that we should make our own history.

Just when everyone was feeling pretty pumped about the tournament, we were soon deflated like balloons when Tugga and Swampy dropped a big bombshell. They said the three words all Australian cricketers fear – and it wasn't 'Warne sex scandal'. No, it was 'total drinking ban'.

The tour party was stunned. Regrets? We already had a few.

BOWLOLOGY

Everyone reacts differently in times of shattering crisis. It was interesting watching the boys' reactions. Some sat there with their mouths open – sort of miming the act of having a beer, I guess. Others were shaking their heads. Junior actually woke up – he must have sensed subconsciously that something was wrong. I looked over at Darren Lehmann, who had actually started crying at the thought of no beer.

Boony questioned whether it was worth going on if you couldn't drink piss – which was weird, as Boony was a selector and wasn't even part of the touring squad. We had to ask him to leave the meeting.*

The players' reaction was best summed up by big Tom Moody. Even as Geoff Marsh was uttering the words 'drinking ban', Moods sensed something was wrong and was already screaming 'Noooo!'

It is fair to say we were not in the best place as we headed into the tournament. If we had discussed the idea months out from the tournament and agreed upon it as a group, fine, but it had been sprung on us and we felt like panicking.

* * *

Anyway, our first game was against the dangerous New Zealand team in Cardiff. We didn't have a lot of support, as our fans were saving their money for later in the tournament. Not the Kiwi fans, however, who flew over early, not knowing if their team would progress to the Super Six stage.

I was fielding down at fine leg, just minding my own business and not trying to bring any attention to myself. But being an Australian player fielding on the fence in front of a hundred Kiwi fans was enough. Sure enough, I was soon copping an absolute caning. There were sheep noises, the old 'Fleming is a wanker' chant – the usual intellectual stuff.

* Boony wasn't actually there . . .

WORLD CUP, CARDIFF, NO REGRETS

One bloke came down near the fence and said, 'Fleming, any chance of a photo?' I saw this as a chance to win the crowd over, so I agreed and started to pose. With that, he threw his camera at me and posed with two girls in front of the big crowd. This got a massive laugh from them at my expense.

I actually acknowledged the play from this bloke and took the photo with a slight twist, and I didn't think any more of it.

Fast-forward eight years to the 2007 World Cup in the Caribbean. I was in a pub, and I heard this Kiwi voice scream out, 'Fleming!' And this bloke in a 1980s New Zealand one-day shirt came up and said I was his favourite Aussie player. Initially I was thinking he was taking the puss . . . sorry, piss.

'I've been waiting eight years to catch up with you,' he said.

'What do you mean?'

'Do you remember the 1999 World Cup game in Cardiff, and a bloke threw a camera at you to take a photo?'

Of course I remembered.

'Well, that was me! I got home and told my mates how I took the puss (piss) out of you and you played along and took a photo of me in front of the Kiwi fans. I couldn't wait to get the photo developed, which I quickly did. But you hit me for sex (six). Instead of a photo of me with two girls on my arm, a big smile on my face and all those Kiwi fans in the background, you took a photo of my feet!'

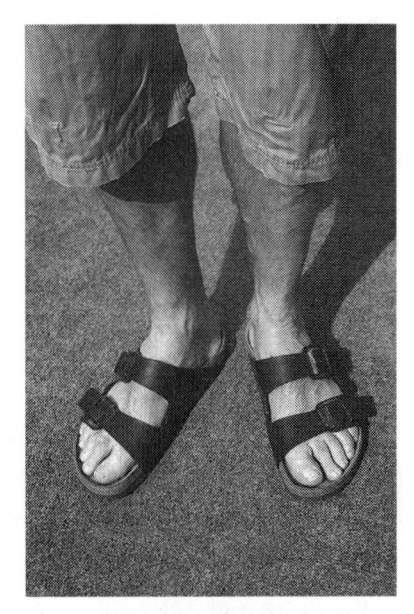

'Cheese!'

With that, the bloke whipped out the print and said, 'I thought it was choice, bro!!'

∗ ∗ ∗

Despite my best efforts on the boundary, we were thrashed by New Zealand in Cardiff, then we lost a close one at Headingly to Pakistan. Our only win early in the tournament came against a full-strength Scottish team that had taken up cricket just two months before the World Cup.

We were in big trouble. In fact, we not only had to win every match from there on, but we also needed other results to go our way. Not only were we losing, we were bloody sober as well.

A crisis meeting was called, and Swampy and Tugga threw it open to everyone to have a chat and get our World Cup plans back on track. Tom Moody – a man who had earned respect for his efforts with bat and ball, and who was comfortably our best haggis hurler (with a world-record-breaking throw of 230 feet) started the meeting by saying we needed to 'erase the zone of doubt' that was eating up the group.

Bevo, probably our most intense player, spoke well, saying we were putting too much pressure on ourselves. We were playing reactive cricket and waiting for things to happen, and we needed to relax and back our skill.

Adam Dale and I had spoken to Steve Waugh the night before, saying we thought our goals were a bit too broad and that we needed a bowling plan cut into three sections: overs 0–15, 16–40 and 41–50. He liked that idea, and Chip and I worked on the strategy, which was big of Chip as he didn't play again on tour, since Glenn McGrath took back control of the new ball.

The drinking ban was relaxed a bit, too.

As we left the meeting, we had a commitment to support each other, to play in the present and to have no regrets. We were actually a solid group, and with this ownership and accountability, things turned around very quickly. It showed that if things don't always go to plan, you should accept it, learn what you can and then move on. The 'zone of doubt' had been erased.

* * *

Like the Terminator from Arnie's famous movie, Glenn McGrath was a fast bowling machine who methodically stalked batsmen and very rarely stopped before he got his man. No one in my time in the Australian team displayed more self-belief and adaptability. His strategy of publicly putting himself under pressure by declaring his targets through the press was brave but effective.

It's easy to see why he was so successful at the top level with the attributes he had: height, pace, bounce and microscopic accuracy, backed up with a good degree of self-confidence and a drive for excellence. He was the complete package.

In his run-up he had a very efficient running style and an action that took minimal effort, with a little jump into the stumps that took him only slightly away from his target of off stump. At 198 centimetres and with a high release, he got maximum bounce out of the wicket. Add to this his unwavering accuracy and it was quite a mix.

McGrath was probably the only Australian Test cricketer ever to have a subscription to *Pig Shooter Monthly*, which he read avidly on planes and buses. (Andrew Symonds killed pigs too, but with his bare hands.) Pigeon was committed to culling the feral pigs on his farm in New South Wales. They were a threat to his sheep and native plants, and could affect his livelihood – much like opposition top-order batsman.

This might have been the inspiration for his well-documented technique of targeting and then dismissing the opposition team's best batsmen. Names such as Michael Atherton (19 times),

Brian Lara (13) and Stephen Fleming (eight) were nominated, then dismissed.

He could recall minute details of every dismissal he ever took, including how the batsman went out, his score, what the weather was like and what he had for breakfast that day. Pigeon loved a kill and cherished each one.

One of the most famous examples of this came in the 1999 World Cup, when McGrath, like a lot of the team, was struggling to find his best form. Before the important game against the West Indies, he wrote a newspaper article in which he admitted he had been down on form. He felt it was time to step up, and predicted that he would get five wickets and knock over the West Indies' best batsman, Lara.

I remember reading the article and thinking, *I couldn't write that . . . What if you get slogged and get 0/60 or 0/70 and you end up with egg on your face?* Best to keep a lid on such carry-on.

But there was no egg on Pigeon's face as he fried the West Indies' batting line-up. They were scrambling for runs against his pace and bounce and accuracy. Result: McGrath said, '*Hasta la vista*, baby!' to the Windies' batsmen.

From 8.4 overs, McGrath took 5/14. He bowled Lara for eight with one of the best balls you will ever see, pitching on middle stump and hitting the top of off stump. He did all this without raising a sweat. It's fair to say the whole team was in awe of that performance.

* * *

Swampy's great legacy was that he started to bring in experts to his coaching panel, such as David Missen, our fitness guru, who later worked with the Sydney Swans and St Kilda football clubs. Another was Sandy Gordon, our sports psychologist. He was a lovely bloke and great at his job. I think he helped Swampy deal with his coaching pressures as much as he helped the playing group.

Swampy had been a loyal vice captain to Allan Border in his playing days, and he conducted tough training sessions. Despite this, he still enjoyed a beer and socialising in the team environment. Public speaking wasn't one of his strengths, though, and he didn't enjoy chatting to the playing group as a whole. You could always pick when he'd had a chat to Sandy Gordon about his presentations. Swampy loved covering butcher's paper with significant quotes.

Before our clash with India, he called a team meeting. He had given us some homework to do – each of us had to assess an Indian player and speak about him. But first we were looking forward to seeing Swampy run the meeting. He usually let Tugga do it, and we knew it wasn't his strong point. On his butcher's paper he wrote: 'The Four Ps – Patience, Partnerships, Pressure, Persistence.' Then he began speaking: 'Okay, if we are going to beat India tomorrow, we need to nail the four Ps.'

Go Swamp! Great start, I thought.

'Right,' he continued. 'Patience – we have to have it. Partnerships – we need to make them. Pressure – we need to keep it going. Persistence – we need to hang in there.'

This was followed by a few seconds of uncomfortable silence. in the room.

'Okay, Gilly, tell us about Tendulkar,' Swamp said, moving on. Short and sweet!

In fact, it was not dissimilar to India's batting the next day, as we used the four Ps to crush them and moved on in the World Cup.

On 13 June we were up against the tournament favourite, South Africa, at Headingly. They'd had the highest win ratio in one-day cricket for the previous two years, and they were a well drilled and skilled unit.

Still, we often felt they could be too structured, whereas we respected flair, particularly in big games. They could bully you when they were on top, but if you could stand up and compete, they had an inflexibility that could work against them. Basically, if it was *Rocky IV*, we were Rocky and South Africa was Ivan Drago.

There was no better example of this than Hansie Cronje, their skipper, who was a very intense and rigid player. You got the feeling that winning meant too much to him.

After a sensational hundred by Hershelle Gibbs, South Africa compiled 271. We were in trouble early in our chase, and I can still vividly remember watching Steve Waugh stride out to the crease with the score at 3/48. He was a captain who led best by example. His determination to win was second to none, and with bat in hand (and red rag in back pocket), there was no way he was walking back to the dressing rooms without winning this game. He was always at his best under pressure like this.

He had been a very influential man around the team even before he was made captain. He was totally ruthless in his approach to the opposition – an attribute he developed after debuting in the mid-1980s in a team still battling after the retirements of Chappell, Marsh and Lillee, and the divisiveness of the rebel tours. Wins were very hard to come by in Tugga's time. He was like a child of the Depression, in that he had to scrap for every piece of bread, and he never forgot it.

WORLD CUP, CARDIFF, NO REGRETS

Steve loved the mental side of the game and was always coming up with lines like 'If your attitude was contagious, is yours worth catching?' and 'Complacency is our enemy'. He loved his players backing themselves, and he in turn would back them to the hilt. Before a series, he would write down a page of team and individual player expectations and roles. This really helped you know what your role was as part of the outfit.

> **Flemo**
>
> **Batting** – make the most of your ability
> – see yourself as a batsman the team can rely on to do well and be consistent.
> – practice your placement – work on soft hands to get singles.
> – if its there to hit, do so, ala, – 1st Test.
>
> **Bowling** – see yourself as the spearhead of the attack along with Pigeon.
> – back your ability to swing the ball and take wickets.
> – switch on from ball one – need more consistency in that 1st spell.
> – be the man in the final overs – back yourself against the batsman – your variety will win out.
>
> **Fielding** – stay alert – look for work – no quiet periods
> – need to hear your encouragement, makes a difference to the bowlers and guys in the circle.
>
> * Take a lead role – now a senior player.

He had a deep respect for the traditions of Australian cricket, but he also challenged stereotypes and pushed us to make our own history. In fact, he created some dressing-room history by making country-and-western music a staple of our rockbox, with Aussie John Williamson his favourite. Let's face it, Tugga was a champion and one of the all-time great cricketers, but he was a god-awful nerd, and nothing said this so much as his love of that bloody song 'True Blue'.

Constant growth was a continual theme of Steve's, not only for the team but for his own game. When his place in the one-day team was threatened, he realised he had to find some more scoring options. Later in his career he developed the slog-sweep – a shot that came to the fore in this innings against South Africa, when he played the one-day knock of his life.

Everybody in cricket knows the story of Tugga hitting a catch to Herschelle Gibbs when he was on 66. Warnie had noticed that the South African had a tendency to throw the ball away before really getting control of it, and he mentioned that in a meeting, noting that Jonty Rhodes did the same. He reckoned that if a batsman questioned the catch, an umpire might just agree. It was one of those 0.001 per cent things that great players exploit, and when Herschelle did fumble the catch, Steve hissed at him, 'You've just cost your team the World Cup.' (Many people think he said, 'You just dropped the World Cup,' and it would have been a better line, but bad luck. Neil Armstrong fluffed his lines too, and nobody cares about that.) Anyway, Steve went on to make his century and prove that poor old Herschelle had indeed cost his side the game.

Thanks to Tugga, we were into the semi-finals, and for once I didn't mind hearing John Williamson. He'd earned the right to play it.

WORLD CUP, CARDIFF, NO REGRETS

* * *

Birmingham was the venue for our semi-final, in which we again faced South Africa. It was also the home of two of the most influential heavy metal bands of all time: Black Sabbath and Judas Priest. There have been calls to name Birmingham's airport after Ozzy Osborne, which I think is a great idea, as long as Ozzy has nothing to do with the planes. Nothing. Put him in charge of the bar.

After our inspired win at Headingly, we were confident that the momentum was going our way and we had a psychological edge over South Africa. Batting first, however, we collapsed to be 4/68, before Tugga and Bevo settled the innings.

I walked out to bat at number 10 after Paul Reiffel was bowled first ball by an Alan Donald reverse-inswinger. As we passed each other, Pistol said, 'Watch out for his inswinger.'

No shit, Sherlock, I thought. *I just saw it on the TV.*

For my first ball I was so conscious of not getting bowled by a Donald inswinger that I decided to go with no backlift at all. I faced up with my bat and pad so close together that a fly couldn't have sneaked through.

Donald bowled a quick delivery. I held up my end of the bargain quite well, keeping my bat and pad close together, but unfortunately it was his outswinger and I missed the ball by a metre.

Very crafty, Alan, I thought. *Bowl the outswinger first ball to set me up for the inswinger second ball.* I was a fellow bowler and was all over his tactics.

Donald charged in, and again I kept my bat and pad close together to stop myself getting bowled leg stump. As I was doing so, I heard my off stump being smashed by a late outswinger.

If I analyse our one-on-one clash from a totally impartial point of view, I probably have Donald winning on a countback. At least I didn't waste balls that could be bowled to Bevo at the other end. Overall, South Africa bowled really well and restricted us to 213, with Tugga and Bevo scoring 50s.

South Africa started well with the bat, too. Gary Kirsten and Gibbs cruised to 0/48, then Shane Warne put his hand up for his country. Warnie was the most dominant personality I played with – he had incredible skills, he was super-competitive, always stalking his opposition, good with the chat and he hardly ever missed out. (He was pretty good *on* the field as well . . .)

All of his arsenal was on display as he spun the game our way with an incredible spell. With his dominant and competitive personality, the bigger the game, the bolder he bowled. He produced a couple of classic 'Gatting balls', first bowling Kirsten with a big in-spinning leggie that landed outside off stump and hit leg, then he bowled Gibbsy with an equally good ball. Both openers gone in two overs. Two balls later, he had Cronje with one that spun off his front foot.

We didn't care how we got them, we were up and their captain was gone. South Africa was now on the back foot at 3/53, having lost 3/5.

Warne's enthusiasm was incredible that day. With each wicket, he screamed, 'C'mon, c'mon,' urging us to ride this wave, flailing his arms like Pete Townshend from The Who playing guitar. He was a rock star in full command. This was his generation and South African batsman were f-f-f-fading away.

The game then swung this way and that, with wickets and runs, until it came down to the last eight balls. South Africa need 16 runs to win and had one wicket in hand. The boundary-hitting warrior Lance Klusener was batting well, but Alan Donald was a number 11 for a reason.

WORLD CUP, CARDIFF, NO REGRETS

In these circumstances, everyone was hoping that a catch would be hit to them so they could be a hero. Klusener hit one in the air to Paul Reiffel at deep mid-on. *You lucky, lucky bastard, Pistol*, I thought. *Take the catch, smile for the cameras and we are into the final.* It's fair to say that Pistol, who had dropped an easier catch earlier off Warnie's bowling, saw things a little differently. He not only dropped the catch but also bumped it over the fence for six!

Watching from deep backward square leg, I immediately thought, *This makes things very interesting.* When Klusener hit the next ball for a single to retain the strike for the last over, it made things very, very interesting. And I was bowling the last over.

I had a white, 49-over-old ball in my hand, and the hopes of my country in my heart. By now South Africa needed nine runs off six balls, and still had one wicket in hand. By the end of my over, we'd either be progressing to a World Cup Final at Lord's or flying home disappointed. It was up to me.

'You ready for the Klusener plan?' asked Steve Waugh. We had talked for hours about Klusener at the previous night's team meeting. Statistics told us that the nuggety left-hander scored 80 per cent of his runs on the leg side, so we'd come up with a plan to bowl yorkers 30 centimetres outside off stump from around the wicket to force him to hit to his *obvious* weakness through the off side. That was not the easiest ball to execute – a degree of difficulty of 10, I reckoned. Once again, our bloody batsmen had come up with the bowling plan.

I was not entirely comfortable with the tactic, but I hadn't expected the game to come down to the last over, as it had in our 1996 semi-final against the West Indies.

I remember thinking, *Just back yourself. You've been in this position a few times before and come through, so just relax.* The atmosphere was electric, with 30 000 Edgbaston fans screaming – and, more importantly, with my 10 teammates urging me on. That made me feel good and gave me a lift.

I ran in for the first ball and delivered a near-perfect yorker at approximately 140 kilometres per hour, about 35 centimetres outside his off stump. Klusener slogged it to the cover fence at about 400 kilometres per hour. The crowd went berserk.

He hit the ball so hard that it ricocheted off the fence all the way back to me, which was bit embarrassing, but I just picked up the ball and my first thought was, *That's a pretty strong weakness outside off stump.*

South Africa now needed five runs to win. As I was walking back to my mark, I was thinking to myself again that Klusener clearly had an extremely strong 'weakness', but this was the semi-final of the World Cup so I wasn't going to change my game plan. And anybody can have a lucky slog.

As I ran in for the second ball, I heard only five or six teammates yell out, 'C'mon, Flemo.' A few blokes had clearly dropped off me. Cheers, boys.

Then things went into slow motion again. I bowled the ball full, just outside off stump, and Klusener smashed it at about 500 kilometres per hour to the boundary. He hit it that hard I swear I heard the ball cry, 'Ouch!'

The scores were now level and the crowd noise was deafening.

I was now starting to have genuine doubts about Klusener's supposed weakness outside off stump. At this stage, he wasn't Klusener, he was the Klusenator. He knew no fear and had no weakness outside off stump. I realised that he had probably scored 80 per cent of his runs on the leg side because everyone was bowling on his legs. Suddenly, I stopped caring that this was a World Cup semi-final – we needed a different bowling plan.

TOP FIVE SPORTING SPEEDS

1. Klusener's second boundary of this over – 500 kilometres per hour
2. Hawthorn superstar Cyril Rioli's closing speed on opponent with the ball – 400 kilometres per hour
3. Klusener's first four in this over – 400 kilometres per hour
4. Sam Groth's tennis serve – 180 kilometres per hour
5. Jeff Thompson's fastest cricket ball ever bowled – 180 kilometres per hour

(Oh, did I mention that South Africa needed to beat us to get into the finals, while we would progress if we drew? A technicality, but one worth noting.)

Deep breaths.

In such stressful times, the professional athlete's mind is trained to kick into action. This is when all your sports psychology themes like positive reinforcement, staying in the present and remaining task-aware are emphasised. In this moment, you need them the most. Every motivational book you've ever read comes flooding back into your mind.

- *How to Score Birdies On and Off the Course* by Tiger Woods
- *Keep It Natural and Win* by Lance Armstrong
- *There's No 'I' in Team* by Jason Akermanis

With such key motivational sayings in my mind as I walked back to my bowling mark, my only coherent thought was, *We're fucked!*

Luckily for me, I looked to mid-on, where our ever-positive captain, the Iceman Steve Waugh, was fielding. The most mentally tough man I ever played with.

'What do you think, skipper?' I asked him.

He paused, then replied, 'I think we're fucked.'

He was obviously reading the same motivational books as me.

He said, 'Any thoughts?'

'Yes, fucking kryptonite!'

Suddenly, my head cleared. I had to take control and bowl him out. All along, I had wanted to come from over the wicket and bowl yorkers across him, as I felt he was backing away to give himself more room. I told Steve my plan and he was 100 per cent with me. 'Whatever,' he said. I think he was already visualising his early flight home to see his family.

In all seriousness, this was another example of Steve Waugh's open leadership style, where he trusted his players to know what to do. Would a more controlling captain have allowed a player to call the shots in such a crucial moment?

I told the umpire, Venkat, that I'd be bowling over the wicket. Tugga astutely brought all the fielders in to stop the single. I looked up and saw Paul Reiffel at slip, and I hoped like hell a catch didn't fly to him.

As I ran in, it was only Gilly who was now saying, 'C'mon, Flemo.' The boys were definitely off me. Feeling the love, I bowled a half-tracker, and Klusener – for the first time in the tournament, if not his life – mis-hit it to mid-on. There was hesitation between him and Alan Donald, and suddenly a run-out was on.

This was a play we had all seen a million times. Everyone knew what was going to happen. The ball would go to Mark Waugh, who would pick it up cleanly and backhand-flick it onto the stumps. Unfortunately, we had Boof Lehmann at mid-on, and his throw from two feet away missed by two feet.

Donald got back in his crease. We had only been practising our fielding for two hours a day for three years, and Boof missed! I thought, *I hope that's not our last chance.* Knowing Darren

WORLD CUP, CARDIFF, NO REGRETS

Lehman, he was no doubt thinking, *Whether we win, tie or lose, we will be drinking piss in five minutes anyway. No drama!*

It was interesting that, after the near run-out and confusion, Klusener and Donald did not talk to each other. Surely they had to commit to a plan and let each other know what they were thinking? If I'd been batting with Steve Waugh or Michael Bevan, I'm sure we would have decided to hit it through the field in the next two balls. If that didn't work and the match came down to the last ball, we would have just run. It's funny how pressure can change and confuse minds.

Before my fourth ball, I visualised my yorker intently. As I ran in, the crowd was going crazy. I had to produce something big for my country. I bowled a superb bat-jarring yorker. I like to think my country needed me and I put my hand up. Belatedly.

The delivery shocked Klusener as much as my teammates. He mis-hit it to mid-off, called 'Yes' and started running. Donald just stared at him like a deer in the headlights. Donald wasn't running but Lance was. This was big.

Mark Waugh fielded and flicked the ball to me – which was dumb, because Lance, Donald and I were now all at the same end. I underarmed the ball down the pitch to Gilly, who was alone at the other end. Donald started running along with it.

Poor Gilly! My throw was so slow that it must have seemed like hours waiting for the ball to dribble down to him. Finally, he grabbed it and broke the stumps, and Donald was run out. We were through to the World Cup final! It's occasions like this that we all play sport for, the euphoria of the win and the celebrations with your teammates.

The team came together in the middle of the pitch, dancing and screaming uncontrollably. We were like kids at a kindergarten, fizzed up on soft drink – we were going nuts. There

BOWLOLOGY

The 1999 World Cup semi-final. Pure euphoria. Look at Gilly running around us to stop umpire Venkat from taking the stumps. Shrewd move from Gilly. Cricket memorabilia is hot property. Although he probably could have grabbed the stumps from his end . . .

was no security at this World Cup, so thousands of people were charging onto the field, and they all wanted one thing – memorabilia. So we grabbed the stumps and ran off like we were in a midst of riot.

People have asked me over the years: why did I underarm the ball?

Was it the split-second actions of a highly trained athlete who realised the danger of throwing the ball over Gilly's head or missing his big right ear? Or did I just realise my inner Trevor Chappell? Maybe the Nerds vs Julios ten-pin bowling match from days earlier had subconsciously influenced my decision-making process?

I have no idea, but I heard Richie Benaud once say it was one of the best decisions he has seen on the cricket field. I'll take that.

In the rooms there was jubilation and relief. It took Paul Reiffel an hour to lift his head from his hands. I walked over for a chat. 'How you going, mate?'

WORLD CUP, CARDIFF, NO REGRETS

Did this Nerd vs Julios ten-pin bowling competition win Australia a World Cup?

'I'm so relieved we won,' he said. 'All I could think about was Ray Finkle from *Ace Ventura* missing the field goal. I didn't want kids to say in years to come when someone drops a vital catch, "Jeez, you had a Reiffel."'

* * *

There were eight survivors from our loss in the 1996 World Cup final, and deep down we all hoped we'd get the opportunity to erase that pain. Our training sessions leading into the final were top-shelf, which led to positive confidence around the group.

We were playing Pakistan in the final. They were a richly talented team, but did not always play as a united group, and we planned to expose them under finals pressure.

We arrived at the mighty Lord's on game day and quickly shuffled opposite the Pakistan team to meet the Queen. I was standing next to Paul Reiffel, who was lined up against Pakistan's wicketkeeper, Moin Khan.

BOWLOLOGY

Gilly reliving the underarm finish.

After the semi-final, I was very popular in the rooms, with teammates wanting autographs and photos. Both Waugh twins were fighting over who would have the first picture with me; Steve won a round of rock, paper, scissors and he was over the moon. (Note: you can see Junior in the background, not happy. Not happy at all.)

WORLD CUP, CARDIFF, NO REGRETS

Moin loved a stoush and could play some incredible shots as a batsman. He was one of the few who could sweep quick bowlers in the death over in one-day games. In the Third Test of our 1994 tour, Warnie had bowled around the wicket to him and got hit for six over mid-off a couple of times, which fired the great leggie up.

When the light had started to fade a tad, Moin had just walked off the pitch towards the dressing rooms without chatting to the umpires, who had then followed him off the ground. Our boys had complained – with good reason – that the light was fine, and that a batsman couldn't just walk off the field in a Test match, but to no avail. Warnie felt particularly aggrieved and started getting stuck into Moin, sledging him as hard as he could.

Moin's cool response was, 'Hey, Warne, you like my sixes? I like my sixes!' And he shadow-batted his big hits over mid-off. This only riled Warnie more, who continued sledging as Moin walked off smiling to the dressing rooms.

So we knew Moin was a stirrer, and he picked an interesting time on the morning of the final to play some mind games.

'Reiffel, Reiffel,' Moin called out to Pistol, who kept his head down and ignored him. 'Reiffel, Reiffel,' he continued.

Finally, Pistol looked up.

'Oh! What about that catch?' Moin cupped his hands and recreated Pistol's dropped catch off Klusener in the semi, then rolled his eyes.

What happened next on the field was a clinical display of bowling and fielding skills that decimated the talented Pakistani team. Some of the catching from Mark Waugh and Ricky Ponting was from another planet. We had a feeling that no one could beat us, as we'd won so many games in so many difficult circumstances to get here, defying sudden death all the way.

BOWLOLOGY

I was our worst bowler in the final, and I remember waiting an eternity at one point for the dangerous Saeed Anwar to change his gloves. Pakistani cricketers are never in a rush. While I was waiting, I thought, *Jeez, he wouldn't want to get out after wasting so much time*. Next ball, he inside-edged an inswinger onto his stumps.

Pakistan was demolished for 132. While we were chasing down that total, I devised a cunning plan for the photos. I figured that if I stayed by Warnie's side, I'd be in every shot. 'Hollywood' Warne hadn't got that nickname for nothing.

I was always happy to play second fiddle to our champions, but now I thought it was time to get my profile up a tad. I shadowed his movements, until he finally sat on the balcony, shoulder to shoulder with me, oblivious to my plan. At last, Boof square-cut Saqlain Mushtaq for four to win the final. It was pure euphoria.

Final win. The boys on the Lord's balcony, and the delayed celebration by myself after ball watching.

WORLD CUP, CARDIFF, NO REGRETS

My Warnie plan worked a treat, too. I was the only player who watched the ball, and therefore I was still sitting down while all the others boys were leaping up.

After a few hours celebrating, we strolled down to the Lord's wicket with all the staff. Punter read out his poem and then launched into a thrash-metal-like version of 'Southern Cross' –

Gilly, me and the Cup.

Moments after the win. Obviously my camera because I'm the only one posing.

with plenty of emotion and aggression. What a close to the World Cup. It had been a bumpy, exhilarating ride at times, and we had peaked on the final day. Best of all, we had 'No Regrets'.

And after our devastating loss in the 1996 World Cup final, we finally got to live out our inner Prince and party like it was 1999!

Aussie fans. Best banner: 'Went away convicts. Came back world champions.'

Self-shooting. Very tough, but achieved. Scorer Mike Walsh and coach Geoff Marsh get a guernsey as well.

WORLD CUP, CARDIFF, NO REGRETS

Teammates, beers and the song. Aussie cricket utopia.

Punter on Moods' shoulders, taking us through the song.

Where's the pooch? Boof pointing to the fake doggy poo that I used to take on tour for a bit of fun. I placed it in the aisle on the plane when we flew back home for our ticker-tape parade in Melbourne, and then we amused ourselves with the confused reactions of fellow passengers as they carefully navigated around it.

Chapter 26
You're So Dizzy

IT WAS LIKE a scene from *Black Hawk Down* – two of our soldiers, Jason Gillespie and Steve Waugh, had been grounded by friendly fire. They were lying on the ground in intense pain, and we had to get them to safe ground.

A few blokes got to Tugga, who looked in a bad way. Blood was clearly visible on his broken nose. Meanwhile, Dizzy was moaning a lot and in a fair bit of pain.

Eventually, we got our two warriors off the field at Kandy, Sri Lanka. Most people were swarming around our skipper, who looked like he had gone a couple of rounds with Mike Tyson. But all he cared about was a photo for his diary!

I was with Dizzy. Someone pulled up his cricket trousers and we immediately saw the problem. His shinbone was actually *shinbones* – there was a clear break. With that, I summoned up my best Craig McDermott impression and yelled out, 'Hooter!'

Finally, the ambulance arrived and we loaded Dizzy on. A little-known fact is that the average Sri Lankan is about a foot shorter then our six-foot-four fast bowler. As the paramedics started to close the door, his leg was still sticking out. Dizzy realised this very late, and I saw the terror on his face and again yelled out, 'Hooter!'

Hooter ran over and stopped the door slamming on Dizzy's broken shin, screaming like James Caan in the movie *Misery*.

We lost the game and went to visit the boys in their Colombo hospital. They were in a very small room, sleeping just inches from each other. As we suspected, our skipper had a broken nose and Dizzy a broken shinbone. It was lucky it wasn't the other way around, actually, as there wouldn't have been enough plaster in Colombo to cover Dizzy's prominent nose.

Unfortunately, Dizzy had a phobia about needles, which was a problem as he needed great dosages of painkiller. The only solution was suppositories up his anal passage. This would have provided a lot of humour for Tugga if only his nose wasn't broken. Whenever he laughed he felt excruciating pain throughout his head.

So, late at night, Tugga would be awoken by Dizzy hitting the nurse's buzzer. A night nurse would roll Dizzy over so he was facing our captain. The big quick, now devoid of any human dignity, would look into Tugga's eyes and relent as the suppository was inserted into his rear end, while Steve would try desperately not to laugh to avoid the pain from his broken nose.

Who said being an Australian cricketer was an easy gig?

Chapter 27
Junior, Nicho and Nine Slips in Zimbabwe

FROM SRI LANKA we flew halfway across the world, as the ACB had an agreement to fly only with only one airline carrier. Forty-eight hours later we arrived in Zimbabwe – about 45 hours more than if we'd taken a direct flight from Colombo.

It was Australia's first ever Test tour of Zimbabwe, and our first stop was Bulawayo, for a tour game against the Zimbabwean President's XI (which I'm pretty sure wasn't picked by Robert Mugabe). Things began nicely. We scored plenty of runs in our first innings, and Pigeon and I started well with the ball, picking up early wickets.

Then big Matthew Nicholson – who had played a Test against the Poms at the MCG the previous summer – came on to bowl. At his best, Nicho was a unpleasant prospect to face, especially on his home pitch at the WACA ground, which was fast and bouncy. His stock length balls often flew to around shoulder height. Nasty. He had a unique action, with his arms and legs going everywhere, not quite the frog-in-the-blender Paul Adam style, but his body parts had to be in perfect sync if the ball was to travel along his Avenue of Apprehension.

Nicho started bowling like the Zimbabwean economy – all over the place. It was like Steve Harmison's first delivery in the 2006/07 Ashes, but on steroids. He was releasing what can best be described as a mix of gutter balls and slam dunks, and he put

BOWLOLOGY

one ball 30 metres over Heals's head. I'd seen fireworks with more control, as ball after ball came flying to down to me at fine leg on the third or fourth bounce. Some deliveries went straight to Mark Waugh at second slip. There was no Avenue for poor Nicho – he was bowling in the Runway of Recklessness

Anyway, we dismissed the Zimbabwean XI but the feeling in our rooms wasn't great. We were still trying to work out what had gone wrong with Nicho, who ended up bowling 18 wides and five no-balls in his 13 overs. Guys were patting Nicho on the back with encouragement, but also looking at each other and shaking their heads.

I had a chat with Nicho and we trudged off to the nets, thinking that their confined spaces might help him get his action straightened out. Nicho bowled about half a dozen balls, none of which made me play a shot as every one of them hit the side net.

'I've had enough,' Nicho said.

'Fair call,' I acknowledged.

Morgues had better atmospheres than our team bus, with everyone pondering Nicho's unfortunate performance. And everyone was really feeling for him. Well, almost everyone. The last to board was Junior Waugh. The laconic younger Waugh was – as usual – taking things at his own pace.

Finally, our bus took off. Junior decided to break the silence and enliven the mood with this icebreaker: 'Well, Nicho, I've got to say, that was the worst piece of bowling I've ever seen.'

At that, there was a tremendous groan from the boys. 'You can't say that,' someone said.

Junior was on the back foot for a moment, then said, 'Well, am I wrong? Am I wrong?' He got no support, but unbelievably went over to the man himself. 'Nicho, am I wrong?'

Nicho just rolled his eyes, and Junior kept trying to rally some support for himself for the rest of the bus ride.

'The yips' is a term for the apparent loss of fine motor skills without obvious explanation. The bowling yips are cricket's version of vertigo. You're unsure of your balance and where the ball will go. Some bowlers affected by the yips are too afraid to release the ball, and many retire with unfulfilled careers.

Not Nicho. Once he got over the yips, he showed plenty of courage. He went back home to New South Wales and had many fine Shield seasons. Even though he didn't add to his solitary Test match, he must have been close to the Aussie squad later in his career.

* * *

So, in October 1999, we played the inaugural Test match between Australia and Zimbabwe at the beautiful Harare Sports Club ground, which was lined with trees and had a wonderful pavilion. There was also a pub at fine leg, which helped cut down the time between leaving the field and having a cold beer – after the day's play, of course.

After bowling Zimbabwe out for 194, we had reached an uncomfortable 7/282 when I walked out to bat. I had no great expectations, as usual, although I'd scored a few runs in the recent Sri Lankan Test series. Batting at the other end was Steve Waugh, who by this time had turned himself from an all-out attacking young batsman into a stronger, defensive player. He would finish his career averaging over 50 and as an all-time great of Australian cricket.

I really enjoyed batting with Tugga. He always gave tailenders a lot of confidence, continually telling us to back ourselves – which, in my case, generally meant slogging.

We had different philosophies on batting. Steve's forward defence was a thing of beauty. He would take a good step forward, in a perfectly balanced position, with his front shoulder and elbow vertical, and then he'd show the full face of his bat and deaden the ball – and the bowler's heart.

He once said that he felt as good playing this shot as when he hit a cover drive to the boundary. This was where we parted ways. For me, every run was priceless, so I'd take the cover drive for four any day.

Anyway, I was feeling good and I stroked my way to 65, with some pull shots and cover drives off Heath Streak, and some smashes back over Henry Olonga's head that were later rumoured to have driven him out of cricket. I'd officially peaked as a batsman.

'You'll only get out if you stop thinking like a batsman,' Tugga said to me. He obviously had more faith in my batting than I did.

The next ball, thinking like a batsman, I tried to block a straight ball. I missed and was out lbw to Streaky, confirming that I really was a tailender.

Tugga went on to score 151 not out and we won the match quite comfortably in the end. We didn't know it as we sang our team song, but it was the start of a record-breaking streak of wins in Test cricket.

Unfortunately, however, Heals wouldn't be there for the record, as the Zimbabwe match was his last Test. He was later named wicketkeeper in the Australian Test team of the century on the back of his feisty batting and nifty glovework. Around the group he was a top-class leader – he had the great ability to mix

STEVE WAUGH'S TOP FIVE TAILENDERS' KNOCKS (WITH HIM AT THE OTHER END)

1. Stuart MacGill, 43 runs in an 88-run partnership, vs England, Melbourne, 1998/99. I was almost as surprised as he was. Because of that knock I trusted him in the second innings, but by then he was back to his true form with a second-ball duck.
2. Colin Miller, 43 off 38 balls in a 53-run partnership, vs the West Indies, Antigua, 1999. He hit two massive sixes off Ambrose that were brilliant. He said to me in the middle, 'They're giving me singles to keep me off strike!'
3. Merv Hughes, 71 runs in a 147-run partnership, vs England, Headingly, 1999. He had orders to block everything – I'd said, 'I'll attack and you defend.' They brought Goochy on and Merv hit him out of the ground. I asked him what he was doing, and he said, 'I was trying to block it but it went for six!'
4. Damien Fleming, 65 runs in a 114-run partnership, vs Zimbabwe, Harare, 1999. Flem's knock was a photographer's delight, especially the Victor Trumper cover drives. This was one partnership dominated by the bowler.
5. Jason Gillespie, 46 runs in a 145-run partnership, vs India, Calcutta, 2001. The human blocking machine's defence was impregnable. Then, after not walking when he'd got an edge, he exploded with some classic cover drives.

---

with both the senior and junior players. He was always proactive in team meetings, but would also take a player aside to ask how he was going. And he had a cheeky jokester side too. All in all, he was the perfect teammate.

BOWLOLOGY

'If only I had got a nick!' Although Warnie (1st), Moods (3rd) and Tugga (6th) with their hands on knees, may have been in trouble.

* * *

During a one-day game at Harare on the same tour, the ball was coming out for me fairly well. Tugga approached me and said, 'I think I've got the cover for your book.' He then proceeded to bring every fielder into a catching position behind the wicket.

Anyway, I think it was only the second time this had been done. My idol, the great Dennis Lillee, had a similar field once in New Zealand in 1977.

My only regret, after bowling to seven slips and two gullys – or was it six slips and three gullys? – was that the batsman played and missed and didn't send a catch through to fifth or sixth slip.

And you were wrong, Tugga – it's not on the cover of my book but shown above.

Chapter 28
Dominators

JOHN 'BUCK' BUCHANAN took over the reins as Australian coach when Geoff Marsh resigned after our 1999 Sri Lankan tour. Straightaway his impact was felt, as he set about challenging our ideas about cricket. He asked a lot of questions about our 'vision' and was one of those 'coloured hats outside the boxes' art-of-inspiration type guys. A little 'out there'. Was more into Confucius than training cones and, man, he confused a few of us. Inspired us, too. He saw himself as a 'performance manager' rather than as a coach, and he was analytical and thought-provoking. Buck worked hard to get the team members to 'buy into' his ideas – which we did, winning his first 15 Test matches as coach.

In one of our first meetings, he drew a pyramid on the whiteboard, part of a four-year plan that had us peaking for the World Cup final in 2003. He felt that Everest was there to be conquered, and we were only at base camp. We were going to take the game to a new level.

We talked through the processes we needed to go through to reach that goal. Everything else would be part of the build-up to that victory. We talked about the legacy of the 1948 'Invincibles', who went through the 1948 Ashes tour undefeated – they were our benchmark. With a team consisting of some future all-time greats such as Warne, McGrath, the Waughs, Ponting, Gilchrist etc., we had star-studded individuals, but how did we want to be remembered as a group? 'The Dominators' was one suggestion, but to get to that level we knew we needed to perform at a high standard for a long period of time.

How would we go from being a very good team to becoming a great team? First we had to ask ourselves some questions such as: Why shouldn't we score at a quicker rate in Test cricket, or use more aggressive fields in one-day cricket? All our standards were linked to our answers. We talked about always being ruthless – complacency was our enemy. We wanted to respect tradition but also to challenge it. This included making some small changes: if we won the toss, we might decide to bowl. And we'd be saying goodbye to the idea of using a nightwatchman much to my relief.

The boys quickly called Buck 'Ned Flanders' because of his similarity to Homer Simpson's neighbour. His public image was as a computer nerd who was meticulous with his timing and preparation. This was partly true – he definitely did love computers and stats. But time management wasn't always his strength.

Our previous coaches, Bob Simpson and Geoff Marsh, had been sticklers about the whole team being on time for our meetings. When Buck came on board, we sometimes had to wait for him to turn up. We'd be there on time and wondering where our coach was, then he'd enter in a panic. Most times he'd trip over Mr Magoo style and his notes would fly everywhere, and we'd watch in amazement as he tried to gather his papers and his composure. He was quite an intense thinker, and really needed 36 hours in every day – 24 hours just wasn't enough.

Not everyone approved of his methods, and he wasn't always successful. His misses included at Middlesex, and the Kolkata Knight Riders in IPL. Some players – such as Shane Warne, Michael Slater and Stuart MacGill – found that Buck's coaching style did not suit their personality types. But his winning percentage of 75 per cent in all games shows that he was a great match for most Australian cricketers playing between 1999 and 2007.

In reality, Buck wasn't the cricketing guru he was built up to be. He was human. His methods inspired loyalty from his supporters and loathing from his detractors. Does a coach make the team or the team make the coach? This is a grey area, but any great team culture needs the right coach as well as the right team.

* * *

In our team meeting the night before the first match of the 1999/00 summer, Buck asked for our goals for the season. We were scheduled to play three Tests against Pakistan and then three against India. There were the usual responses from our group to
- win each series
- bowl consecutive maidens with the ball
- target the Pakistan/Indian top order (Pigeon)

I responded that I wanted to sing the team song six times in a row; as soon as the words left my mouth I sensed a vibe from my teammates that I'd finally gone totally bananas.

Nevertheless, my two goals for every game were to 1. be the best bowler in the game, and 2. sing the song.

But I felt, with the talent in our group, why couldn't we win every Test?

A great initiative from Tugga was inviting former Aussie players to present new players with their baggy greens. The first man to do so was the Invincible Queensland opening batsman Bill Brown, who played 22 Tests between 1934 and 1948. It was his job to put the caps on two very different players before the Brisbane game. Scott Muller was making his debut. He would only play two Tests and unfortunately will be remembered for the infamous 'can't bowl, can't throw' line from ... Joe the Cameraman. The other young fella lining up for his first match was one Adam Gilchrist, a wicketkeeper batsman who luckily Joe thought 'could bat and keep a bit'.

Interestingly, Brown was the first batsman run out at the bowler's end before the ball was bowled. In the summer of 1947/48, he was dismissed for 18 when the Indian spinner Vinoo Mankad held onto the ball he was about to deliver and whipped the bails off at the non-striker's end. Brown was backing up well out of his crease and so was given out. After this incident, cricket officials knew they needed to name this mode of dismissal to give it some relevance. Had the bowler 'Mankadded' the batsman, or had the batsman 'Browned' himself? They eventually settled on 'Mankad' as they felt it sounded slightly better.

Anyway, I brought Gilly into the game on day one with a couple of outswingers in the 'Fleming Freeway', which Wasim Mohammed and the 'Woodchopper' Ijaz Ahmed nicked through to him behind the stumps. I always liked to look after the new guys. Then, in our innings, he proceeded to make a breathtaking 81, belting a top-class Pakistan attack to all parts of the Gabba. In the dressing rooms, all members of the Aussie group thought the same thing: *We've got a good one here.*

Gilly's debut Test innings was ended by an unbelievable delivery from Shoaib Akhtar, an outswinging yorker at 160 kilometres per hour that hit the base of off stump. After watching that incredible delivery, I severely lowered my expectations of myself with the bat. Where I had initially hoped to score a few runs, I was now in furious negotiations with the higher being to see if maybe he could see clear just to let me get out of there alive.

Gilly got cheered off, which was good as the Gabba crowd had booed him when he walked out to bat because he had taken the place of Ian Healy, a legend in the side. Fair to say that after one knock not even the most loyal Queenslander could give a XXXX* for Ian whatshisname.

I strode out to the batting crease at sloth-like pace – unlike Shoaib's first ball, which had broken the sound barrier. I experienced post-traumatic stress even before the ball pounded into my front pad and hit me dead in front. I was plumb lbw. *You beauty!* was my first thought, followed by a searing pain in my shin. But, god wasn't letting me off that easy.

Much to my distress, I looked up to see the umpire calling a no ball. I tried to walk, but to no avail. I was stuck there.

I didn't even see the next two balls – there was just a red blurry thing flashing down the pitch. After the fastest three balls I had ever faced, I was out lbw – even though this time it was too high. But we still had a big lead of 208 on the first innings.

Wasim Akram was my favourite bowler in my era. In fact, Bowlology is based on his exquisite abilities. In Pakistan's second innings, I came on to bowl from the members' end and bowled a very slow warm-up ball, which Wasim smashed down the ground for four. He then gave me a few words as he ran past. That got me a little fired up, and for the next ball I did my best Wasim Akram impression. The kookaburra ball started on leg stump, then swung late, reverse-style, and clipped his off bail.

'I'm back, *baby!*' I shouted to Wasim in my best Austin Powers impersonation. Wasim looked at me in a bemused way; there had been nothing in our confrontation that indicated I would

* Like the beer.

use an Austin Powers reference. After I had cleaned up Shoaib as well, I had 5/69.

As you are probably realising by now, for me cricket was never about personal milestones, but team success. However, when I knocked over Shoaib Akhtar to complete our win, I had my Man of the Match speech prepared by the time we left the field. But in another *batsmen run the bloody game* decision, when the time came to declare Man of the Match in this Test, they read out Michael Slater's name.

Lets analyse the stats here just to see why I was peeved.
1. There were 1297 runs scored and 30 wickets taken.
2. I took 9/124, around a third of the entire wickets taken in the match for a tenth of the runs.
3. Slats got 169 and 32, about a sixth of the total runs.

Surely, in a game dominated by batting, the bowler should have got the biscuits. The members of the Fast Bowlers Cartel were not happy.

I'm not a bitter person and I moved on . . . eventually. About a week later I did get a sincere apology from the Man of the Match adjudicator, who shall remain nameless.*

* It was journalist Martin Blake.

❋ ❋ ❋

The night before the Second Test, in Hobart, the Australian team had the pleasure of having dinner with four members of the 1948 Invincibles, one of the greatest cricket teams of all time:
- Bill Brown: An opening batsman who played 22 Tests, he averaged 47 and was known as a beautiful timer of the ball.
- Bill Johnston: A tall, left-arm swing guru who played 40 Tests and took 160 wickets at an average of 24.
- Doug Ring: A leg-spinning all-rounder, who played 13

Tests, averaging 22 with the bat and 37 with the ball. He also starred on the legendary *World of Sport* television program on Sunday mornings on Channel Seven.
- Arthur Morris: A master opening batsman, later named in Australia's team of the century, he played 46 Tests and averaged 46.

They all provided great entertainment – and maybe, in hindsight, some positive vibes for our incredible Test win over Pakistan.

Pakistan had a *reasonable* bowling line-up for this Test: Wasim Akram, Waqar Younis, Shoaib Akhtar, Azhar Mahmood and 'mystery spinner' Saqlain Mushtaq. So they had express pace, new- and old-ball swing, and an off-spinner who spun the ball both ways. In poker terms, they had a bowling royal flush.

The match was evenly balanced after both teams' first innings. When I came to the wicket I was facing Saqlain, who was on a hat-trick. In our team meetings it had been emphasised that we had to watch out for his 'doosra' – the delivery that looked like an off-spinner but spun away from the right-hander's bat. As instructed, I played for the doosra and was luckily given not out, as I somehow batted away his off-spinner with my pad. A few balls later he got me for a duck anyway with another off-spinner.

Pakistan set us a target of 369 runs to win, and on a wearing day-four pitch, it seemed like we had more chance of seeing a Tasmanian Tiger than of singing our victory song. But by the end of the day's play, we were 5/188, with Justin Langer on 52 and Gilly on 45.

If those two had been in AC/DC, Gilly would have been Angus Young – with brilliant, flashy solos – and JL would have been Malcolm Young – playing solid chords in the background but hard as rock. Gilly's batting was breathtaking and daring, and

SAQLAIN MUSHTAQ

The plucky Pakistan off-spinner was in fact my batting nemesis. If I was Austin Powers, Saqlain was Dr Evil, with all his varieties. A quick review of facing him:

1. The first ball I faced from him, at Headingly in 1999, I hit him inside-out over cover for three. I didn't know it was the doosra, I just hit it on length. Basically eyes-closed stuff.
2. At Hobart, when I was walking out to bat, I met Steve Waugh, who cautioned me about Saqlain's doosra. Out second ball, lbw to his off-spinner for a duck. In the next Test, in Perth, I was out for another duck, lbw again to his off-spinner but played for his doosra.
3. In the one-day series at the MCG, I was chipping Wasim and Shoaib around, then Saqlain came into the attack. I tried to hit him over cover, like at Headingly, but it was the off-spinner again. I ran down the pitch and did the splits as I missed the ball. As I tried to edge my back foot behind the crease (in the process almost ripping myself in half), Moin Khan had the ball in his gloves. He watched my back leg edge closer to the batting crease, slowly and painfully, and smiled, knowing I wasn't going to get back. Eventually he took a bail off. Back in the dressing rooms, Ponting and Gilchrist were sitting next to each other with their heads down. Even though I couldn't see their faces, I knew they were pissing themselves laughing at me. I glanced up to see the replay of me doing my best gymnast impression and couldn't help but join them.
4. At Trent Bridge for a one-day game against Pakistan in 2001, I decided it was time to destroy my nemesis. Dizzy and I were batting and making a good fist of winning the game. I was facing Saqlain again. I decided two things: if the ball was thrown up, I was going to slog-sweep, and if was darted in,

then I was slogging it straight down the ground. After a couple of slog-sweeps, Saqlain darted one in the slot and I gave it everything. It came straight off the middle of my bat and went over the sightscreen for six. It was my first six for Australia — and my last. In fact, it was my last scoring shot for Australia. And if you look at Saqlain's record after that shot, he was never the same bowler. Points won to Fleming.

---

even his teammates just had to watch every ball. He was the core of the Australian team on the field but was just as important off it, with his sense of fun and clear reason.

With the bat, he was 'Errolesque', to quote British author Benjamin S. Johnson's ode to Errol Flynn. Like the actor, when he got going he was brave and dynamic, bringing a devil-may-care attitude to the crease. Who else could walk in on a pair against the English in Perth, nearly get caught first ball and then proceed to amaze the cricketing world over the next 56 balls and score the second-fastest century in Test history?

No one personified the baggy green better than Gilly, and he was a role model not only for all cricketers but also for all sportsmen. He had a real respect and passion for the game, he worked hard for his success, and he loved nothing more than a teammate's success. He cherished sitting down with a beer and telling stories and laughing at others' anecdotes.

Within the team, he was always an easygoing teammate who loved all the little intrigues of each player. His instinct was to find something funny or quirky in his teammates. He often took an earphone from a teammate's iPod to find out what music he was listening to, so he could judge his mood and attitude.

Like the man he succeeded, Ian Healy, Gilly had a genuine ability to lead, with his strong work ethic at training and on the field. But he could also switch off quickly, celebrating hard after a win or making the environment as friendly as possible for newcomers to the team. After a big win he always left in his whites, with his baggy green sitting proudly on his head.

Justin Langer was as tough as nails. As a player, he knew his limitations, but what he lacked in height he made up for in character. Belligerent and determined, he was one of the toughest batsmen for the opposition to dismiss. Yet he was continually under pressure for his spot – until he combined with his great mate, Matty Hayden. Then we had Australian cricket's first 'bromance', and also one of Australia's great opening partnerships.

JL loves his martial arts and has a black belt in karate. He once sparred with world lightweight champion Vic Darchinyan; apparently Jeff Fenech liked his style. On one tour of New Zealand, Buck asked all the players to give a five-minute presentation on their passions. JL decided to demonstrate nine different moves that could stop an attacker in his tracks and stun him to silence. The touring group all agreed that it was in our best interests never to tour without JL – and that he could bat where he wanted.

So, on day five of the Hobart Test in late 1999, we rocked up to Bellerive with five wickets in hand and needing 181 runs to win. Cricketers being a superstitious lot, everyone had to resume the same positions they had sat in the night before, when Gilly and JL had begun their partnership.

Attack was the name of the game, and this was right up Gilly's alley. He quickly started to punch the boundaries, while JL was in his Yoda state, watching the ball like a hawk. He copped one Shoaib thunderbolt – a full toss – on the thumb. My immediate thought was, *Oh, no, that's a break for sure*. JL simply smiled at Shoaib. Tough little bastard almost looked like he enjoyed it.

As the runs flowed, our confidence in the dressing rooms

began to lift. JL eventually got out for 127, by which time we were just five runs short of victory. Then Gilly hit the winning runs off Saqlain; well, that was what Warnie thought. Gilly played the shot and our crazy leggie just ran down the pitch and hugged him while we screamed from the room 'FINISH THE RUN!' The message eventually got through and we had pulled off one of the more amazing wins, a victory that gave us the belief that we would win no matter what the situation.

* * *

We won the Third Test against Pakistan as well, so we went into the three-Test series against India in good shape. The first match was in Adelaide, and after two good batting displays we had set the Indians a target of 396 runs on the last day and a half.

By day five, our pig-shooting enthusiast, Glenn McGrath, and I were running through India's strong batting line-up, which included Laxman, Tendulkar and Dravid. I was bowling from the Bradman Stand end as it was into the breeze; as usual, Pigeon had taken the option to bowl down-breeze.

Souruv Ganguly was a beautiful driver and cutter of the ball, but I knew they were his only shots, so I decided to come around the wicket and bounce him. Trying to bowl too quick, I delivered my worst ever bouncer. Ganguly got a bit of bat on it and Adam Gilchrist dived full-stretch down the leg side to take an unbelievable catch. Gilly was an underrated wicketkeeper, but because of his height and reach he took some magnificent catches. This was one of his best.

The next batsman was Ajit Agarkar, who, the cricket grapevine had whispered, had pretentions as an all-rounder. On his first ball we realised that it was only a rumour, as he drove a widish, fullish ball straight to Steve Waugh in the gully. Remarkably, in his next six innings against Australia, Agarkar made a combined total of no runs – the Olympic rings!

So I found myself on *another* Test hat-trick! I wasn't that nervous as I'd done this Test hat-trick stuff before. (Have I mentioned my hat-trick on Test Debut?) Then I started thinking if I got another one, I could be the only person in the history of Test cricket to take two hat-tricks! (I later discovered that both Jimmy Matthews of England and Hugh Trumble of Australia had done so – and Matthews' two hat-tricks came on the same day!)

Then it occurred to me that there were probably just two great honours in Australian Test cricket.

The first was the greatest honour – to wear the baggy green. Even now, there have only been 430-odd players to don the cap, so each one is part of an elite club.

The second great honour that every Australian Test cricketer strives for is to get an *individual* Tony Greig piece of memorabilia!

Now, I'd only been part of some *team* memorabilia pieces, and we had to divide that cash by 12 so it was never a lot. But if I could take this second Test hat-trick, Tony Greig would no doubt be on the phone very quickly. After only four easy repayments I'd be able to retire a millionaire.

I was a common sense kind of guy, and I knew I was never the biggest name going around in the Aussie team. So I had to get a famous teammate to take the catch. That would generate more public interest and more cash – maybe enough so that I could send my kids to private schools . . .

There was only one man who fitted that bill in my era: Shane Keith Warne. If I could get an edge from Javagal Srinath's bat into Warnie's safe hands, then the money would flow in.

I knew I had to generate good bounce from a very flat Adelaide pitch – it was so flat that I *only* had 8/92 at this stage! So I brought in a bit of Bowlology. Instead of releasing at ten-thirty for my stock late-swinging out-winger, I decided to release at 12 o'clock to maximise the bounce from this flat, flat deck. I was hoping to find the splice of Srinath's bat and thus create an easier catch for the great Shane Warne.

I was pretty pumped up as I ran in for the hat-trick ball, and everything went into slow motion. I released it at 12 o'clock and hit the pitch hard. Srinath, surprised by the extra bounce, fended and nicked the ball behind. It flew straight at Warnie's forehead.

By then I was running down the pitch, screaming, 'Tony Greig, here I fucking come!'

Warnie reacted slowly. He raised his big mitts up in front of his face, and the ball cannoned into his palms and went over his head for a run.

I couldn't believe it. I fell to my knees, trying to understand what had just happened. All of a sudden, there was a hand on my shoulder.

It was Warnie. 'Flemo, think of the positive,' he said. 'I saved four runs.'

Unsurprisingly, I didn't see that as much of a positive. 'Maybe I should have bowled a mobile phone down there,' I said. 'You would have snaffled that.'

People sometimes ask me whether I was disappointed. No, I never even gave it a *ninth* thought. I'm on the honour board in the Adelaide Oval dressing room, and I like to go there and stand under my name and wait for blokes to notice. It says 'D. Fleming, 5/30 vs India, 1999/00' – but how good would '6/29, including a hat-trick' look?

So you would think Warnie would have looked after me after I talked him through his hat-trick in the 1994/95 Boxing Day Test.

Regrets? Not me. I moved on (in 2012).

BOWLOLOGY

Warnie putting in jeopardy the private-school plans
of future generations of Flemings. Why, Warnie, why?

※ ※ ※

Anyway, we won that match and the next two – making it six from six. I had called it early but I'd been right. We sang the song six times in a summer for the first time ever, and our celebrations reflected the size of the achievement.

We wanted to do something memorable to honour our historic summer. I'm not sure who first suggested singing the song in our jockstraps, but by then many hours had been spent drinking the beer sponsor's finest, so our decision-making processes were obviously blurred.

At about one o'clock in the morning we ventured out onto the SCG pitch to sing the song, wearing only our jockstraps or bike shorts. Punter led us into the song, which we belted out a couple of times.

Suddenly, the silence of the night was broke by an almighty *whack!* A bum-slapping sniper had let rip with an open-handed

DOMINATORS

The Dominators: Not to say we were arrogant, but we posed for this in the warm-up on day one.

smack on a teammate's raw behind. Soon, in a scene reminiscent of the opening of *Saving Private Ryan*, teammates were running for their backsides' lives. There were blokes copping whacks from everywhere, and bum-slappers trying to get in first before copping a whack themselves. Blood-curdling screams were heard all the way to the safety of the dressing rooms.

Once inside, we quickly tallied up the casualties. Red baboon-like bums were in the majority, as everyone got their clothes on as quickly as humanly possible. This was followed by a lot of standing around as we drank more beer; sitting down was not an option.

Not long afterwards, the SCG security staff turned up at the rooms. Immediately, we thought we might be in some trouble, but in fact they had brought us some snaps from their security cameras of the jock-strapping madness minutes before.

Chapter 29
Streakers and Albatrosses in New Zealand

I'D NEVER BEEN to New Zealand before, and nothing prepared me for it. In a word, the New Zealand public fucking hated us. No doubt this wasn't helped when Warnie was asked at a press conference, 'What do you think of New Zealanders?'

'Really, they're all just frustrated Aussies,' our spin king replied.

Our tour in 2000 started badly when we played our first one-dayer in Dunedin, a big university town on the South Island. The signs weren't great early, when some students, bored by the 10th over, set fire to the couches they had brought in and chucked anything they could find at us – bottles, foodscraps, Split Enz LPs. Bevo even copped a fish! It wasn't technically a flying fish, but it did a great imitation of one as it landed near our one-day batting machine.

A chant broke out near me while I was fielding down at fine leg: 'Fleming's a wanker!'

'If that's the way you think of your captain, imagine what you think of me?' I called back. That went down like a lead balloon, and the abuse went to a new level.

'Wanker, wanker!'

Dunedin is traditionally regarded as the coldest of New Zealand's major cities, and so it doesn't seem a natural fit for male streakers. But one local man thought he would lighten up proceedings by having a run.

STREAKER'S CHECKLIST

- Ditch clothes
- Get over fence without catching any of your dangling bits
- Run like you stole something
- Once on field, avoid Andrew Symonds . . . He hits *hard*!
- Take on biggest security guard and run like crazy to other side of field, while being chased by other security staff. Make fools of them by jumping fence in one leap
- Keep running. Jump over back fence; avoid damaging the *frank and beans*

The first four points of the Streaker's Checklist went to plan. But the Dunedin security guards were a bit laid-back, and they seemed as happy as the crowd to sit back and watch the streaker go about his business.

Meanwhile, the bloke was running like crazy, really putting in the big ones. He was at the top of his game. The uni students were cheering him on, and so now were most of security staff, who definitely weren't going to chase him.

After a couple of minutes of Matt Shirvington–like pace, the lactic acid began kicking in. Our streaker stopped and doubled over, trying to suck in as much oxygen as possible. Streakers by nature are sprinters – they don't train to run middle-distance. He was gone.

For the first time in streaker history, the streaker had actually *fatigued*! Finally, the ultimate insult: play restarted before he had staggered off the ground.

STREAKERS AND ALBATROSSES IN NEW ZEALAND

※ ※ ※

This was John Buchanan's first international tour as coach, and he liked to put us out a bit. He instituted activities such as getting the players to talk about their passions in front of the group. The titles of some of these talks included the following:

- Haydos: Fishing Coral Trout – firm, fleshy and big fillets!
- Punter: The Joys of Greyhound Training
- Me: The Comedian Stephen Wright – 'Can you get amnesia and déjà vu at the same time?'
- Blewy: Bodybuilding for Beginners – focusing on the calf muscle
- JL: How to Be an Assassin

Buck would often quote from Sun Tzu's *The Art of War* as we prepared for games. He might as well have been speaking Martian to Andrew Symonds and Ian Harvey. On match day, he'd get players to recite their own poems about the day of cricket ahead – which resulted in us realising that cricketers can't write poems.

The day after our one-day streakathon game in Dunedin, we had a day to kill. Buck gathered the group together.

'I've got a real treat for you guys today,' he said proudly. 'We're going on a trip by bus to a remote spot outside Dunedin, which is *the* nesting spot for the royal albatross. It's the *only* mainland breeding colony of these massive seabirds in the world!' He said this with as much excitement as his monotone voice allowed.

It's fair to say this was met with less enthusiasm by the playing group; we felt he had lost the plot like an Adam Sandler movie. But off we went, in two buses, in search of the royal albatross. Two hours into our drive, the natives were restless. Luckily, I was in the rebel second bus, led by Warnie, who, realising that his and Buck's planets were not going to align, said, 'Seriously, let's fucking turn around.' Another 20 minutes went by. 'Fuck it,' Warnie said. 'I'm turning us around.'

There were no arguments from the boys on the bus.

The ill-fated first bus, led by Buck, eventually arrived at their destination. Andrew Symonds related the scene to me: 'There were just thousands of what looked like seagulls flying around. Buck hadn't told us that the royal albatross looks like a large seagull, so we didn't even know if we were seeing large seagulls or small royal albatrosses.'

Small royal albatross? Large seagull?

KEY STATS FROM AUSTRALIA'S TOUR OF NEW ZEALAND, FEBRUARY–APRIL 2000

- 365th Test wicket taken by Warnie, breaking my hero Dennis Lillee's Test record wicket tally by an Aussie
- 14 one-day international wins in a row by Australia (a record)
- 10 Test wins in a row, one behind the great West Indies team of 1984
- One fatigued streaker (streaking was soon banned in Dunedin by the World Streaking Federation)
- Zero sightings of the royal albatross

Chapter 30
AC/DC Caught Backstreet Boys Bowled Kenny Rogers

WE ARRIVED IN India in 2001 brimming with confidence, having won 15 Test matches in a row. We'd beaten India 3–0 at home, and now we had to conquer them in India. It was our Holy Grail – no Australian team had won a series in India since 1969/70.

Buck was generally a very composed, if not dour, speaker, and he rarely broke out of his deep monotone voice, not dissimilar to the economics teacher in the movie *Ferris Bueller's Day Off* when taking attendance: 'Bueller? Bueller? Bueller?'

In New Zealand, however, he had challenged us one morning, and on that occasion he'd chosen his moment well. He really let us have it, questioning our motivation and passion for the baggy green cap. He knew we were going to win, he said, but that wasn't enough – it was about maximising all our skills. Great teams *dominate*. Most of the guys were quite stirred up by this, and we went out and crushed the Kiwis.

One spray that didn't work came after a warm-up game in India early in our tour. Our lead-up matches hadn't gone well, and Buck had a crack at a few players, including Glenn McGrath and me (it was fair, in my case) for playing too angry. We had to get back into our roles, he said. He then turned to Mark Waugh, who generally didn't pay a lot of attention in team meetings, preferring to let his actions on the field speak for him. He woke up when he heard his name mentioned.

'What's this bloke talking about?' Junior asked the bloke next to him.

Buck then turned to Shane Warne, pointing out that there was some room for improvement in his bowling. Warnie didn't say a word, but you could see that was the end of any relationship between our coach and our star leg-spinner. Like Ned Flanders and Homer Simpson's relationship, it was never going to work.

Next was Michael Slater. But our nuggety opening bat came out swinging – much like the way he batted – and he yelled straight back at Buck. The rest of us were stunned. I just remember looking at Buck as we finished the meeting. I think it had already hit him that his spray hadn't made the impact he wanted it to, which was to inspire and challenge us. Instead, it had been divisive. He had singled individuals out, and he hadn't read his players well enough. He looked shattered.

Despite this, we convincingly won the First Test, played in Mumbai, wearing black armbands in memory of the greatest cricketer of all time, Sir Donald Bradman. I reckon Sir Don would have been proud of our team effort, but especially with the batting of Matthew Hayden and Adam Gilchrist. Having come together with the score at 5/99, they both scored centuries – Haydos 119 and Gilly 122.

It was a career-defining innings and series for big Haydos. He had dominated domestic cricket for years without transferring that form into the Test arena. He was averaging in the mid-20s after a dozen Tests, spread out over seven years.

We sometimes called him 'Jurassic' early in his career, after the movie *Jurassic Park*, thanks to his tall barrel-chested frame, and he turned into a T-Rex on this tour, blocking, sweeping and hitting bowlers over the top as he mastered batting on Indian pitches. Overall, it was great to see him fulfil his massive talent.

Few know that he actually tried his hand at bowling, to make himself more attractive to the selectors. For such a huge man, he had a very effeminate run-up – almost like he was running on eggshells on his tippy toes. As he approached the crease, he rocked back onto his back foot – he'd obviously been coached to do that as a kid. There were occasions, as I watched him from mid-on, that I thought he'd rock back so far that he'd fall back away from the stumps, which tends to hinder your wicket-taking options.

※ ※ ※

Mowbray's own Ricky Ponting is a legend – the best Aussie batsman and fielder of his era. He was one of the greatest attacking batsman of all time when in full flight. He could hit a length ball on the up back past the bowler, or pull the same length behind square leg. His Avenue of Apprehension was the size of a 20-cent piece.

He was a leader of the team from a young age, an unselfish teammate and an exuberant encourager on the field. You always heard him shouting encouragement and celebrating wickets more passionately then anyone else on the field. Sure, he was quite hairy and had nerdish qualities, but he was our singer of 'Underneath the Southern Cross I Stand'.

That's not to say we didn't have our disagreements. One of the team's favourite flicks was *Wild Things* with Matt Dillon, Neve Campbell, Denise Richards and a great cameo – as always – from Bill Murray. I think most guys would agree that, on the hottability scale, Denise Richards packing out her bikini was the pick of the girls. No, Punter preferred the gothic Neve character. Give me a break, Punter!

However, I did appreciate him watching the *South Park* movie with me about a dozen times on our 1999 tour of Sri Lanka. To this day, we still refer to ourselves as Terrance and Phillip, the rear-end-unstable comedy duo from Canada who are regulars in the show.

Punter and I also loved our AFL, often kicking the ball for hours around training and watching games on tour when we could. His beloved Kangaroos played in the 1998 Grand Final. We were in Pakistan at the time and had to wait two days before we could watch the game. We committed to not finding out the result so we could watch it live. Of course, our bloody teammates told us the result, but it said much about our love of the game.

We even played the Big Dipper Footy Quiz – named after the Hawthorn Brownlow medallist and legend Robert DiPierdomenico – on tour in Sri Lanka. Darren Lehman had brought it with him, and we played while having a couple of cold beers in Colombo before the 1999 Preliminary Final between Carlton and Essendon.

Punter is one cricketer I believe could have made it to the top in Aussie Rules. He had great skills and is really tough – a perfect midfielder. But when it came to goalkicking, I reckon I had him covered. The challenge was issued and accepted.

In Mumbai after training, we set up some goals. I went first and kicked four goals and two behinds from my six kicks. Punter started badly, not kicking a major until his third attempt, but then he slotted a hat-trick. So with his last kick he needed a goal to take the contest to a sudden-death kick-off.

He started his run-up and laid his right foot into the pigskin. The kick looked good off the boot and he started his celebration – a little early, for my liking, as it faded to the right. Punter claimed the goal, however, so we were at a stalemate.

Luckily for me, a worker at the ground who was painting the stand behind us was watching our battle with great interest. He came up to me and said, 'Fleming, don't let him stiff you. It did indeed miss to the right.'

Punter conceded.

Bang! Victory for Fleming – and a good inclusion into a future Big Dipper's Footy Quiz, I might add.

Q: Who defeated Ricky Ponting in a goalkicking completion in India in 2001?

A: Yours truly.

Thank you very much, Dipper.

※ ※ ※

With our win in the First Test, we had pushed our winning streak to 16 wins in a row – an amazing effort. But it came to a screeching halt in the Second Test, in Kolkata, thanks to some amazing batting from the classy V. V. S. Laxman and Rahul 'the Wall' Dravid, along with some penetrating spin bowling from Harbarjan 'the Turbanator' Singh.

Confidence was sky-high, as we were coming off a convincing 10-wicket victory in the First Test in Mumbai. How could anything go wrong, you might ask yourself? Well, let me tell you. The selectors decided to go all funky and make a change for Kolkata. The bleeding lunatics may as well have handed the series back to India then and there. That's right, they did the unthinkable and dropped ME.

In truth, I bowled poorly in Mumbai. We experimented with my bowling cutters, which worked a bit, but probably I should have been bowling swingers. A week later I saw some footage on TV and noticed how wide I was bowling on the crease. We had come to India straight out of a one-day series in Australia. In one-day cricket when the ball wasn't swinging on flat tracks

I liked to bowl wider on the bowling crease and angle the ball into the batsman, cramping them for room and to minimise the risk of getting cut, but I'd continued this in the Mumbai Test match. Nobody had picked it up, not even the clown doing it.

It was disappointing being 12th man but the boys played brilliantly during the first couple of days at Kolkata and looked a sure thing to take a 2–0 series lead on day three. Australia enforced the follow-on with India still lagging 274 runs behind our first-innings total. As a faithful 12th man, I started to get the beers on ice in our esky for the lads to replenish their body fluids while celebrating our 17th win in a row.

No one could have envisaged what happened next: V. V. S. (Very Very Silky) Laxman and Rahul Dravid combined for a staggering 376-run partnership. Laxman had generally struggled against us in the past – apart from one hundred he scored in Sydney, an innings in which we'd set very aggressive fields – so this was a massive innings for him. In hindsight, I now wonder whether allowing him easy singles in the first innings had given him some confidence and freedom, as he looked a different player in his second dig. Always a beautiful timer of the ball, his batting against Warnie was particularly amazing. V. V. S. was flicking our leg spinner through mid-wicket from the footmarks against the spin for four, then doing the same next ball through the cover area, with the spin, timing, execution and skill of his batting from another planet.

Dravid we regarded as a very good defensive player early in his career but one who didn't damage at pace on the scoreboard, hence his nickname 'the Wall'. Well, it was like Germany 1989 as the Wall fell down and then blossomed into a classical stroke player, driving and cutting his way to a hundred, then flourished to be an Indian all-time batting legend and great bloke as well.

They got to the 350-run mark for their partnership. Our poor boys had been toiling in the heat for days, and wickets looked as likely as David Boon sipping tea on a flight to England, when Haydos, Alfie and Slats got a trundle. I decided to start unloading the beers from our esky and happened to pass by a mirror and catch my image. I looked into my eyes and said, 'Good one to miss, Flem, good one to miss.'

India then snatched the unlikeliest of victories by 171 runs. Rumours are that Lazarus rang the Indian dressing rooms and conceded, 'Now *that* is a comeback.'

Our streak had come to a dramatic halt, well, the team's streak had. As far as I was concerned mine was still going.

* * *

I was a member of our social committee, and I thought the boys might need a lift. So Darren Lehmann and I decided to organise a trivia night with beers and pizza to keep morale up. We didn't want to test the boys too much, so the questions were basically all on general sport, movie trivia and music.

Now, I had played in Australian teams that were very harmonious, but one source of friction was always what music was played on our rockbox after a win. There were three distinct factions in the Australian cricket team.

You had the hard rock guys: Dizzy and Kasper and me. David Boon was also a real headbanger who loved his AC/DC, Led Zeppelin and Deep Purple. When I first made the team I influenced him with some Motley Crue, Pearl Jam and Red Hot Chili Peppers music. Being a new guy in the team, my influence was minimal on the rockbox. If *Blood Sugar Sex Magik* by the Chili Peppers was on, the other boys would chuck it off after about 30 seconds. But if Boony put it on, we'd at least get three or four songs as he was a legend. So I really missed Boony when he retired.

I loved pumping up some hard rock before going out to bowl. I felt it influenced the way I performed. Well, before we went out to bowl in the sixth one-dayer in India in 2001, our very own Mr Pop, Warnie, was mugging our ears with some stomach-churning Phil Collins. I pulled John Buchanan aside. 'Buck, do you expect me to go out there and bowl fast swingers and be aggressive with "Easy Lover" going round in my head? Do you?'

Unfortunately, it turned out to be 'Another Day In Paradise' for the Indian batsman as they smashed me all over the Indira Priyadarshini Stadium.

'Are you happy?' I asked Buck, reflecting on my eight overs resulting in 0/53. If you read the *Wisden* reports from that match, they might say my line was this, or my length that, but now you know the real reason I was off my game.

KASPER'S TAKE ON THE MUSICAL TASTES OF THE AUSTRALIAN TEAM

I have to say that music played an important role in my cricket career. It was invaluable in the countless airports, planes, buses, hotels and dressing rooms that are so much a part of a cricketer's life on tour. With many personalities on a team comes many music preferences. However, although no two bowling actions are the same, in our music tastes we fast bowlers were united. We loved the hard stuff.

Whilst I liked the typical 1980s hard rock, I was an unashamed lover of 1990s grunge. The fast bowler has always fallen into a minority group within the team, and so has suffered relentless persecution from batsmen over the years. Perhaps it was this that drew me to the melancholic symbolism of grunge music.

KASPER'S TOP FIVE BANDS AND ESSENTIAL ALBUMS

1. Pearl Jam's *Ten*: I bought this on the strength of hearing the first single, 'Alive', and I was amazed at the hidden classics that filled the rest of this CD.
2. The Stone Temple Pilots' *Purple*.
3. Soundgarden's *Superunknown*.
4. Green Day's *Dookie*.
5. The Foo Fighters' *The Colour and the Shape*.

Who would have thought that each of these outsiders would show consistent form over many years and still be performing today? Even after 20 years, these bands continue to produce arguably their best work, and they now have wider audiences than when they began. I love the symbolism of the longevity of their performance and ability to perform on all conditions without much reward — just like fast bowlers, really.

I just wonder what Joshua Kadison is singing about today.

Then there were those who liked the pretty-boy bands: Shane Warne, Brett Lee, Greg Blewett and Michael Slater. The worrying thing was not only that they knew the words to songs by Boyzone and the Backstreet Boys, they knew all the dance moves as well.

For me, the boy-band lowlight was a Sydney Test match against India. I was looking for some musical inspiration, so I checked out our passionate opening bat Michael Slater's CD collection and found a disc by Britney Spears. Less than a year later, Slats was dropped. Tell me: is there a correlation there?

TOP FIVE APPALLING PRETTY-BOY SONGS PLAYED BY MEMBERS OF THE AUSSIE TEAM

1. 'Jessie' by Joshua Kadison: Justin Langer loved this song. It is just a simply appalling song. Jessie wants Josh to go to Mexico with her and their cat. Poor cat.
2. 'Barbie Girl' by Aqua: The lead singer was quite cute. Crap song. Why doesn't Ken get a song, by the way?
3. 'Everybody (Backstreet's Back)' by the Backstreet Boys: Slats' and Binga's band. A song about the fact that you are *back* for your third single? You're kidding, right? Nope. They had already stopped trying.
4. 'The Macarena' by Los del Rio: Sorry, but the rock boys – Kasper, Dizzy and I – couldn't participate in the pretty-boys' dance to this song after a Test win. That was unAustralian.
5. 'She Bangs' by Ricky Martin: A Warnie fave. The late AC/DC lead singer, Bon Scott, passed away choking on his own vomit. I almost did the same the first time I heard this song.

Last but not least, we had the disturbing group of the country-and-western boys. This posse was led by Steve Waugh, who was into Kenny Rogers. He also thought John Denver was pretty hip and was obsessed with John Williamson.

AC/DC CAUGHT BACKSTREET BOYS BOWLED KENNY ROGERS

When Steve became captain, it wasn't hard to work out who was desperate for a game, because there was an increasing number of requests for his favourites.

'Hey, Tugga, have you heard Dolly Parton's new one?' Justin Langer might ask.

'What about some James Taylor to get us in the mood, Tugga?' Matty Hayden would slyly suggest.

They weren't fooling anyone.

Back to our trivia night. For once, I too had a hidden agenda – I wanted my bloody Test spot back. So I planted a question for the skipper and tour selector Steve Waugh. He would answer the Dorothy Dixer and be happy with me and reward me by letting me use the new ball in the Third Test.

The first half a dozen questions went by and Tugga hadn't answered a single one. *This cunning plan is working a treat*, I thought.

Then I asked, 'Who was a *gambler* and was also the *coward of his county?*'

Now, what do you think the answer would be? Kenny Rogers? Of course it is.

Tugga threw his hand up like he was Horshack from *Welcome Back, Kotter*. 'Ooh, ooh, ooooh, pick me!' said our captain and selector Steve Waugh. *I might as well put my baggy green on now*, I thought. *This plan is working to perfection!*

Tugga answered excitedly: 'Tommy.'

Everyone was a bit stunned.

'No . . . the answer is Kenny Rogers,' I replied hesitantly.

Tugga protested, explaining that he was correct. Apparently, in the song 'Coward of the County', the yellow coward is in fact named Tommy.

BOWLOLOGY

After some more uncomfortable silence, I spoke for the group: 'I'm sorry, Tugga, that's too sad that you know the real name of the guy in the song. I can't pay that.'

Tugga wasn't happy, and it wasn't the smartest thing I ever did. I never played Test cricket again.

Chapter 31
Foccor

WITHOUT DOUBT, the most popular game played between the Julios and the Nerds was the short-lived but dynamic sport of Foccor.

The following was taken from the *Foccor Monthly* magazine from the Ashes tour of 2001 (copyright © Damien Fleming and Wade Seccombe):

Foccor was born on the Ashes 2001 tour out of sheer frustration over the mundane warm-ups run by our fitness advisor, Jock Campbell (alias 'the Fitness Nazi'). It had to happen! An angry band of cricket rebels, sick of the ritual of dull games that neither challenged or motivated, formed a breakaway warm-up sport, a hybrid game of soccer and Aussie Rules. No, not Gaelic football. It was soccer with an Aussie Rules ball, making the bounce of the ball a little bit more unpredictable.

There has since been a massive resurgence in our pre-match activity, and it is hard to understand how this new sport has not yet taken the world by storm. It is a game for the people that were bred on anger and a complete lack of belief in those in charge of our warm-up activities.

To gain a greater insight into this great game called foccor, an understanding of its background is vital. The first question that must be raised is who was supposed to be conducting this warm-up ritual that had gone from bad to worse over the past 12 months, and led us to the point where we would rather jab ourselves in the eye with a training cone than go through another one of his cockamamie drills? Honestly, if you asked schoolkids to do the stuff he had us doing, they'd ask if they could go to the library. Or an isolation cell. All the blame must lie squarely on the shoulders of the Fitness Nazi.

What was he doing? Why was he being paid?

On this momentous day – thankfully, for our soldiers of fortune – the Fitness Nazi was away. Historical records do not say exactly why; some say illness, others suggest guilt over a previous misdemeanour in a warm-up activity, still others a paper cut. Nonetheless, his absence created the chance for other people to take control.

The Fitness Nazi had a paranoia of injuries from fun games like Aussie Rules, rugby and soccer. All those traditional pursuits had been replaced by stretching, running and more running. Yawn. (Pant!) The past 12 months had been a difficult period, and team spirits were waning. Questions were being asked.

Damien Fleming – known as the founding father of foccor – was quoted recently in an exclusive interview with Foccor Weekly *asking, 'Has any side had to suffer such gross incompetence and neglect with regard to warm-ups as our side has over the past 12 months? It has been a long, cold, heartless period. It felt like a life sentence.'*

Despite a lack of assistance from the Fitness Nazi – indeed, because of his absence – this band of young men, led by Fleming, managed to rally together and introduce foccor to the world. On the 10th day of August, 2001, foccor was born.

It was a morning unlike any other. The cold, sleeting wind blew in over the South Sea. Only the brave (where was the Fitness Nazi?) ventured outdoors. The brave and the contractually obligated. When Fleming suggested marrying soccer and Aussie

Rules by using the Sherrin instead of a round ball, the world changed forever.

As we now know, no goal is easy in foccor. Defence is regularly turned into attack, and attack into defence. It is a game of skill and passion, and only the brave compete. Ball control has been taken to a new level.

Will they ever go back to their old warm-ups? I don't think so – foccor is here to stay.

Only time will tell what effect this game has on the masses, but already there is a suggestion that the introduction of foccor will have the same historical significance as Hillary conquering Everest or Bannister breaking the four-minute mile, while the Fitness Nazi may well, in years to come, be referred to in the same breath as Hitler, Mussolini, Hannibal Lector and all those boy-bands. Well may we say 'God save the Queen', because nothing will save the Fitness Nazi.

RESIDENT PRO SIMON KATICH ON THE FOUR COMMANDMENTS OF FOCCOR

When Chairman of Selectors Andrew Hilditch told me my Australian career was over in 2005, I knew I had to take not only my game but also my training habits to a new level. And, yes, Bob Simpson helped me with my batting technique, but for my footwork, balance and mental toughness, there was only one way to go – foccor.

1. Because an Aussie Rules ball bounces differently to a soccer ball, you need

to expect the unexpected. When you do that, the expected is expected.
2. Try to be ahead of the game, so that by the time that moment has come you've already played it.
3. Foccor is a tough game, and you should always give 100 per cent (unless you have a big night on the piss, in which case anything up to 80 per cent is acceptable).
4. It doesn't matter whether you win or lose, it's how you play the game. But if your team is struggling and you can win by cheating, that's acceptable. After all, no one likes a goody two-shoes. Or losing.

After his career-saving Foccor training camp, Simon Katich averaged 50 while opening the batting for Australia — a sure sign that foccor works for elite athletes.

Later on our 2001 tour of the UK, we travelled to Ireland for some matches against the locals. Bad weather forced the abandonment of the cricket, so we treated the big crowd to the first away international game of foccor. They loved it!

If there was one country born to enjoy foccor, it was the Irish, considering their mish-mash hybrid of games.
1. Gaelic: Aussie Rules with a soccer ball.
2. Hurling: Hockey, lacrosse, soccer.
3. Life: Guinness, potatoes, poetry.

Unfortunately, the Fitness Nazi was jealous of foccor's popularity among the playing group and banned it from Australian cricket warm-ups, but he couldn't suppress the game in Ireland. Years later, I was commentating in that great, green, Guinness-drenched land and, to my disbelief, I saw some groups of kids playing foccor.

FOCCOR

The great game of foccor. Massive in Ireland.

A COMMENT FROM JOCK THE FITNESS NAZI

Hello, it's Jock Campbell here from www.jockathletic.com. I will certainly never speak out of school, nor dob in a teammate, but it was our team manager, Steve 'Brute' Bernard, who put an end to the game of foccor. He wanted a share in it — he was greedy! Just like Flemo. Not me! I despise all those self-indulgent cricketers — it's all 'I' and 'me' all the time. You can read about it on www.jockathletic.com or in the *Jock Athletic* online magazine. Or you can just pop in to see me at Jock Athletic. I'm here!

What was the question again?

The foccor vibe was that big I was asked to write about it for the Fourth Test preview magazine.

257

***

The AFL *Footy Show* filmed a show in the UK during our 2001 Ashes tour. Dizzy and Glenn McGrath were invited onto the panel, and I was at the show's bar with Trevor Marmalade. Warnie was, as usual, a main guest, along with Sir Ian Botham and Danni Minogue.

During the show, they played footage of us down south of England, and Trevor had some fun with our interviews and training. I started to get stuck into Warnie about how his favourite song at the time was 'It's Raining Men' by Geri Halliwell – pure pop drivel. Surely, Aussie blokes should like a bit more rock. I really bagged him.

Host Eddie Maguire rudely cut me short, saying, 'Well, Flem, you'll enjoy our next segment after the break . . . "It's Raining Men", by the lady herself, Miss Geri Halliwell!'

It was live TV and I was pretty embarrassed. Later, I walked backstage and the first person I saw was Geri Halliwell.

'Hi Geri,' I blurted out. 'How are the Spice Guys going?'

'We split up two years ago!' she replied coldly.

Bad luck, I thought. *I prefer All Saints anyway.*

Chapter 32
Sackings

SACKED! AND, LIKE Lloyd Christmas when he gets robbed by a sweet old lady in a motorised cart in *Dumb and Dumber*, I didn't even see it coming. There was no sweet little lady in my case – just a ruthless Cricket Victoria, and the new state head coach, David Hookes.

I'd met with Hookesy a few weeks before for a coffee in South Melbourne to chat about the Victorian team. I'd always got along well with Hookesy, who was 'clearing pickets' in World Series Cricket when I was a boy and a charismatic batsman for South Australia. He was always the big wicket when we played against the South Aussies until 'Boofa' Lehmann blasted his way onto the scene.

Hookesy had a cutting wit. Once spinner Tim May asked the great South Australian captain if he could move Peter 'Sounda' Sleep to a new fielding position.

May: 'Hooksey, can I have Sounda a little bit more backward?'

Hookesy: 'No, Sounda can't get any more backward.'

At our meeting, while he didn't have his arms wide open saying he desperately needed me, he did say that the team lacked experienced bowlers. At any stage, if he'd said, 'Flem, you might not be in the first Eleven,' it would've been fine. I would have looked around for another state and the split would have been amicable.

At my contract meeting a couple of weeks later, I arrived with a five-page document on what I thought Victoria needed to do to become the dominant state team in Australia. (You see, I would never have got dropped for not doing my homework.)

Well, it's fair to say I could have saved my time (although I am proud that I use all of two fingers when typing and can crank out about 13 words a minute), as we didn't even make it to the first page of my *Blueprint to Save Victorian Cricket*. It seemed that item one on the selectors' version of *Blueprint to Save Victorian Cricket* read:

1. Dump Fleming.

Chairman of Selectors Michael Sullivan told me there was no contract on offer for me in the first round, but that I could continue to train with the squad. They might give me a second-round offer.

I was stunned. The little old lady was driving off with my career at four kilometres per hour and I couldn't do a thing. I had not seen this coming. In my preparations, I'd thought about the Victorian team as a whole, and I'd never considered the possibility that *my* spot was under threat. I eventually asked why, and I got the Marcel Marceau treatment. I then turned to Hookesy. 'You're the coach,' I said. 'Just tell me, mate.'

Their stonewalling really hurt. I had just come off my Australian contract a couple of weeks earlier, although I'd been told that I was still in the national selectors' thoughts for the World Cup in South Africa at the end of the summer. Now, this meant I was basically on the dole. There aren't a lot of jobs for swing bowlers at Centrelink. Also, as a sportsman I was always looking for feedback so I could improve my game. But everybody sat there with their mouths shut.

'There is still chance of a second-round contract,' Cricket Victoria's CEO, Ken Jacobs, said again. I remember saying that was just lip service, and again I asked Hookesy why I was out.

SACKINGS

He mumbled something about the selectors' 'different criteria' these days. I was really disappointed, as Hookesy had a reputation as a guy who told it how it was. I was getting verbal donuts.

And I was ropeable when he later went on TV and his own radio show and announced that he had been the one who made the decision to axe me and Colin 'Funky' Miller – something he wouldn't say to my face. I found out the next day that they'd deliberately not given me any reasons because they feared I might sue them for unfair dismissal. This pissed me off further, as I would never have thought to sue. I think it said much more about them than about me.

After the meeting, I went home and told Wendy that I hadn't been offered a contract. She was just as stunned as me. It was a crap day.

So this is where I was at:

1. Thirty-two years old and with no job.
2. Still recovering from a shoulder operation.
3. Dealing with parenthood for the first time. Our young son, Brayden, was just six months old (One massive positive was that Brayden kept smiling the whole time, which put things in perspective.)
4. In debt. We had just taken out a big mortgage to buy a townhouse, and now it looked like I would have to find a job interstate.

The supportive calls and texts I got from friends and teammates really gave me a lift. I had a few beers with most of the Victorian players in South Melbourne that night, which reaffirmed my faith in cricket and cricketers.

My manager and friend Peter Thomson gave me a lot of support and mapped out a plan. I was in a bit of trouble as far as getting another job was concerned, since Cricket Victoria had sacked me so late. There were only a few days left before all state contracts had to be finalised, and most sides were already settled.

This was obviously well planned from Victoria's point of view, but I wished they had put that amount of business nous into providing the playing group with good coaches, medical staff and decent training facilities.

South Australia and Western Australia both started to talk to me about playing with them, so things started to look up pretty quickly, but thinking about shifting interstate and leaving our families behind when we had a young child was still a bummer. I had always imagined that if I were to play in another state it would be Western Australia, as I was born there and enjoyed bowling at the WACA.

In fact, I'd had two serious offers to go to Perth – in the 1993/94 and 1997/98 seasons – but each time I'd been told by my Victorian coaches and Cricket Victoria officials that it was best to be seen as a one-state player, which now sounded reasonably ironic, given the situation I ended up in.

Eventually, I went with South Australia – Hookesy's old state – and I was always eternally grateful for the opportunity to play there, even though my career for the Redbacks was as brief as the Knack's greatest hits (I did like changing the words of 'My Sharona' to 'Cold Corona' during post-match celebrations).

Adelaide had been a happy hunting ground for me, and some of my best mates played for South Australia – Blewy, Boof and Dizzy. Greg Chappell, a great thinker about the game, was the coach, and I had always enjoyed his company. The clincher was that they had a full-time physio for my high-maintenance body. (Unluckily for me, the physio turned out to be more of a fitness guy...)

SACKINGS

Hookesy passed away in early 2004 in the most tragic way. The Bushrangers went on to win the Sheffield Shield months later, in honour of their coach. They had appeared to have a great mix, with Hookesy' and Greg Shipperd's coaching nous and a talented group of players.

A couple of years later, I was asked to play in a charity day in South Australia for organ donation – a cause that Hookesy had championed. On the plane, I found myself sitting next to his widow, Robyn, and we chatted all the way to Adelaide – she was a lovely lady.

As I was writing this book, I came across an article Hooksey had written about me after my first season for Victoria. Maybe my sacking was a payback for a prank Merv and I had played on him after one of my first games in the FAI Insurance Cup. We were having a couple of beers when Merv told Hookesy – who loved his Aussie Rules – that I was playing for Hawthorn that year at centre half-forward, as a back up for Dermott Brereton. Hookesy was initially very wary, noting my lack of height (I was 181 centimetres or 191cm with mullet) and weight (63 kilograms), but Merv was very convincing.

FLEMING

VICTORIA surprisingly finished at the bottom of the Sheffield Shield table last season. The most significant area of struggle was their fast bowling.

Former Australian opening bowler Simon Davis was discarded, promising fast bowler Denis Hickey lost form (perhaps a victim of overcoaching) and newly appointed captain Simon O'Donnell didn't bowl at his best.

After languishing in club cricket for most of the season, Hawthorn footballer DAMIEN FLEMING was introduced during the limited-over matches late in the year.

Fleming is a medium-fast bowler with a nice high arm action, a good follow through and a typical VFL aggressive streak. Aggression is an attribute many Australian Rules players contribute to cricket teams. Not the 'knock 'em down, run through 'em' aggression, but a professional approach to training and on-field desires.

In his short stay in the team Fleming has shown he not only possesses a natural bowling ability but the approach and manner required to succeed at first class level.

— David Hookes

Being a shy kid, I hadn't really wanted to be part of the crank, but with Merv putting pressure on me I agreed. Yes, I told Hookesy, I was at Hawthorn and things were going pretty well.

No one thought anything about it till the next season, when Hookesy wrote an article (see page 263) about five players to watch out for in the 1989/90 season.

He certainly got me back for that one.

Chapter 33
Coaching Cricket Academy

MY SHOULDER NEVER felt right in my season with South Australia. Late in the pre-season in 2002, I travelled to the UK to play for the Warwickshire Bears to get some games under my belt before the Australian season. To be honest, I was looking to exert myself a bit more than the 18 balls I bowled against Yorkshire in my *only* game in the UK. Flying over in luxury business class, I awoke to find I couldn't move my neck, and my shoulder blades felt as if they couldn't hold up the right side of my upper body. I had actually stood out a game for Victoria prior to this after we won the toss and batted. While we had been batting I'd had the same feeling and had been diagnosed with a slipped disc in my neck. So I really tried to get through the game with the Bears but ended up walking off the field again, humiliated that my body had let me down once more. I was starting to get so frustrated, spending my time in rehab and really only playing some cricket *in between* injuries.

Was I injury prone or prone to injury? Please find my career injury audit following:

1986/87 My first shoulder injury. Missed virtually a whole season at 16 years of age. Sign of shoulder problems to come, but had no diagnosis back then, and definitely not a mullet-related head banging injury.

1987 to mid-1993 The golden years. Had the usual string of lost toenails, aching muscles, the odd sore back from carrying the attack, but hardly missed a game.

1993 Playing for the great Enfield in the Lancashire league in the UK, I tore two hamstrings and suffered ankle strain all against Michael Bevan's team, Rawtenstall. I proceeded to be run out three times batting with a runner. On all three occasions all three batsman finished down the same end.

1993/94 Another hamstring strain. I was getting quite good at them. The start of shoulder tendonitis.

1994/95 Continued shoulder problems and tendinitis. Right hamstring tear in Fourth Test vs England. And to even things up I then had a left hamstring tear in same game. Left West Indies tour early for a shoulder stabilisation operation.

1995/96 Tore hamstring in second game. I often did this clever move of getting a new injury while coming back from a different injury. This time it allowed me take my mind off my shoulder for a month while I focused on my hammy tear. Right knee operation after World Cup.

1996/97 Tore my thigh muscle twice and missed first half of season.

1997/98 Early season hamstring injury, then a relatively quiet summer injury-wise.

1998/99 Another ligament shoulder strain bowling during the MCG test. Played a couple of ODIs. Out for two months.

1999/00 Despite painful knee tendonitis, played every Test of the summer for the only time.

2000/01 Missed seven months while in rehab for tendinitis in both knees. First game for the mighty Bloods, South Melbourne Cricket Club, on a flat pitch, my dwarfish slow medium pace Victorian teammate Simon Dart hit my glove while I was batting. I got that black feeling. I knew it was broken, and it wasn't just any finger – it was the middle finger on my bowling hand. Later, I slipped a disc in my neck while sleeping, missing the first half of the season.

2001/02 Tore rotator cuffs and hamstring; underwent second shoulder operation.

2002/03 Second slipped disc in neck and third shoulder operation.

Somehow I actually bowled well in the first couple of 50-over games and took wickets in my first innings in Shield cricket against Western Australia. I even chatted to Boony, who was an Australian selector. He felt he had some good news for the other selectors, in regards to my bowling, which was a big lift. This lasted less than a day when, after getting out, I decided to do a warm-up in the Perth nets before our second innings bowling stint. After a couple of balls I had that familiar electric shock sensation in my right shoulder. I played the next couple of games, bowling no more than medium pace and in pain. So I was under the knife again for another shoulder stabilisation operation.

I had spent my whole life in physical pursuits, with my body and mind committed to one thing. So when I did retire, I knew there would be a huge vacuum to fill. My mind and body would be separated, and I knew there would be a bloody huge hole in my days, my heart and my head.

So I decided to be my own man, forge my own path, be the individual I had always prided myself on being. Yes, I joined the media. 'G'day, Junior . . . Morning, Kerry . . . How are you, BJ? . . . Geez, AB, you're looking well . . . Is that you, Warnie?'

And, just to add another unpredictable twist to my post-cricket career, I dabbled in a bit of – you'll never see this coming – coaching!

Teaching young sportsmen was something I thought would provide me with a great challenge. I looked forward to gathering the lessons I had learned as a member of high-achieving teams such as Australia, and passing them on to under-achieving outfits such as Victoria. I'd had plenty of ups and downs in my career, so I thought I'd identify well with blokes who were struggling. And I had spent a lot of time observing great players in the sides I played with and against, noting how they went about their roles. If I could pass that knowledge on in the right way, it might help accelerate a young player's career by a couple of years.

Sometimes, the penny just has to be put into the right slot for it to drop. I hoped coaching would prove to be a rewarding path for me – and, as most of us will admit, it would keep me under the security blanket of cricket. The nets, the dressing rooms, the outfield – these were the places I had spent the best times of my life. Oh, and there were a few pubs and restaurants here and there that held some good memories too.

While I was in rehab I happened to see an application for the fast bowling cricket academy. Even though I was still contracted to the South Australian Redbacks, I'd known for a couple of years that I wanted to go down the coaching path. Why not start while you're still playing? I rang Matthew Drain, a former grade player now working at Cricket Australia, who I knew well, enquiring about the position. He was a little coy with me for some reason. Then he mentioned that this phone call was very spooky as he had just come out of a Cricket Australia meeting less than half an hour before, and two current players' names had been mentioned for the role and I was one of them! At that time, I was hoping to keep playing for South Australia and do the coaching job in the winter, but I was told I had to take the leap and retire from cricket if I wanted to start building my new career.

But now Troy Cooley had resigned as fast bowling coach to work with the England cricket team, while Wayne 'Flipper' Phillips had just resigned from the academy to take the job as head coach of South Australia. My job was going to be a mixture of marketing and overseas player development, and coaching the young fast bowlers.

Flipper was the former wicketkeeper-batsman who – while sporting a great mullet – had scored a hundred on his Test debut against Pakistan. He was also one of the funniest, driest men I have ever met. Some 15 years after his retirement as a player, his gloves and bat had disappeared but his mullet remained. He was the bogan version of Robert Smith, the lead singer of the Cure, who to this day still has the same haircut and bad makeup he had back in the early 1980s.

At the age of 44, Flipper had applied for the 1992 AFL National Draft, offering his services as a clever half-forward or fast-leading full forward – anything to give himself a chance at the big league. This was declined.

As I was taking over Flipper's role, I was keen to catch up with him. In fact, it was a pretty bizarre situation. I had wanted to ask him about his former role and whether I should take it, but he was telling me not to take the job, and to continue playing under him for South Australia instead.

BOWLOLOGY

Eventually, I accepted the coaching position. Flipper was to hang around for a week to mentor me and ease me into the role. Part of Flipper's overseas program involved bringing Indian and Bangladeshi players to the academy on scholarships – a great cause, but also a situation with the potential for a shady immigration scam.

The Indians groomed Flipper by sending a couple of players, who trained at the academy and then went home. This went without a hitch, and soon the Indians had gained his trust. It was time to execute their plan.

They contacted Flipper and said they were sending five players over to Adelaide for training. Flipper did the usual airport pick-up. The Indians did arrive, but he couldn't find them. He thought at first that they'd got lost. Then he fretted that they'd got into trouble. Eventually, Flipper realised they had disappeared, Ronnie Biggs–style, somewhere into our vast continent, although as far as anyone knows, they haven't recorded an album with the Sex Pistols.* After that, a long, bureaucratic and mind-numbing military checklist was needed to allow any cricketer from overseas to attend the academy.

Like a good mentor, Flipper took me aside on my first day and mentioned that it might be worth having a chat to the four Bangladeshi Academy cricketers that I would be coaching for next two months. So I sat down with them and their team manager, introduced myself and proceeded to chat cricket. I could see in these cricketers' eyes that they were hooked.

I started off with some lessons I'd learned while playing with superstars such as Steve Waugh, Shane Warne, Glenn McGrath and Adam Gilchrist. With every new story, the boys seemed more and more engrossed in what I had to say.

Next were my theories on preparation, and how perfect practice would give you confidence before a game, so that

* *The Great Rock 'n' Roll Swindle*

COACHING CRICKET ACADEMY

you could just let it happen in the match situation . . . I was so impressed by the way these young cricketers were soaking up my information that I continued, knowing that I'd got lucky in my first coaching role with a good group of guys who really wanted to improve their cricket.

After about an hour, I'd pretty much gone through everything I could possibly pass on to these boys. I shook their hands, looked them in the eyes and thought, *This is exactly why I wanted to get into coaching. Passing on knowledge to help young cricketers get the best out of themselves.*

As I walked back into my office, I found Flipper there. He shook my hand and said, 'Great work – you're a natural.'

So I was pretty happy with myself after day one. Later that night, in bed, I was reflecting on the day and something didn't seem right. But I just couldn't put my finger on it . . .

When I arrived at Henley Beach for work the next day, the first man I sought out was Flipper. I finally tracked him down in the canteen, which he called his 'other office'. He was doing a crossword, which was apparently his other job.

'Flipper, can I have a quick word?'

'No worries, mate,' he said. 'What's up?'

'Flipper, I'm going to come right out and say it. Do any of the Bangladeshi cricketers speak or understand English?'

With a dead face, looking me right in my eyes, he replied, 'No.' Then he went back to his crossword with a big smirk on his face

Eight across. Person born outside of wedlock. Seven letters . . . Bas . . .

Chapter 34
Bowlology

I CAME UP with the concept of Bowlology while I was still a coach at Cricket Australia's Centre of Excellence. It all started when I was doing some radio work. We were doing a report on a former Green Bay Packers NFL player called Reggie White, who had just passed away. His nickname was impressive: 'the Minister of Defense'.

Something clicked. Yes, I could continue to pass myself off as a regulation fast bowling coach, like the hundreds of others around the world, or I could come up with concept that would set me apart. And it was also an opportunity to refer to myself in the third person – yes, Flemo would like that. And then it hit me: who would a budding fast bowler rather get mentoring from – a fast bowling coach or the Bowlologist? No contest. The Bowlologist was born.

Let's look at the pillars of this modern-day coaching phenomenon and some great examples of the bowling art. The six deliveries of Bowlology are the physical, the technical, the mental, the skills, the in-game tactics and the performance.

The Bowlologist

BALL 1: THE PHYSICAL

Height, build, strength, fitness, flexibility, stability, recovery

Curtly Ambrose, the physically imposing West Indian fast bowler who used his 200 centimetre height to great effect, with acute bounce and accuracy at good pace, is the epitome of the big, strong, fast bowling type. He wasn't the friendliest bloke on the field – you had as much chance of seeing him smile as you would of seeing Marlon Samuels as best man at Shane Warne and Liz Hurley's wedding. He was always menacing, as there was always a threat of real physical harm. And as I was allergic to pain, he was my natural enemy. When facing Curtly, it felt like when you lean back on a chair and catch yourself just before you fall. Well, that was how it felt if you survived. Curtly retired from cricket to play bass in his and Richie Richardson reggae band the Big Bad Dread and the Baldhead. Blewy and I watched them in Antigua once and was surprised by cricket's 'Silent Bob' Curtley doing the soundcheck 'one, two, tree ... cool, man', 'one, two, tree ... cool, man'.

BALL 2: THE TECHNICAL

Safety, efficiency, run-up, gather, delivery stride, release and follow-through

Alan Donald – known as 'White Lightning' – had the whole package. He was a biomechanist's delight and had almost perfect form. He had a beautiful running technique (except when running between the wickets ... Should I bring up the World Cup again? Oh, okay, not this time.) His run-up was very athletic, like that of a 400 metre runner at his best. He would take off into a compact gather and jump straight towards off stump. And he had a good release, with his wrist and fingers behind the ball – which gave him swing – before he finished his action off with a powerful follow-through, ending only yards from the batsman.

Then he'd postscript the whole thing with one of those 'I'm a crazy South African' stares, which he has since handed on to Dale Steyn.

BALL 3: THE MENTAL/EMOTIONAL
Vision, game plans, self-awareness, belief, passion, ball-by-ball focus, checklists

Glenn McGrath's aim was always to be the best bowler in the game. He accumulated wicket like Paris Hilton did boyfriends, and was rarely flustered in pursuit of another positive statistic, as he was one of the most efficient fast bowlers of all time. Like Richard Hadlee, Pigeon had such incredible self-belief that he could name his targets in print and then back it up on the field. He's in the running to play the Terminator in the fifth movie instalment.

Merv Hughes was all about putting in 100 per cent and never giving up. He had a massive heart – almost as big as his head. In fact, if Phar Lap had his heart the famous horse would have won five Melbourne Cups (but been slightly less popular around the stalls, for obvious reasons). Merv's teammates admired his drive and passion to push himself to the limit, time and again – even when his body was crying out for a rest. He's also a member of the exclusive club of Australian Test players who have taken a Test hat-trick and made a Test 70. Merv, I will book our usual table for two at next year's reunion (Warnie never turns up).

BALL 4: THE SKILLS
Stock balls, pace, swing, cutters, bouncers, yorkers

Like a game-show host (and most teenagers I have met), Wasim Akram had all the answers. Express pace off a short, bustling run-up, plus superb accuracy. He swung the new ball and the old ball like they were boomerangs, he had a bouncer that lifted you off your toes, and then he could smash your little piggies with yorkers that were like exocet missiles. He also had a few pretty good slower balls too. Bowlology's Buddha, he is worshipped daily by graduates of the program.

BALL 5: THE IN-GAME TACTICS
Reading the pitch, assessing batsmen, setting up wickets, cues, ball-by-ball review, adjusting pace, line and length
In Arnie Schwarzenegger movie terms, if McGrath was the Terminator then Shane Warne was the Predator. His mantra was 'If it bleeds, we can kill it', and he sniffed out any weakness in batsmen's games. The master of the hunt, he was well prepared, with great skills in his arsenal. He spun a web around most batsmen he came across, whether bowling to their weaknesses or playing on their insecurities. The cunning bastard would sometimes bowl to a batsman's strength, so his confidence lifted and he became more daring in his strokeplay, then Warnie would knock him over with his leg-spinner, wrong'un, flipper, zooter, zinger – take your pick. A magician.

BALL 6: THE PERFORMANCE AND REVIEW
Wickets, maidens, strike rates, runs per over, partnerships
Bowlers win Test matches. And, at the end of the day, it is by your performance that you are measured and rated. Remember, relax and work on the previous five balls, and just let it happen in the game, confident in the knowledge that you have done all the work.

In the golfing comedy *Happy Gilmore*, when Happy is standing over a putt and looks a bit worried, the sports psychologist says to him, 'You've done the work to get to here. Just send him [the ball] home. He's got his bag packed and his airline ticket. Just send him home.'

BOWLOLOGY

❈ ❈ ❈

Well, that's a short explanation of Bowlology. It's impossible to cover the total program in one page, but I'll leave you with one last quote from the Bowlologist: 'The goal of the program is to get the bowler (the graduate) to the stage of development where, when the umpire asks him what he bowls, he'll say, "Right-arm Sizzler." When the umpire asks what he means, the bowler will reply, "I'm like a smorgasbord – I've got the lot."'

Also, I'd like to take this moment to refute some rumours doing the rounds about Bowlology. Katie Holmes did not leave Tom Cruise and Scientology for Bowlology. This sort of gutter-press rumours doesn't help the Bowlology cause. We're not a sect or a cult, more of a sult.

(And for those interested, Katie's outswinger is coming along nicely.)

For more Bowlology tips download the app from itunes or www.bowlologist.com.

Chapter 35
Transition from Player to Commentator

AS I MENTIONED earlier, when I was nearing the end of my cricket career, I began looking forward to doing something completely original for a retiring sports player: I was going to try my luck in coaching or the media. A real shock there.

So, after two years at the Cricket Academy, I started working for the ABC Radio and Fox Sports cricket commentary teams. These days, I analyse every commentary stint just like I would a bowling spell. Commentating has been better for my body, and I haven't missed a game through injury yet. Playing gave me the satisfaction of doing something special, both as an individual and as part of a team, and I've found that there are some parallels in the media.

INITIATION

As a player, my initiation to the Victorian team in the late 1980s was as 12th man. Back then, the Victorian team was still in the Dark Ages of human relations towards 12th men in general – and towards one long-haired, mulletted 18-year-old heavy-metal-loving kid straight out of school in particular.

For four days I'd be at the beck and call of my teammates, carrying bags, finding errant cricket balls, doing hours of throw-downs to intense batsmen or making sure the beers were cold for the fast bowlers. Once, when Geoff Lawson was made 12th man, Rod Hogg said to him, 'Think of the positives – same pay, no pressure!' I remember thinking, *Give me the pressure any day.*

My initiation with ABC Radio was a little different – and a little classier. At my first Test match, in Hobart in the 2005/06 season, everything was going well. I had a good rapport with the doyen of the team, Jimmy Maxwell, and Glenn Mitchell and I had a good laugh at Kerry 'Skull' O'Keeffe – the only guy I know who refers to me as 'Flemee'. I also listened with interest to Peter Roebuck's views on the cricket world.

Halfway through the Test, I was on air with Glenn Mitchell, and he announced with great enthusiasm the ABC Grandstand trivia question for the Test. Being a big trivia fan, I was delighted and listened intently.

He read the question out: 'Which Australian Test batsman has the highest percentage of lbw dismissals in his career?'

Crikey, that's a bit obscure, I thought. *If this is the standard for the summer, I'm in real trouble.*

Glenn gave me some clues. 'A lower-order batsman, and handy with the bat.'

'Warnie,' I said straightaway.

'No,' said Glenn.

'Paul Reiffel?'

'No.'

'Merv?'

'No,' Glenn said, before adding, 'He was quite brave with the willow.'

That counts me out, I thought. 'What percentage are we talking about here?' I then asked.

'Thirty-seven per cent,' Glenn said. 'Nearly double the next worst, former Aussie opening batsman Bruce "Stumpy" Laird.'

'Who coached this bloke?' I said. 'Didn't he know how to play straight?'

TRANSITION FROM PLAYER TO COMMENTATOR

Everyone in the box laughed. (Maybe a bit too loudly, in hindsight . . .) Glenn strung the quiz out for another 20 minutes, until finally he read out my name. There was no coming back and I put my head down in shame – not 37 per cent shame but 100 per cent – not only of getting stitched up on air, but also of my woeful batting technique.

CURRENT TOP FIVE AUSSIES WHO LET THEIR PAD DO THE TALKING, WHICH LED TO THEM WALKING

(Minimum of 20 Tests for Australia)

1. Damien Fleming 37%
2. Shane Watson 28%
3. Bruce Laird 23%
4. Arthur Morris 22%
5. Dean Jones 22%

Note: Ed Cowan shares 37% with me, after 17 Tests pre-2013 Ashes (By my calculations if Ed falls lbw four times in 10 innings in England I've lost me title. Play straight, Ed.)

Stats provided by Ric Finlay from Tastats

---

* * *

There are plenty of ways to get a buzz as a player, whether it's taking wickets, scoring runs or celebrating wins. I loved getting wickets, although I didn't appreciate that it took me up to 60 balls to get one, but it's a tough game. So when I finally dismissed a batsman, I made the most of it. The beautiful sound of the ball hitting the stumps or taking an edge and flying towards the keeper or slips was as good as hearing Eddie Van Halen's riff on the song 'Panama'.

The closest thing to getting a wicket as a cricket pundit is predicting when and how a bowler will dismiss a batsman. When your prediction happens, you get a real lift and you feel the satisfaction of being able to read the game.

Both as a player and as a commentator, preparation is the key to going into a game confident that you have done everything you can. But even when you think things are going to plan, the game can surprise you.

For me, this was highlighted in the Second Test of 2006/07, played in Adelaide against the Poms. At the end of day four, both teams had batted once and England was 1/59 in its second dig, so the chances of a result were about the same as the chances of Danny Green and Anthony Mundine pairing up to go on *Dancing with the Stars*. With the match headed for a draw, I prepared myself with every story I have ever written, ready for a long day and some debates with my fellow commentators.

Within 20 minutes of play on day five, my expectations had changed. Warne's energy and the reverse-swing the quicks were getting at the other end combined to snare a brace of wickets, and suddenly the English looked tame at the crease. With England tentative, the positive Aussies now sniffed an unlikely victory. Due to a heavily booked flight schedule, Jim Maxwell and I had to shoot off early to catch our flight or face a couple of extra days in Adelaide.

Like a scene from *Ronin*, we got a quick taxi fare to the airport, listening all the while as our colleagues talked through the tight last session. England had been knocked over for 129, leaving Australia a target of 168 runs from 36 overs. We rushed through to the Qantas Lounge at the airport. All possible scenarios were on the cards: Australia might win, draw, tie or even lose.

TRANSITION FROM PLAYER TO COMMENTATOR

We settled at the bar as, with four wickets down, Hussey and Clarke nudged closer to the target. The atmosphere was intense, with the packed crowd cheering every run. And when Hussey finally hit the winning runs off James Anderson to complete one of Australia's greatest victories, everyone in the Qantas Lounge bar was as happy as teenage girls front row at a One Direction concert.

※ ※ ※

One of the highlights of working for ABC Radio is that I am constantly realising what a big country we have. The ABC reaches everywhere, and we get plenty of emails, SMSs and tweets from avid listeners all over the country, from the Kimberleys to Port Arthur.

I was in the box during a match between Australia and New Zealand at the Adelaide Oval. Mitchell Johnson was having as much trouble swinging the ball as Big Merv would performing *The Nutcracker* ballet.

Jim Maxwell read out an email from a listener named Matthew in Adelaide: 'Do you think Johnson cocks his wrists too early, and that this affects the ball's movement in the air and the timing of his release?'

'So, Flem, what's your analysis?' Jimmy asked me as Mitch started his run-up.

Now, when you are giving special comments, you have to finish your comments before the bowler releases the ball so that your teammate can describe what happens. Mitch was halfway through his run-up when I began answering, so I didn't have a lot of time.

'Okay, I'll have a look at his cock right now,' I blurted out quickly. 'Of the wrist.'

BOWLOLOGY

The whole commentary box broke up laughing. Only Jimmy, the veteran caller who had seen and heard everything before, kept his composure.

Johnson bowled the ball through to keeper Brad Haddin, completing the over.

'No, it looked good, Jim,' I said, barely keeping my composure. 'Pretty good.'

'The wrist position? Is that what you're talking about?' Jim enquired.

'Yes, Jim, his wrist looks good . . . I didn't see that one coming.' Then I lost it completely.

'Well, that's one for the Christmas party blooper tape,' Jim said coolly.

Chapter 36
The Corridor of Uncertainty

I WAS TALKING once to Sir Richard Hadlee at a beach cricket function. He mentioned he wasn't happy with the term 'corridor of uncertainty'. I have a deep respect for knights (especially Hawk footy legend Peter Knights) so the next time I was on ABC Radio's cricket commentary I told the listeners about my proposal to ban the term. I was sick of these old clichés. So I came up with my own alternative – the 'avenue of apprehension' – which I then used so much that it became a new cliché.

I realised that I had to come up with some fresh alternatives. Following are some suggestions from ABC Grandstand and Fox Sports fans over the years.

FOR BOWLERS

Avenue of Uncertainty	Alderman Alleyway
Lillee Laneway	Hadlee Highway
McGrath Motorway	Ambrose Autobahn
Snick Street	Snickville
Road of Risk	G Spot
Bermuda Corridor (since it might disappear)	
Passage of Paranoia	Lane of Pain
Gate of Fate	Hesitation Lane
King Street (aka the Avenue of Temptation)	
Discomfort Zone	Anxiety Avenue
Line of Indecision	Channel of Caution/Concern
Aisle of Apprehension	Pathway of Perfection

BOWLOLOGY

Temptation Alley
Gateway to Guesswork
Boulevard of Bewilderment
Driveway of Disaster
Corridor of Carnage
Promenade of Plumbness

Doorway to Departure
Boulevard of Broken Dreams
Promenade of Procrastination
Tarmac of Terror
Back Road to Bamboozled
Runway of Recklessness

FOR BATSMEN

Promenade of Plunder
Causeway of Clubbing
Highway to a Hundred
Freeway to Fulfilment

Highway of Hammering
Boulevard of Boundaries
Freeway to Fifty
Boulevard of Big Bash

My all-time favourite is the Strip of Vindaloo – because you don't know if there are any runs in it or not.

Please take the time to fill in your own Bowlologisms:
1.
2.
3.
4.

Tweet them to @bowlologist, and together we'll take your innovative ideas and I'll make them mine on air.

Chapter 37
The Fast Bowlers Cartel

BESIDES DIFFERENT MUSICAL tastes, there were other factions within the Aussie cricket team – and the most notable was the Fast Bowlers Cartel. It has a long history, having been evident even on Australia's early tour to England in 1882. The great fast bowler Fred 'the Demon' Spofforth documented it in his diaries, even alluding to some growing separation within the playing group during their two-month boat trip to the UK.

18 June 1882
The batsmen who call themselves 'the Platinum Club' like to hang with the first-class customers, sharing cigars and caviar, and they talk incessantly about their batting averages. Our opening pair, Bannerman and Massie, dine together exclusively and practise shaking their hands for when they celebrate their 50, 100 and 150-run partnerships.

Our keeper, the nifty John Blackham, is getting into fine form for some on-field byplay by arguing with staff and picking apart the dressing fashion of fellow passengers. He even laughed when a waiter dropped some cutlery and a wine glass. 'Call yourself a keeper?' he said. I've just found out that our reserve keeper has never kept in his life – I overheard a teammate saying about the chap, 'Can't bat, can't bowl, can't keep.'

One of our members, who I don't know a lot about, seems to be playing around with deliveries that appear to be moving left and right at a slower pace! He has some of our batsmen in a complete spin! A peculiar chap, he has recently dyed his hair blue, and has a ring not on his finger but in his ear. I might give him a wide berth for the rest of the trip.

The quicks, Garrett, Boyle and I, have spent a lot of time in each other's company to keep each other sane. Beer, music and jokes are our bond. We have early morning workouts in preparation for our long spells in England, backed up by late sessions on the fizz preparing for the celebrations when we beat the Poms. We have called ourselves the Fast Bowlers Cartel.

Imagine my surprise when I read the Demon's diary and saw how relevant it was to my era!

BATSMEN
A very intense race of cricketer, they love talking about their batting averages and their massive batting contracts over skinny mocha lattes. The opening batsmen form bromances, their drink of choice is the Vodka Breezer, as it helps them keep their skinfolds low for their women's magazine photo shoots. Batsmen are generally Julios – they love colour, flicks or tints in their hair. Their music of choice is pop, R&B or extra-soft rock.

WICKETKEEPERS
Before Adam Gilchrist, these were blokes who couldn't bat or bowl as kids but aspired to play cricket, so they would don the gloves. Keepers choose to talk a lot of crap on the field, and they generally take it upon themselves to be the on-field *motivators* (sledgers). Their chat doubles in intensity whenever the opposition wicketkeeper comes in to bat, and their ultimate pleasure in a game is to see an opposition keeper score a duck or let a couple of byes through. No one else in the game actually cares much about that. To be fair, they do take catches for

the FBC, so they can sometimes get honorary membership, as Gilly did.

SPINNERS

Wow, what a weird mob they are! Maybe because spinning is such a character-building art. Balls delivered at an average of 80 to 90 kilometres per hour struggle to intimidate batsmen – unless you're playing on a real dustbowl, and even then it's only mental anguish, not physical threat. We've seen a plethora of extreme characters in the last few decades: Greg 'Mo' Matthews (so called because of his likeness to Australian comedian Roy Rene's character Mo McCackie), Shane 'Showbags' Warne, Tim 'Doink' May (after the WWE wrestling clown), Stuart 'Magilla' MacGill (Magilla Gorilla) and Colin 'Funky' Miller (after the Tone Loc song 'Funky Cold Medina') – an honorary FBC member for his outswingers.

FAST BOWLERS

Laid-back men of the people, often put down by the aforementioned groups, who question the FBC's intelligence and treat its members like second-class citizens. Fast bowlers are hard workers, often sending down 30 overs in extreme conditions, and they're happy with just a beer and a good chat at the end of a day's play. The myth about their intelligence has been totally debunked over the years, as many FBC members have gone on to hold prominent positions in cricket, as CEOs (James Sutherland, Tony Dodemaide, David Gilbert and David Johnston), Cricket Australia board members (Michael Kasprowicz), captains of the Fox Sports commentary crew (Brendon Julian) and umpires (Paul Reiffel). This group basically keeps cricket surviving and thriving.

Two of my best FBC mates were Jason Gillespie and Michael Kasprowicz. We shared a great love of fast bowling, hard rock and comedies. Kasper is a top bloke, honest, hard working and great company. His greatest legacy – besides *probably* being Poland's greatest ever cricketer – came at Edgbaston in 2005, when he gloved a ball from Andrew Flintoff down the leg side to Geraint Jones, who took the catch to win the match for England by three runs, keeping the Ashes series alive. Kasper knew that, under the rules of cricket, he was not out, since his glove had not been on his bat when the ball struck it, but he calmly put his bat under his arm, shook the Poms' hands and walked off the ground. Once in the dressing rooms, he grabbed a beer and rewarded himself with a little smirk, knowing that he had just saved Test cricket.

Jason Gillespie is one of the great men of Australian cricket. I loved his company – and not just because we shared a prominent nose and a mullet. In many ways, he reminded me of Merv Hughes. They were both awesome bowlers but even better men, unselfish, honest and fun to be around. You could always trust them to do the right thing. Dizzy battled some major injuries to take over 250 Test wickets, and at his peak he was the most hostile Aussie quick of our era. He also had one of the funniest laughs ever, which meant everyone else had a strong incentive to make him laugh.

SOME OTHER PROMINENT FBC MEMBERS OF MY ERA AND THEIR FBC ROLES

- Glenn McGrath, President
- Jason Gillespie, Fashion Consultant
- Merv Hughes, Diet Consultant
- Craig McDermott, Treasurer
- Brett Lee, Female Consultant

THE FAST BOWLERS CARTEL

*   *   *

You have to have some sympathy for fast bowlers. They get no bat contracts to compensate them for the tremendous strain they put on their bodies to send down each delivery. Ricky Ponting was paid millions each year to wield the willow for Australia, but the only money Glenn McGrath made was from bat companies that paid him *not* to use their gear.

I have always worked feverishly and passionately for FBC recognition, and I've had a couple of great ideas along the way.

One that got though:

1. Hold up the ball to the dressing room and the crowd after a five-wicket haul, just like batsmen raise their bats after 50-run milestones. Surely the hard-working FBC should get some acknowledgment as well?

And here's one that fell as flat as a pancake:

2. Anyone batting at number eight or lower should raise his bat after scoring 30 runs.

Well, as Meatloaf almost sang, one out of two ain't bad.

That's not to say that the FBC members didn't love their batting. Some of the highlights of our careers came when we scored runs after the top order had collapsed. Lindwall, Lillee, McKenzie, Walker and Thommo did it on numerous occasions, and I did it in Brisbane against England in 1998/99, when I smashed a match-winning 71 not out in a *drawn* Test match.

I had joined Heals in the middle. He'd already made a fantastic hundred, and he soon left, replaced by Stu MacGill. I pulled Darren Gough for consecutive fours in front of square leg early in my innings.

'Flem, what is going on with your batting today?' the English opening bowler asked.

'I seriously don't know,' I said, as puzzled as anyone else was.

And when I hooked Alan Mullally for four – looking just like Gordon Greenidge – the tall left-arm seamer claimed I was the wrong colour to be playing shots like that.

MacGill departed, and Glenn McGrath joined me at the crease.

Now, I had a couple of goals. One was, obviously, to score a Test hundred, but the second was too score eight more runs. If I could do that, I would pass the highest Test scores of three of my Victorian teammates. Merv's was 72, Shane Warne's 74 and Paul Reiffel's 78. With just two more boundaries I would win bragging rights.

By this time, McGrath was not the ferret he was early in his career. We had a quick chat and he committed to digging in and helping me pass some milestones. A couple of balls later he tried to slog off-spinner Robert Croft into the Brisbane CBD and was bowled. I swear that wasn't part of the plan we had orchestrated not five minutes before.

As we walked off, I raised my bat to the crowd. It was probably the greatest 71 not out at the Gabba against the Poms in the late 1990s in a drawn Test match. I thought about questioning Pigeon about his shot selection, but I stopped myself, knowing that I was an equally unreliable tailender and I would let him down at a later date when *he* was near a personal milestone.

* * *

Early in his Australian career, Dizzy was the youngest member of the FBC and also had the lowest Test score. He used to cop a bit of stick about that, and it frustrated the hell out of him.

Paul Reiffel had a 78, Hughes a 72, Bichel a 71, myself a 71 not out. We'd ask Dizzy what his highest score was, knowing the answer – 'A four-hour 25!'

Unlike his fellow FBC members, who were unreliable strokeplayers, Dizzy was a dour batsman. When you talk about signature shots, Ponting had his aggressive hook, and Tugga his poetic back-foot cover drive. Dizzy had a solid forward defence.

In one Test match, our captain, Steve Waugh, called Dizzy and me aside in the rooms. I think this conversation explains a little bit about our different batting styles.

'If we're trying to win this Test match, Flem, you bat at number nine,' Tugga said. 'And if we're trying to save it, Dizzy, you bat at number nine.'

Point made.

But it still wasn't yet Dizzy's time to shine. In a match against New Zealand in 2004, Dizzy played a great knock to score 54 not out. But at the other end was Glenn McGrath (who, later in his career, perfected a lovely deft leg-glance after he learned not to glance it onto his stumps), and he scored 61! When Pigeon was finally dismissed the pair went back into the rooms, and before Dizzy even had his pads off McGrath turned to him and said, 'Hey, Diz, what's your highest Test score?'

Even though he had broken his drought and scored a Test 50, he still couldn't get any respect!

※ ※ ※

Fast-forward to 23 April 2006, a black day in the history of nightwatchmen. Dizzy was sent in by the cowardly Ricky Ponting at number three at the end of day one. He was using a nightwatchman against the mighty Bangladeshi cricket team.

Now, the nightwatchman's job is to simply survive to stumps, in order to protect the batsman at the other end. Generally, the

BOWLOLOGY

lower-order batsmen who are used in this way are unreliable but flamboyant, and so they usually like to play their shots the next morning to get some quick runs before they're knocked over.

This tradition was treated with great disdain by Jason Gillespie. He showed blatant disregard for the nightwatchman fraternity by out-batting the batsmen and overstaying his welcome.

Unlike Shane Warne, who was inducted into the Nightwatchmen's Hall of Fame after getting sent in as a nightwatchman in a county game with an over to go. That evening he patiently played his role beautifully throughout his whole innings, which lasted all of two balls, when he was stumped for six!

Well, after another day's play, Dizzy was 100-odd not out. Overnight, I awoke to a text message from him which read: 'Flem, how did you go in the nervous 90s?'

By the middle of the next day he had scored 201 not out, and Ricky Ponting finally declared the innings closed. Dizzy

The Fast Bowlers Cartel average stock balls, 1994 to 2001 – all very similar, right in the 'avenue of apprehension', apart from two glaring omissions.

had passed the highest Test scores of Mark Waugh, Darren Lehmann, Ian Chappell and many other legendary batsmen. Apparently he'd been telling Mr Cricket exactly this in the middle every time he passed someone.

Another text message arrived: 'Flem, did you fatigue much in the 180s?'

Well played – what else can you say? Although I am currently petitioning the International Cricket Council to reclassify this match as a non-Test as it was against Bangladesh.

Chapter 38
ABC Radio, Richie Benaud and the Chinamen XI

WHAT IS CRICKET commentary Bowlology? If we are looking for Bowlology in the box, we are looking for the ideal blend of

1. former player
2. preferably an expert all-rounder (knows bowling and batting; sorry, Heals, wicketkeepers need not apply)
3. an innovative and respected captain
4. insight
5. poise
6. wit
7. rapport with fellow commentators
8. a great sense of style (it's all about the jacket).

The only man who ticks all these boxes is, obviously, Richie Benaud. He is the greatest commentator of all time, whether he is wearing the cream, the white, the off-white or the beige suits. He opened up the summer's cricket coverage from the time I first remember watching cricket. And now, as I'm working in the media, I have an even greater appreciation for the work he has done.

The ABC Radio and Channel Nine boxes are generally very close, and I bump into Richie every now and again. I must admit,

I'm still daunted by his presence and usually get by with a quick 'G'day, Richie'.

One time I was commentating a one-day series for the ABC and things were getting a little boring in the flat middle overs, so I was trying to think of some things to say. Brad Hogg had recently announced his retirement, and Simon Katich was also on the field, both left arm wrist spinners. While 'the Kat' didn't ever bowl in an ODI, his hairy left arm wrist spin was better than you think. He was a good bowler and had a serious wrong'un ... if he had a better body he could have been a valuable weapon but his back/neck were so bad the team called him Stifler after the character from *American Pie*. The Kat is the only cricketer I know who carried his own pillow because hotel ones could render him a cripple by morning.

This got me thinking about whether I could pick a Chinamen XI, because they're as rare as real men from China playing cricket.

And there was also the bigger question: Who came up with the term 'chinaman'?

Straightaway I selected my old teammate Michael Bevan, who once took 10 wickets in a Test match against the West Indies. Then, obviously, there were Hoggy and Kato.

Ian Chappell, who was a huge cricket nut, heard about my quest and started to contribute. He suggested the West Indian Roy Fredericks, a fast-scoring opening batsman who bowled chinamen. For the rest of the day, every time I got off mic, Ian was there with another idea. 'What about Denis Compton?' he said. 'A great English bat, but he bowled left-arm wrist-spin. And don't forget one of our great opening batsmen, Arthur Morris.'

Chappell seriously knows his cricket history. And we were building a solid team.

Later, as I walked out of the box, I saw the former Indian all-rounder Ravi Shastri and the Pakistani (and Bowlology guru) Wasim Akram. 'Did you guys play with any chinaman bowlers?' I asked. They both said no.

I turned to go back into the box, when all of sudden I felt a great presence near me. I turned and it was Richie. He was just *there*. And he spoke.

'Ah, the chinaman. Ellis Achong, a West Indian cricketer of Chinese descent, played six Tests between 1930 and 1935. His stock ball was one of left-arm orthodox spin, but in the 1933 Manchester Test match he was bowling to Walter Robbins. He delivered a left-arm wrist-spinner and completely deceived Robbins and had him stumped. Robbins was given out by Joe Hardstaff senior, the square leg umpire, and he was quoted as saying to Hardstaff, "Fancy that getting done by a *Chinaman!*" '

And then, as quickly as he had appeared, Richie disappeared again.

Baseball great Ted Williams once said that he wanted to be able to walk down the street someday and have people say, 'There goes the greatest hitter who ever lived.' Richie would never aspire to that sort of adulation, but he is the greatest cricket commentator ever. Period.

THE CHINAMEN XI

1. Arthur Morris, two wickets at an average of 25. Also picked in Australia's team of the century.
2. Roy Fredericks, seven wickets at an average of 78. Once smashed a Lillee and Thomson attack for 169 runs off 145 balls in Perth.
3. Gary Sobers, 235 wickets at an average of 32, with swingers, pace, offies and chinamen. Pretty handy with the bat as well!

BOWLOLOGY

4. Denis Compton, 25 wickets at an average of 56. Also won the FA Cup, playing for Arsenal as a winger.
5. Simon Katich, 21 wickets at an average of 30. Also made it to the semi-finals of *Celebrity Master Chef* with his signature dish, crispy salmon with wilted spinach and mashed potatoes.
6. Michael Bevan, 29 wickets at an average of 24. The only Test cricketer with the middle name Gwyl.
7. Johnny Martin, 17 wickets at an average of 48. Once dismissed Kanhai, Sobers and Worrell within four balls.
8. Ellis Achong (captain), eight wickets at an average of 47.
9. Lindsay Kline, 34 wickets at an average of 22, including a Test hat-trick.
10. Chuck Fleetwood-Smith, 42 wickets at an average of 37. On the field, he would sing, whistle, practise his golf swing, and imitate magpies and kookaburras.
11. Brad Hogg, 17 wickets at an average of 54, with his trademark tongue out while bowling.

12th man: Paul Adams, 134 wickets at an average of 33. Known as 'the frog in a blender'. His head pointed skywards at the moment of delivery.

Chapter 39
Beach Cricket

EVEN THOUGH I believed I was a competent cricketer on grass, it wasn't until I represented my country on the sand in the XXXX Gold Beach Cricket series that I truly felt complete. Beach, sun, beers, the XXXX Angels and playing with and against a host of cricketing legends – it was all a massive buzz.

1. It gave me the chance to play with and against some of my cricket idols (Dennis Lillee, Jeff Thomson, Sir Richard Hadlee and Sir Vivian Richards).
2. I got to play again with a lot of my former teammates (Darren Lehmann, Jason Gillespie and Michael Kasprowicz).
3. It gave me the chance to find out that most opposition players were actually good blokes (Graeme Hick, Adam Hollioake and Nathan Astle).

The series was like indoor cricket on a drop-in pitch. There were no lbws, you lost runs for each wicket, and there were 30-metre boundaries. We played on beaches throughout Australia – Coolangatta, Scarborough, Maroubra and Glenelg produced plenty of sixes and packed crowds, and the ball swung like a taped tennis ball for the bowlers.

The competition went for three years, and everyone involved had an absolute ball.

BOWLOLOGY

Aussie beach cricket dream team – AB and me.

THREE THINGS I LEARNT FROM BEACH CRICKET

1. Bat with your captain – it guarantees you a game in the side. My batting partner and captain was the great Allan Border – we were known (to ourselves) as 'the Dream Team'.
2. Now that you've got a close relationship with your skipper, manipulate the times that you bowl. I had a wonderful first season with the ball, as I constantly bowled to and knocked over former *bowling* greats such as Joel Garner and Courtney Walsh. Also, I very sensibly batted against noted *batsmen* – such as Desmond Haynes, who bowled little drifters, and South African–born Englishman Robin Smith who bowled a lot like the bowling figurines in Fred Trueman's Test Match board game, just not as accurate.
3. Create a nickname that sticks. With my ability to bowl out Garner and smash Smith for six, I became known as 'Sobers of the Sand' (self-proclaimed).

BEACH CRICKET

The man with the most steel in the beach cricket series was Sir Vivian Richards. Even at close to 60, he was still the coolest dude playing. He looked about 40, with the build of a boxer. When he hit the ball it was still smokin'. But I did have one embarrassing incident with the great man.

A couple of years earlier, whilst I was in England for the 2005 Ashes, I played cricket for a travelling Harlem Globetrotters–style cricket team called Lashings, run by David Folb. Lashings was mostly made up of ex-West Indian players, such as Richie Richardson, Gordon Greenidge, Jimmy Adams and Vasbert Drakes, but there were a few others like Herschelle Gibbs and Chris Harris. They would travel around and play league teams and schools throughout the UK. I hadn't played a lot of cricket in the previous few years – well, none – but I was told the games were not taken all that seriously.

In our first game we played against the county team Glamorgan, who took the match pretty seriously. It's fair to say my bowling had dropped off a bit. So much so that after the match, Folby quietly asked me if I wouldn't mind keeping the runs under 12 per over, which in hindsight wasn't an unreasonable request.

Anyway, I was really enjoying playing with all these legendary ex-players. Easily the most popular player we had playing in my second match was the former English spinner Phil Tufnell. 'Tuffers' had become a media superstar after winning the reality show *I'm a Celebrity – Get Me Out of Here* (which, ironically, is what he used to say when he walked out to the middle to bat in a Test match).

Tuffers was flying high this day. There were many beverages flowing and he was assisting the DJ by singing and dancing and generally floating around larger-than-life. At one point, still quite early on in the day, he said to me, 'Flem, if this all goes to shit, I'd still be prepared to work on the roads, if that's what it takes to provide for my family.'

What the fuck is he talking about? I thought.

The day continued, and Tuffers had a few more beers and kept socialising. He wasn't really concentrating on the cricket match. Every now and again he would repeat to me, 'Seriously, Flem, if this all goes to shit, I'll be happy to work on the roads. If it means providing for my family'

We went out to bowl, and it was tough. Tuffers was just making up fielding positions for himself and generally showing no interest whatsoever in the game. At one point a batsman cut the ball out to point, where Tuffers was lying comatose, not moving at all. Then he miraculously recovered, got up, tripped over his feet, arose again and threw the ball in. Gradually, Tuffers was spending more time in the crowd than on the field. Folby wasn't happy.

After the game, Tuffers started to come down from his big high. The rest of us were having a few beers in the dressing room, and Tuffers got flatter and flatter. He was sitting by himself, drifting in and out of sleep.

He stirred and spotted me, and looked up sheepishly. 'Whatever you do, Flem, don't let me work on the roads,' he said. 'It would fucking kill me.'

Anyway, besides being probably the worst player ever to have represented Lashings, I was now part of a team heavy with West Indians. Whenever I'd taken a wicket for Australia, there had generally been a pat on the back, maybe a high-five, before we got on with things. The West Indians did things differently.

Celebrating a wicket with eight West Indians was totally intimidating. I soon discovered that they had not only invented the higher-five, but they'd taken it even further. There were many different levels of high-five-ology.

BEACH CRICKET

There were low-fives, high-fives, air-fives, sometimes over their heads or around their backs, butterfly-type finger rotations and fist-pumps. I was like Gary Cherone as lead singer of Van Halen after David Lee Roth then Sammy Hagar – truly out of my league in regards to high-fiving with these West Indians.

In fact, I started to get the high-five yips, and actually dreaded getting a wicket. Eventually, like Baldrick from *Blackadder*, I created a cunning plan, in which I'd make sure I was running so late for the wicket celebrations that the high-fiving was finished and I wouldn't send another palm into a teammate's face.

Fast-forward back to the beach cricket. It was a Thursday and I was having breakfast by myself. In walked Sir Viv, who I was still very much in awe of. We locked eyes in recognition, me of his magnificent cricket career, him possibly going to order eggs off me.

A voice in my head reminded me that Sir Viv was Antiguan, just like Lashings captain Richie Richardson. I knew from experience that Richie's trademark was the fist-pump – maybe it was an Antiguan thing?

Viv reached me, and his right arm started to extend. I reacted by closing my fist for the pump. A horror story was unfolding right there and then.

As my fist connected with Viv's hand, I realised that he'd gone for a traditional handshake. I punched his open hand quite hard. I shat myself, feeling like a complete idiot, and I left without saying anything. Over the next few days I tried to work up the courage to talk to Viv about it, but the longer it went, the harder I found it to confront him. I now had Sir Viv yips.

Later that summer I was in Perth, commentating the cricket for ABC Radio, and I told the story of my high-five disaster with Viv. The next day, the beach cricket teams were on a bus on our way to the beach for our game. Viv was up the back.

Acceptable Hand Greetings

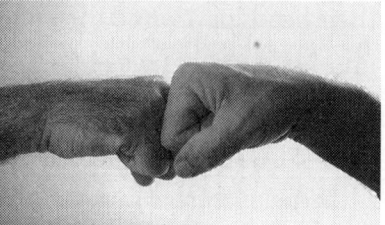

Traditional handshake

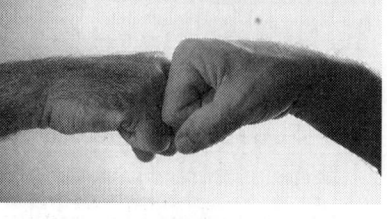

Fist pump

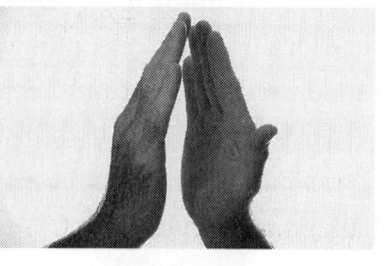

The high bro

High five

Unacceptable Hand Greetings

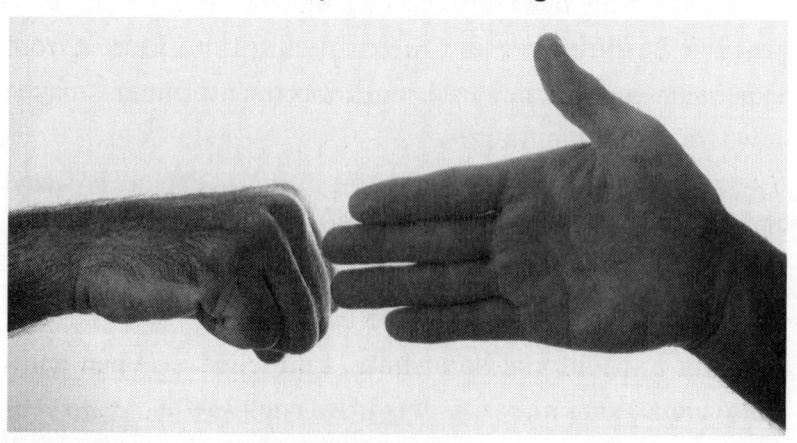

'Hey, Damo,' he called out to me. 'I heard you commentating last night on the cricket... Very interesting.'

I shrunk into my bus seat like a deflated balloon and reflected on his open-ended statement. Had he heard me retelling my high-five story or was he just complimenting me? I don't know and I have never asked him.

Chapter 40
Pitch Reports, Aussies with Hat-tricks and Test 70s Club

THE FOX SPORTS commentary crew has a lot going for it. In any successful team, you need talent, a common goal and team players – and we pride ourselves on thorough statistical preparation and hard work (except for Junior, who does most things pretty naturally). Importantly, we have a natural rapport as ex-teammates but more importantly, we were all different types of players – batting all-rounders (AB, Blewy and Junior) and bowling all-rounders (BJ and myself ... just) – and distinctively different personalities.

Brendon Julian: Has there ever been a better 196 centimetre, left-arm swing bowler TV presenter with two first names? I don't think so. BJ is the undisputed captain of the commentary crew – well, that's what we tell him, anyway. He inspires and challenges the group, and he's always there with a hip to cry on (as I can't reach his shoulders). His thick flowing hair can be as wayward as his left-arm swingers, but you would never know. In fact, scientists have noted that there are holes in the ozone layer above every cricket ground in the country and are baffled by this. The reason is that BJ uses crates of the stuff to keep his hair just right. At times the studio is so dense in this

Greg Blewett, Mark Waugh, Jess Yates, Allan Border,
Brendon Julian, Sarah Jones and me.

mist, which he applies during every ad break, that we can't see or breathe. Because of this, gas masks are part of our Fox Sports commentator kit.

Allan Border: He's gone from being Captain Grumpy to being everyone's favourite in the crew, our very own Uncle Al. I love commentating with the man who played 156 Tests and 273 one-day games – which, as he often mentions, meant that he did over 1000 warm-up sessions.

AB rarely slips up in the commentary box, but one rare moment came during a Victoria vs New South Wales game at the MCG. Doug Bollinger was charging in to bowl but collapsed just before his take-off step. He was lying on the grass, motionless.

I could see that AB was keen to say something, but he was a little hesitant. Eventually, he blurted out: 'Dougy looks like that guy from that movie . . . *Breakfast at Bernie's*!'

PITCH REPORTS, AUSSIES WITH HAT-TRICKS

The box erupted with laughter, and I just managed to respond. 'Is that like the guy from *Weekend at Tiffany's?*'

Mark Waugh: When you talk about the hard men of Aussie cricket, Junior's name is never mentioned. But as a commentator he is hard as fingernails. He's a legend of the game – witty, insightful and with instinctive knowledge of cricket. He calls a spade a shovel, he speaks the truth and he often says things that the rest of us are dying to say but hold back because of political correctness or respect for the player who has just stuffed up. Junior shoots from the hip, Rambo-style, which is great.

We were commentating on a Ryobi Cup game together around the time West Aussie Batsman Damian Martyn retired. I thought I would pay my respects to Marto's fabulous career and give Junior a rap at the same time. 'Junior, if I had to pick an ideal batsman from a spectator's point of view, I would have you gracefully glancing the ball through the leg side and Marto eloquently driving through the off side.'

I thought that Junior would thank me for the rap and acknowledge what a great player Marto was, but in typical Junior style he told it straight. 'I was pretty strong through the off side as well, Flemo!'

Junior gold.

We have a similar relationship to Dwight and Jim in the US version of *The Office*, in that there's a little bit of rivalry in the commentary box. I'm not sure where it comes from. Maybe in the back of my mind I'm remembering how Junior's catching in the slips was always safe as houses – except when I was bowling! The worst was in a one-day game in Adelaide against the West Indies. Second ball, I got Darren Ganga to nick the ball to second slip, and do you know what was waiting for the ball? Not Junior's safe hands but the middle of his back. He claimed afterwards that he 'lost the ball in the crowd', but really I think he was protesting about my bowling or something like that. Luckily, it bounced off his back and into Warnie's hands, but fair dinkum!

Junior can become infatuated by certain players – generally those in the New South Wales Blues' colours, such as Moisés Henriques and Sean Abbott. As for the rumour about restraining orders, well, there haven't been any issued . . . yet.

Mike Hunt: He played a big role when Fox Sports' cricket coverage met the movie *Porky's* during our 2009 Ashes coverage. There was a rain delay, so we filled in some air time in our Sydney studios while our host, Nick McArdle, wrapped up the scenes in the background.

'Who are all the guys out there? Umpire bodyguards or ground staff?' I enquired, just throwing it out there. Actually I knew one of the groundsmen who was on camera.

'Mike Hunt! It's Mike Hunt!' I heard Junior yelling out, as I had my back to him and he started giggling. 'He was on the ground staff at Lord's when I was there.'

I automatically realised we could have some fun. I turned to Nick to continue, but he had lost it and put his head on the desk laughing.

I refocused on Junior. 'What, do you know him?' I asked. 'Did he do something to you?'

'You didn't reckon I knew his name. It's Mike Hunt.'

The whole studio had broken up laughing by now – cameraman, producer etc. – but I held it together long enough for one last line.

'Who is it again?' I asked.

'You know his name.' he replied, and I thought that was the end of it. 'It's Mike Hunt,' Junior barely spat out.

PITCH REPORTS, AUSSIES WITH HAT-TRICKS

I turned back to Nick, who was still laughing with his head on the desk. Then miraculously he popped his head up and said, 'Let's go to a break. Hopefully we'll be back . . .'

As soon as we got off-air, of course, Junior blamed me for it all as I had asked him the question

Greg Blewett: Blewy is BJ's mini-me. A good-looking, tanned rooster, but unlike BJ he brings high fashion standards to the box. The open-neck shirt, slacks and trendy shades make him look like he is continually auditioning for an Old Spice commercial. He says he's a passionate South Australian, and yet he has never grown a mullet or commentated while wearing moccasins. But then he still hasn't forgiven Melbourne for stealing Adelaide's Formula 1 Grand Prix, so he's allowed to be a little anti-Victorian.

* * *

Fox Sports Cricket is also a leading innovator in world sports broadcasting:
1. With two lovely and knowledgeable female boundary-riders, Jess Yates and Sarah Jones.
2. By attaching microphones to players, such as Shane Warne during the Big Bash, and have them talk viewers through their upcoming dismissals.
3. Using breathtaking shots from the air of the ground and the crowd from the Foxcopter.
4. Use of 'third eye' vision from the umpires' hats and the batsmen's helmets – great initiatives for the viewer.
5. And, impressively, the biggest height difference between co-hosts in world sports – the six-foot-nine BJ and the five-foot-four AB.

BOWLOLOGY

Pitch reports are a staple of any pre-match. In cricket, there are many ways to do a pitch report, and the late Tony Grieg probably covered the entire range – from his 'weather wall', which measured player comfort levels, to the way he stuck his keys into the pitch.

In Test and Shield cricket, the pitch deteriorates day by day, so it's always interesting to talk about how this deterioration will affect the day ahead – whether there will be inconsistent bounce, or how much spin and reverse-swing will play a part. In one-day and Twenty20 cricket, however, the pitches are generally as flat as an ice rink, so there's less to talk about.

The most enjoyable pitch report I have done for Fox Sports was in Hobart. My old roommate Merv Hughes joined me, so I took the chance to promote the exclusive group we were part of.

'Thanks, BJ,' I began. 'It's brass-monkey weather down here in Hobart, cool conditions with a little bit of rain hanging around. I'm down here with Merv Hughes. Well done on your Fox Sports debut, but better than that, it's a chance for us to catch up for a reunion of our club, isn't it?'

'Yes, Australians that have taken Test hat-tricks and scored a Test 70s club,' Merv agreed.

'We inducted Shane Warne last year into our club . . .'

'But Warnie never turns up,' Merv noted.

'Yeah, he never does,' I said sadly. 'Who else can we induct? What about Dennis Lillee? He scored a Test 70.'

'No, he didn't take a Test hat-trick,' Merv said.

'Damn.'

'Lindsay Kline?' Merv suggested.

'Yeah, he got a Test hat-trick,' I said. 'Oh, but he didn't score a Test 70 . . . Okay, back to the game today. The pitch they're using is the same one used for the fantastic game last week. Merv, you've have had a look – what do you think?'

PITCH REPORTS, AUSSIES WITH HAT-TRICKS

'With the rain overnight – and the covers have just been taken off – I reckon it will be a little bit tacky,' Merv said. 'It will be a new-ball wicket with plenty of life in it.'

'What's the secret to bowling with the new ball on this pitch, taking into account that you played two one-day games here for Victoria and *didn't* get one wicket?'

'Yeah, but I did hit a guy in the head,' Merv answered. 'Which I thought was better than getting a wicket! With the new ball you have to be aggressive, you have to look to get two, three, four wickets in the first 12 overs.'

'And what does the team batting first have to score to win the game?'

'Two hundred and seventy-eight would be a good score,' Merv replied.

'Two hundred and seventy-eight?' I said. 'A very specific score. But no worries. What about Max Walker – can we induct Max into our club?'

'Well, he did score a Test 70 . . .'

'Yes, but he didn't get a hat-trick. Damn it! Back to you, BJ.'

* * *

Merv, Warnie and I want to be clear here: we want to be inclusive, not exclusive, so if you do play Test cricket, take a hat-trick and score a Test 70, you're in our club. (Peter Siddle, I know you're reading this – yes, you've taken the hat-trick but with a highest score of 51 you're still 19 runs short of the club.)

Chapter 41
A Bit Like My Bowling, eh, Steve!

IT'S FAIR TO say that, as I was a low-profile, injury-prone swing bowler, sponsors weren't jumping out of their skins to have me advertise their products on TV ads. Plenty of cricketers lapped up the opportunities for a bit of extra cash in exchange for trying to look convincing while endorsing products, much to their teammates' amusement, from 'Boony Dolls' to Greg Matthew's memorable catchphrase: 'Advanced Hair – Yeah Yeah!', which was a classic.

My favourite, however, was Mark Waugh's advertising of an anti-dandruff shampoo, and I once quizzed him about it.

'Junior, you know you have to believe in the product you're endorsing,' I said. 'Did you have dandruff before you used this shampoo?'

'No,' he replied, 'but I haven't got dandruff since I started using it.'

Kasper and I always wanted to do an ad for Subway sandwiches. We would both be naked, and we'd each have a Subway sub positioned where our cricket box would normally be. I would have a six-inch sub and Kasper would have the foot-long, and my line, as I was looking at Kasper, would be: 'Wish I had a foot-long . . .'

We were *ideas* guys, but we were also pretty undesirable ideas guys.

BOWLOLOGY

When I was growing up, my schoolmates and I were big fans of the D Generation and *The Late Show* from the Working Dog guys. So when I received a call from them to see whether I would get involved in their fabulous TV show *Thank God You're Here*, I jumped at the chance. (To be fair, it was a small jump as I was suffering from knee tendonitis at the time.)

Santo Cilauro from Working Dog explained the reasoning behind *Thank God You're Here*:

When I was in Grade 5, a VFL star in an ill-fitting tan suit came to my school to explain the importance of saving money. I was stunned. I grew up in an era where footballers played on Saturday, then spent the rest of the week pruning trees for the council, digging holes for the Board of Works or, at best, running the local pub.

But this guy was different – he was a spokesman for the National Bank!

Soon my astonishment turned into confusion. As the champion half-back began telling us how a savings book works, I could see the beads of perspiration starting to form on his forehead. By the time he got to the concept of compound interest, he was drowning in his own sweat.

Clearly, he had tried to memorise the entire spiel in his Ford Escort on the way in.

What the performance lacked in polish, it more than made up for in doggedness. The air of stiltedness that hung heavy in the classroom didn't stop me from joining their Xmas Club (with a bank book in my team colours!), but it certainly started my lifelong love affair with the sportsperson out of his/her depth while endorsing a product.

Thank God You're Here is not a show about comic improvisation – it is a 'celebration of bullshit'. The central question

A BIT LIKE MY BOWLING, EH, STEVE!

is 'How much can you get away when you have no idea what you're talking about?'

Enter sports star.

Unfortunately we couldn't convince Damien to get into an ill-fitting tan suit.

Below is the first script for the *Thank God You're Here* mock sporting ads and the chance to see how much bullshit I could actually verbalise selling products. You can check it out on YouTube.

I had to endorse the Australian Synchotron:

> You know, choosing the right sub-atomic particle analysis facility is a little bit like medium-pace bowling. That's why, when I need high-resolution photon delivery, I head straight for the Australian Synchrotron. This place has *nine* different beam lines, including powder diffraction and X-ray absorption fluorescence. Now, that is unbelievable!
>
> You know, over the years I've seen too many people select the wrong multi-wave linear accelerator systems. You've got to have megahertz accuracy! Just check out these dispersion rates. *[Looks into microscope.]* They've done it again!
>
> Whether I'm after protein micro-crystal or a small molecule X-ray diffraction, the Australian Synchrotron is fast and it's accurate. Bit like my bowling, eh, Steve? *[Thumbs up from a technician.]*
>
> That's why I head for the Australian Synchrotron. *Howzat* for electron imaging performance!

All in all, we recorded nine ads, in which I plugged a variety of products, including these gems:

BOWLOLOGY

- 'In the last year alone, Sovereign Super is proud to have wiped out nearly 17 per cent off the value of members' assets. Wow! That's impressive under-performance...'
- 'Selling primary sedimentation tanks, with circular aeration units or membrane bioreactor modules, Aquatec Maxcon has a solution for my *every* sewerage need...'
- 'With Surginex, I know I'm getting precision-engineered, ISO-accredited equipment that's both reliable and accurate. Bit like my bowling, eh, Steve?'

I loved those 'bit like my bowling, eh, Steve' endings where Steve and I would give the camera a cheesy thumbs-up. It's an affirmation that I reckon could help me through life, especially when times get tough, just like when I was getting 0 for 100 in a test match and I'm a bit flat. Steve would be in the dressing rooms with his thumbs-up.

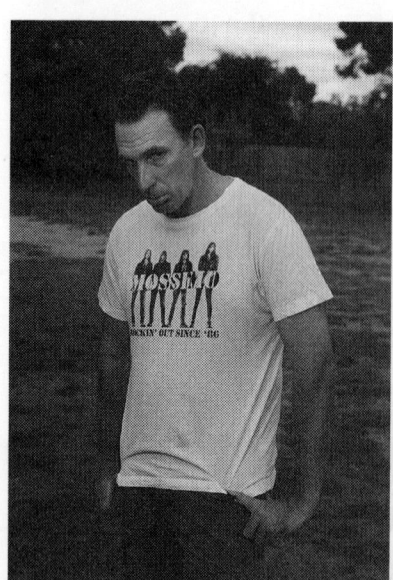

A bit flat...
until I see my mate, Steve.
(My actual neighbour, Steve Collet.)

Chapter 42
My Mate Oscar

AS DIFFICULT AS it is to imagine, when I was reviewing my four life goals in 2007, I had three fails! One was that I still hadn't starred in a Hollywood blockbuster film. Little did I know that my Oscar was about to be handed to me on a silver platter.

The Oscar statues (believed to be named after Sylvester Stallone's classic 1991 movie of the same name) are presented at the Academy Awards as a reward for excellence in a variety of fields – best movie, best actor, best screenplay and so on.

Over the summer of 2007/08, when I was commentating for ABC Radio, we were inundated by comments reviewing my performance in the movie *Slumdog Millionaire*. I was puzzled and had to wait until later in the summer to watch it.

The experience is explained in this *Sunday Age* article by Pete Hanlon, 6 March 2009, after *Slumdog Millionaire* won multiple Academy Awards.

HOLLYWOOD STARS IN FLEMING'S EYES
Damien Fleming has always been the consummate all-rounder: swing bowler, cavalier batsman shoved too far down the order to give full expression to his talents, illuminating commentator, 'bowlologist' extraordinaire, heavy metal aficionado and general wag. Now, he is proudly telling anyone who'll listen that his CV is bulging with yet another accolade: Oscar winner. 'Mate, I'm big! This TV and radio stuff, it's just something to keep me ticking over until I get to where I'm inevitably going – and that's Hollywood! I'm just

treading water until the next blockbuster.' When *Slumdog Millionaire* won eight Academy Awards last month, all the attention was on its cast of largely unknown Indian actors, but the role of a key player shouldn't be lost. Fleming takes up the story: 'In the big scene, the really big scene, with the mafia guy at home – and this probably got them over the line for the Oscar – the mafia guy's getting hassled by his missus and he goes, "Shut up, I wanna watch the cricket!" Tendulkar's batting, he gets a hundred, and guess who's commentating? "Oh, Tendulkar, he's a sensation," I say, or something like that anyway, and then you hear me for about 90 seconds. Mate, I'm an Oscar winner! I'm dirty that I couldn't go to the red carpet because we were recording the last *Inside Cricket* on Fox. I actually said on the show, "Make the most of this, boys, Hollywood beckons."'

It's a Private Joke

Fleming's conviction was hardened by the fact that none of Rameez Raja, Laxman Sivaramakrishnan or Daryl Cullinan – his fellow commentators from the match in question (which was India vs South Africa in, of all places, Ireland) – were deemed worthy of a run in *Slumdog*. 'In the movie, the other commentator – who doesn't say as much as me by the way – he's an actual actor who they've got in to do the voiceover, but they've kept me in!' The whole episode has caused much mirth, not least when Fleming and his wife Wendy went to see the film. 'I've known for a while, but my missus forgot about it when we went and saw it. It's at a really emotional time in the movie, and she's wetting herself laughing. The audience are all looking at her and obviously thinking, "Why is this lady laughing herself silly at a really emotional scene?"'

Hulk Hogan's Got Nothin' on Me

One movie does not a Hollywood Boulevard handprint make. But further rave reviews came while Fleming was sitting at home recently working his way through a few scripts – 'mainly voiceovers for now, like your *Shreks* and *Madagascars*' – and his mate and old adversary Chris Cairns contacted him by Skype from Dubai, where he now lives with his Australian wife. The former Kiwi all-rounder had been watching the movie *Hansie*, a portrayal of the life of the late, disgraced South African captain Hansie Cronje, made by his brother Frans. 'Cairnsy's watching it, and in the middle of the movie it's the World Cup semi-final (at Edgbaston in 1999), and Fleming comes on to bowl, and they're all excited, and it goes to me . . . and I'm about six foot five! I've got long, blond hair and massive muscles! They go through the whole last over, and there's Fleming, looking like Hulk Hogan. I told you I was big!'

In honour of the award, during the Sheffield Shield final on Fox Sports I did the pitch report on a red carpet with my Oscar in hand.

Finally, I'd achieved a life goal. My movie CV is now bulging, and I certainly don't want to be pigeonholed into Indian dramas featuring cricket voiceover work. Those movies are a dime a dozen these days. And as Clint Eastwood says, you're only as good as your last movie. (Actually, Clint never really said that . . .)

Chapter 43
After the Bounce

IT'S FAIR TO say that when Fox Footy's boss, Rod Law, rang me and asked what I was doing for the winter, it was a call from out of the blue. It turned out he had an idea to get me involved with a show called *Before the Bounce*, since Billy Brownless had moved on.

As a keen Hawks fan, the chance to work with Jason 'the Chief' Dunstall (one of our greatest full forwards and four-time premiership player) and Danny 'Spud' Frawley (longest-serving St Kilda captain) was too good to pass up. My main role was to referee (or attempt to referee) the sporting challenges between these two super-heavyweights in a segment called 'Yesterday's Heroes Challenges'.

From gymnastics to rugby league, hockey, circus performing, clay-pigeon shooting and gymnastics, the boys tried every sport imaginable. The Chief had bulked up a little since retiring, living on a diet of pizzas and soft drink, but he was still a very skilled athlete and very competent in all sports, so it seemed an unfair battle against Spud, who nevertheless called himself 'Mr Natural'. His bravado was a bit reminiscent of the way Muhammad Ali used to try to build up his confidence before a fight, as Spud didn't really having a sporting bone in his body – bedsides his right fist, which used to punch leather and full-forwards' heads while he was playing full back for St Kilda. But he was a goer and hung in for every contest, knowing that the Chief could explode at any minute and lose concentration. If he did, *bang*! A Spud win.

YESTERDAY'S HEROES SNOOKER CHALLENGE

One of our contests involved the Aussie snooker champion Neil Robertson. At practice, the Chief showed his natural competence, and Neil was impressed. But Spud was more used to pub pool in Ballarat, not snooker. We started the challenge and the Chief wiped the floor with Spud: one–nil to the Chief.

The second challenge was simple: hit the white ball from one end of the table and make it stop as close to the cushion at the other end as possible. In the trials, the Chief had great touch, while Spud was hitting them everywhere. But the word 'Action' sparked the Spud to life. He went first and hit the ball within millimetres of the cushion. Straightaway the Chief's body language changed. He was not happy, and it showed. In his anger, he hit the ball too hard and lost the challenge. It was now one-all, and the 'Chief-ometer' – a measure of the Chief's anger – was starting to go up.

The third challenge was trickshots, which meant hitting multiple balls into the pocket at the same time. The Chief, hurting after losing the second challenge, started poorly, and Spud coolly sank the ball to win the challenge. Our cameraman tried to get a shot of the ever-ungracious Chief, but all we saw was the door slamming shut as he left the room.

* * *

A decision was made in 2012 to move the show from Friday nights to Sunday nights. After hours of debate about a name change that was both catchy and time specific, we eventually emerged exhausted but motivated as we had cleverly decided to

A screenshot of me with my wheel mentor, the legendary Baby John Burgess.

rename the show from *Before the Bounce* to *After the Bounce*. See what we did there?

Sunday night has always been variety night on TV, and Rod was keen for the show to reflect this. Of course, it was natural for me to get a wheel to spin for a contest. My wheel had some problems on its debut show. We gave it a big build-up but unfortunately when push came to shove I found myself the game's master of a wheel that was perfect except for one thing: IT WOULDN'T SPIN!

The bloody thing was sent back to the workshop for some minor adjustments and returned the next week where I was relieved to find that it did what a wheel should do and spun. Only problem was now it wouldn't STOP SPINNING.

I decided to get some mentoring from one of TV's big guns and wheel specialists, the legendary 'Baby' John Burgess. He gave me plenty of sound advice, but unfortunately none of it was relevant to wheels or to TV entertainment in general. But while the segment lasted, I got a tremendous buzz each time I spun Australia's and probably the world's best wheel.

After a while, the show's producers became keen for a new segment, and the Chief came up with a role for me with the segment 'Turn It Up'. This gave me free rein to analyse and question any issues in the AFL, sport and society.

A TYPICAL 'TURN IT UP' SEGMENT

Traditionally, Aussie test captains aren't Julios or SNAGS or manscapers. When you think of AB, Tubby or Ian Chappell, you think of fine batsmen, tough, uncompromising skippers who managed the team dressing room with a few beers after play.

With the announcement of Michael Clarke, the 43rd Aussie captain, we have seen a break in that tradition. He's our first Generation Y skipper and fine wine and personal grooming habits may well now be the dressing-room banter, but that still doesn't excuse the anti-Clarke bandwagon that's been out in force. His preference of a chilled chardonnay over a cold beer has turned noses.

Turn it up, Australia!

C'mon, Aussie, we believe in giving everyone a fair go. His 5–1 record while in charge during the one-day international series against England proves he can take the reins, even under intense pressure, and he showed intuition with his bowling and fielding changes.

He looked after his mates, too – through his Twitter account he got Steve Smith a cracking date for the AB Medal!

Let's say no to the tall-poppy syndrome. Clarke didn't take over the team that S. Waugh or R. Ponting took, we are fifth in the world in Test cricket. Let him be measured by the wins and his batting record, not the amount of tattoos, Twitter followers and models he's had on his arm. There's nothing more un-Australian than not giving a bloke a fair go.

Turn it up!

AFTER THE BOUNCE

In truth the best thing about my 'Turn It Up' segment was the intro, which was so good that the segment just had to stay.

After three years of doing Fox Sports cricket and *After the Bounce*, I thought I needed a rest and it was time to enforce my own rotation policy. Now former Aussie basketball great and fellow Hawk fan Andrew Gaze has taken 'Turn It Up' to a new level and height – he's seven feet tall, while I'm only six feet.

Chapter 44
Finish Life Goals Review

AT SOME STAGE you have to settle down, but when it comes time for cricketers, it can be a little more complicated than most. Let's face it, when you have spent most of your early adult life trapped in dressing rooms with other men, sharing rooms with Merv Hughes and chasing cricket balls around the planet you aren't really that well equipped for the Other Game.

Still, you've got to make the best of what you've got and when I was introduced to the beautiful Wendy O'Donnell by her sister Shelley at the Star Bar in South Melbourne, in 1996, where I was halfway through my regular Sunday night nightclub trifecta (Depot, Star Bar and then the Tunnel), I knew that it was going to take a bit more than my natural charm to make sure this girl didn't slip away.

And she ticked a few boxes:
- Good-looking sort
- Sporty – she was playing state netball
- Liked the footy – her brother Gary played for Essendon and while that would normally sound some alarms she barracked for the Hawks as a kid, so she was vulnerable for a team swap
- Didn't mind cricket – she grew up playing at Ringwood Cricket Club, where her dad, Graeme, was the president and her mum, Bev, basically ran everything

- Liked the right music – she'd attended Kiss's 1980 concert at Waverley Park
- Movies – she generally let me choose them. Gold!

My eventual proposal occurred a couple of years later, and was a classic of the kind (keep in mind, guys, what a daunting prospect a proposal is . . .)

We were in bed on a Sunday morning. I actually had in my mind that this was the day, and I was thinking about how I should do it. At dinner or lunch? Should I get down on one knee? How would I get the flowers into the restaurant without Wendy knowing?

At that moment Wendy broke the silence. 'You know how I like to plan the day and you fly by the seat of your pants? What do you want to do today?'

'Well . . .' Big pause and deep breath. 'What do you want to do for the rest of your life?'

After a few seconds, which seemed like an eternity, Wendy replied, 'Have you *thought* about this?'

Whoops. (Cue needle scratching the record.) What I really didn't want to hear at this point was a question in answer to my proposal. I just wanted an answer – preferably a yes.

After what seemed like another eternity, she said yes. The arvo was now planned and structured – we were getting an engagement ring!

❉ ❉ ❉

I have never given up on cricket, it's one of those games that doesn't let you go and, while I no longer play it, I do get to enjoy it from the commentary position. I'm also a board member of Melbourne Stars and the parent of junior cricketers. One thing I do miss from my playing days, however, is a particular split-second sound that I used to hear every so often. To me, it was as magical as the opening riffs to AC/DC's 'Black in Black'.

When you bowl a great outswinger, you know it by the way it flies from the tops of your middle and index fingers – it has a real snap to it. As the ball flies down the pitch with its stable seam, the batsman sees it sitting there begging to be driven through the covers, but if everything is right, the moment he makes that decision, the ball begins to swing away from where it was. The bat, already committed to a meeting, comes through its arc but instead of smashing the delivery manages only to give it a little flick with the outside edge.

That's the noise I miss.

That and the time freeze that follows as the ball begins its slow journey toward the wicketkeeper's waiting gloves. The anticipation is exquisite. It's like you have an explosion of euphoria a millisecond away, everything is in slow motion, but already your adrenaline has kicked in and you are halfway up in the air just waiting to unleash all those great emotions.

That's what I miss, well, that and a massive win.

Naturally in life you search for those outswinger moments and they come, but these days it's more likely to be from predicting a mode of dismissal while commentating or sinking that big putt (after three earlier attempts).

Life is a little more vicarious, but just as good. When son Brayden gets a wicket with his outswinger, daughter Jasmine shoots a big goal at the basketball or presents me with one of her drawings (she is a great artist), or when the youngest, Isobel, took her first steps and spoke her first word ('dad', second word was 'dad...dy'), or seeing my parents become grandparents, I get just as big a rush.

These are all wins, and may there be many more!

BOWLOLOGY

The Fleming outswinger is getting passed down generations — just have to work on Isobel's grip.

FINISH LIFE GOALS REVIEW

* * *

I want to finish with some life Bowlology shown to me a few years ago by Brayden, which really put things into perspective.

Weetbix had brought out some cricket cards, mostly of current players but with some older players in there as well. I was lucky enough to get a card. We are all Weetbix eaters, so Wendy and I would check the packets for one of my cards, planning to put it on the top for Brayden to find. Eventually, after our garage was full of Weetbix packets we found a D. Fleming card and packed it on top one night.

The next morning we waited for Brayden to wake up and open the pack, which he did. Immediately, he grabbed my card, screaming, 'Dad!' It's hard to express how I felt at seeing my son so pumped up to find my card. He proudly took it to school to show his friends who thought it was pretty neat having a dad with a Weetbix card.

This certainly was a massive life outswinging win.

A couple of days later, I asked, 'How's my card going?'

'I swapped it,' he said calmly.

'What?'

'I got a Sir Donald Bradman and an Adam Gilchrist card for yours,' he continued. 'Don averaged 99.94 and Gilly hit 120 sixes, and you only hit one.'

As disappointed as I was, I thought it was a very shrewd move by the young fella. He is going to do well.

Chapter 45
Australians with Hat-tricks on Test Debut Club

Australians with Hat-tricks on Test Debut Club AWHOTD

February 2013
Moises Henriques
Test cricketer on debut

Dear Moises,
Firstly, congrats on your selection to make your Test debut against India. You are part of an elite club – you're only the 432nd bloke to play Test cricket for Australia over 136 years – so you should be proud.

Speaking of elite clubs, are you aware of the most elite of clubs – the Australians with Hat-tricks on Test Debut Club? We just had our AGM last night. There were a lot of laughs, plenty of drinks and stories, and a bit of karaoke later in the night. I picked up the bill . . . as I'm still the only member.

So consider this an invitation to join the AWHOTDC. You have a rare opportunity to join the club over the next five days. All we require is three wickets in three consecutive balls – and it doesn't matter if you spread them out over a couple of overs, as I did, or over three

BOWLOLOGY

overs and two innings, like the great Merv Hughes. They just have to be in the next five days.

Quite frankly, I'm sick of winning the club's golf day every year. I've thought about introducing a tennis match, but obviously we need someone to return serve. There have been 70 players who've had the chance to join the club since my debut, so it's disappointing that no one has.

That's not to say there haven't been some near misses: Nathan Bracken against India at the Gabba, Patrick Cummins against South Africa in a man-of-the-match performance, James Pattinson against New Zealand at the Gabba. They all bowled valiantly and took two wickets in two balls on Test debut but they failed to get the all-important third wicket. Possibly the pressure of joining the AWHOTDC was too overwhelming. I'd like to bend the rules, but two wickets in consecutive balls just doesn't constitute a hat-trick.

Good luck, Moises. I'm really looking forward to swinging the tennis racquet with you.

Yours sincerely,

Damien Fleming
President, Secretary, Board Member, Treasurer, Player Representative, Union Member and Sponsor of the Australians with Hat-tricks on Test Debut Club

Acknowledgements

Big Bowlology delivery to all my ex-teammates and people off the field, such as Peter Mathieson and Craig Slocombe, and all at Springvale South – Go Bloods!

Craig Ortland and John Stones and company at Noble Park – great premiership in 2005/06 when we had Malvern 9 for 15 in the final.

Ossie Wright, thanks 'Champ', for all your help, mate, and to the late Joan Holdsworth who helped save our club, South Melbourne; hope the club thrives down in Casey – Go Bloods!

Thanks to Dean Waugh (why did it take an hour to drive to East Torrens in my first game?) and Jamie Panelli (for not listening to my bowling advice) at Kensington, the mighty Browns.

Apologies to my mate Chris Davies – you might not have nicked the ball, but I needed at least one wicket for the Browns to get a bowling average.

Thanks to Amersham cricket club (UK) and Damian Hartley (The Ghost), Michael Deveney (how good was Manhattans?) and everyone at Enfield CC in the Lancashire League in the UK.

To all my ex-teammates I played for with the mighty Victorian cricket team – thanks for the ride, it was fun and laughs – Hodgey, Herby and Sakesy and co. – especially at Coppin Street team meetings. Special mention to the Coppin Street crew and roomies Geoff Allardice (Joffa, you didn't think Harvs and I would be interested in the naked Twister next door?), Ian Harvey (is your dog coming back?) and Michael Foster (Fossie, why did you eat my elegant rabbit?).

Also, to the coaches and off-field staff – Muddy Waters, Steve Sandor, Peter Kremer, Steve Lausson and Anthony Stewart.

South Australia – wish I'd played a bit more, but appreciate the chance.

Warwickshire (18-ball career) – sorry to Denis Amiss, but looking forward to the past player functions with the Bears.

Thanks to John Harmer, my under-19 coach and the man who gave me a cricketing biomechanical/Bowlology degree at the Centre of Excellence.

And thanks to Peter Thompson, for all your help and guidance. I will overlook your botched Joffa gag at my wedding.

And for those who have worn the baggy green and yellow cap for Australia, I salute you.

A shout-out to the mighty Hawthorn Football Club and Noble Park Football Club.

MUSIC – TOP 10

AC/DC – *Back in Black*
Faith No More – *Angel Dust*
Foo Fighters – *The Colour and the Shape*
Ace Frehley – first solo album, self-titled
Hellacopters – *High Visibility*
Kiss – *Dynasty* and *Alive* albums
Metallica – *Ride the Lightning*
Motley Crue – *Shout at the Devil*
Nirvana – *Nevermind*
Red Hot Chili Peppers – *Blood Sugar Sex Magik*

ACKNOWLEDGEMENTS

The Fleming crew: Wendy, Isobel, me, Braydon, Dianne, Ian, Justin, and Jasmine in front.

MOVIES – TOP 10

Ace Ventura: Pet Detective
Blazing Saddles
Caddyshack
Dumb and Dumber
The Hangover
Monty Python and the Holy Grail
Naked Gun
National Lampoon's Vacation
There's Something About Mary
This Is Spinal Tap
Wedding Crashers

Thanks to Jimmy and everyone at ABC Grandstand, and Susie Robinson who has moved on to improve her golf handicap.

And to BJ, Blewy, AB, Junior and the fantastic crew and staff at Fox Sports.

Finally, thanks to Peter Lalor, a true all-rounder: journo, author, beer critic, distance runner and Alice Cooper fan, whose help for this book was indispensable. Thanks, mate. And to everyone at The Five Mile Press for getting *Bowlology* to the masses . . . maybe!